When The African Bus Came Down

Elaine Bosman

Illustrations by Paul Bosman

© 2015 Elaine Bosman. All rights reserved.

I have tried to recreate events, locales and conversations from my memories of them. In order to maintain their anonymity in some instances I have changed the names of individuals and may have changed some identifying characteristics and details.

FOR PAUL,

MY PARTNER IN ADVENTURE

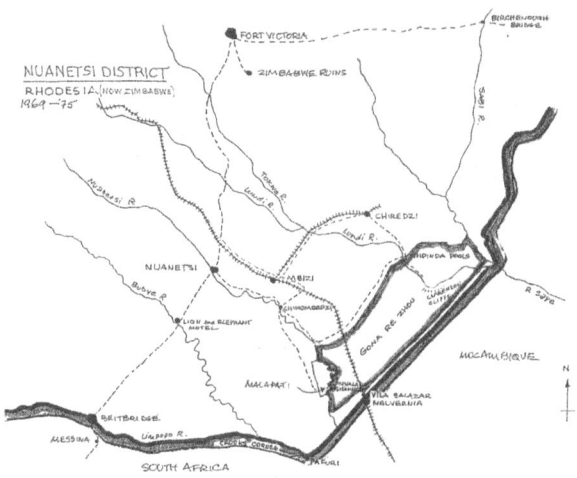

Introduction

About 1652, when Jan van Riebeek landed at the Cape of Good Hope to establish a supply station for ships carrying spices to Europe from the Far East, various tribes began moving south. At the same time, Europeans were colonizing in the south and moving north. It was inevitable that they would meet and ultimately clash.

It has always amused me that, although whites have resided in southern Africa about the same length of time as have these migrating tribes, white people whose families in Africa may date back as many as several hundred years never refer to themselves as "Africans" - it is a designation reserved for black people. Whites refer to themselves as "Europeans." In the context of this narrative, "African" refers to a black person and "tribesman" and "tribal" refer to the people who have not yet had much contact with civilization and who have not, for the most part, assumed a western style of dress. In the South Africa where I grew up, a white person seldom had contact with a black person who was not in an unskilled position. Almost every home had live-in domestic help. There was always a gardener and a housekeeper. If there were children there would also be a nanny. Television was not introduced until the mid-seventies on the pretext of trying to establish which system was most suitable for South Africa. In truth, it was to keep people who had not traveled outside Africa ignorant of world affairs and even what was happening within South Africa. The local radio stations were government owned and generally broadcast what was, in their view, good for people to know. When television did come, it was only in the evenings and it came as a surprise to many South Africans that there were articulate black people since they had always encountered only menial workers.

One hardly ever knew the last names of Africans, and just referred to them by their first names, in contrast to the formal way – Mr. or Mrs. – in which one addressed an adult white person with whom one was not familiar. South Africa had always had the social segregation that arose out of the different lives they lived; it was economic more than anything else, but it became law in 1947 when the Nationalist government came into power and apartheid (literally separatism) became law. A white and a black person could not legally marry and it was a punishable offense to cohabit. This law was called the "Immorality Act." White and black lives seldom intersected socially but when they did occasionally they would find they had enough in common to want to be together. Many lives were ruined by the stigma of having been found guilty under the Immorality Act.

At one stage, Africans were referred to by the government as "Bantu," a variation on the Zulu word "abantu" which is the word for people. The singular was "umuntu" and was abbreviated to "muntu" when speaking of one person. Because of the perceived connection to the government, Bantu and Muntu became anathema to liberals who saw this as a derogatory form of address, but it was how black people referred to themselves.

For the government, there was the problem of keeping black people in their so-called homelands where they had been settled. In rural areas, there was little chance of employment and they naturally gravitated to the cities. To live in a city, one had to have an identity document called a "Pass," which had a photograph and fingerprint of the individual and it was issued by his local authority and not readily given. To be found without a passbook or even without the necessary stamp was reason for arrest. The police would raid an employer's property in the middle of the night, rouse the occupants, and if a husband was visiting his wife who was there legally, and he wasn't, he would be arrested and taken away. This often happened without the knowledge of the employer.

For office and business workers where housing was not provided, Africans lived in a "township" that was some distance from the city. They had to commute by bus or by train to get to work and they often had to walk several miles to get to whatever transportation they used. Buses and trains were inadequate for the population they served. Once they got to the city, they may have had to take another bus so, for workers to get to work on time, they frequently had to leave home three or four hours before starting work.

Government schools were free to white children and compulsory. Instruction was either in English or Afrikaans depending on the pupil's home language. A child who was more fluent in Afrikaans had to be educated in Afrikaans. The government had found that a child educated in English had access to the classics that had not yet been translated into Afrikaans, and it opened a wider world for them. They became anglicized. For families who wanted their children to be bilingual, the option was a private school, which was generally more liberal. Black children had to buy their own books, school was not compulsory, and they were educated in Afrikaans only, although many of them learned English on their own. The townships usually were without electricity and water had to be brought to the home in a bucket from a communal tap. One has to admire minds such as Nelson Mandela's that came out of their primitive schools. English universities were open to black students and this allowed for an interchange of ideas, which often led to a better understanding of the plight of the Africans. As a result, English universities were seen as a hotbed of communism. The major threat to South Africa was perceived as communism. There were no doubt communists, but the vast majority of white and black intellectuals did not agree with apartheid. People were told that Nelson Mandela and the other "political prisoners" on Robbin Island were out to overthrow democracy in South Africa. What better way to ensure that the Nationalist government remained in power? We had several friends, otherwise caring people, who voted for the Nationalist party.

African children studied by lamp light. If they were particularly bright, they ended up at university but had to take a train or bus to get there. Most white students were taken by car, had the luxury of electricity in their homes, and had access to radio, newspapers and magazines to broaden their outlook.

On the whole, employers saw themselves as caring of their workers. They provided basic accommodation in a unit separate from their house, a uniform to be worn at work, and they paid medical expenses, very often for the extended family as well but they were grossly underpaid for the work they did. They generally worked from six in the morning until after dinner was served at night with a three-hour break in the afternoon. They also had a three-week paid vacation. At that time, they brought in a substitute worker who was not nearly as quick or intelligent as themselves. They did not want the temporary worker to replace them permanently. Considering the fact that they were always in the home and overheard conversations and arguments, met visitors, and were generally part of the daily life, one would think they would be an integral part of the family, but they didn't have the interaction one would expect. On the part of the Africans there was also aloofness. They didn't usually confide in an employer. Perhaps experience had taught them that silence was golden!

In recounting our time at Malapati, it was to keep the memory accurate and alive for our children and their children. It was a life few people ever experienced and most of which is now gone forever. Our eldest son, Christopher, kept all of the letters I had ever written to him and they were a valuable source of material. He and his brother Simon provided a lot of the action. My husband Paul had grown up in the wilderness areas of the Bechuanaland Protectorate, now Botswana, where his father had been Director of Agriculture for the British government. During school vacations, he had traveled extensively with his father into wilderness areas unencumbered by the restrictions of living in a city. Some areas were so remote that on one occasion his father had asked a local what the road conditions were like farther north and the man had replied, "I don't know. You were the last person to come through here twelve months ago."

Having experienced that, it was difficult for Paul to settle to any other way of life. He constantly hankered for the bush, and our vacations as a family were generally to some remote place. It was Paul's deep-seated longing to get back to nature that made me realize his life was not complete in a city and we would have to think of a way to find that. My childhood had been more urban and although I enjoyed wilderness, I was inherently a city dweller. I knew little about wildlife and unknown sounds set my heart pounding. I was to learn a lot during my time at Malapati.

Chapter 1

I often dream of Africa. It is where I was born and raised. We now live very happily in the United States but a large part of me is still in Africa. Thirty years later, I look back on an interesting and developmental phase of my life in what was then Rhodesia (now Zimbabwe). Africa has changed beyond our wildest expectations. It sometimes seems like another lifetime and another world. Much of what we knew has gone forever. We were glad to have been a part of it and there is a certain sadness that what we knew is no more, but we also recognize that what has come to pass is what we had hoped would one day happen, just not the way it happened. For us, it began in 1969.

As the magician waved his wand and pulled a rabbit out of the hat the children squealed with excitement. It was Simon's eighth birthday party. "Can you make a horse?" asked Christopher who was twelve. I came to the magician's rescue. "We have Misty, we don't need another horse. What about a guinea pig instead?" A wave of the wand produced a guinea pig.

I wished life could be that simple. I would wave a wand to let everything remain as it was. I looked at my beautiful home with its acre of sweeping lawns and the colorful flower beds. I was so reluctant to give it all up. We were about to leave to go and live in a wilderness area in Rhodesia.

We lived in Johannesburg - the city of Gold - which had sprung from a small mining community in 1886 when gold had been discovered in South Africa to a sophisticated city of sky scrapers. It became one of the 50 largest metropolitan cities in the world and the source of a large-scale gold and diamond trade.

I loved every aspect of this concrete jungle. I enjoyed its facilities. The bustle and activity stimulated me and the very concrete structures, reaching up to the sky, were to me a triumph of Man's ingenuity. The jagged skyline of high rises, sometimes swathed in an ethereal mist, were to me quite beautiful. To my husband, Paul, who was an artist, it was a monument to those who had come to plunder the earth, bringing with it all the attendant devastation, and he saw my 'ethereal mist' only as the pollution it was.

It is difficult to know just when we decided to give up city life and all that went with it and to go and live in the bush. Paul had grown up in Botswana and he had spent his teenage years free of the restrictions of suburban living. He had shown a talent for drawing at an early age and it had seemed natural for him to study art, first in Johannesburg and then in London. The necessity for earning a living had drawn him to city life, but he never lost his hankering for the sounds and smell of the wild.

Paul was now a Director of an advertising agency, probably one of the most vibrant professions. As he progressed, the tensions and pressures mounted until it seemed he would soon be another casualty to a heart attack. The competitiveness pervaded all our lives. It seemed to be a part of living in an affluent community. When we had been planning Simon's party, I had suggested having our gardener lead Misty around for the children to have rides. "Gordon had a pony for his party. Can't we have a magician?" Parties were no longer a simple affair of a cake with candles and games in the garden. There had to be entertainment and the object was to have something different, which in truth meant something better than the last party.

At first I hadn't taken Paul seriously when he talked of leaving advertising to go and live in the bush. Most of our friends had a private dream of building a boat to sail round the world; to grow apples or buy a country inn. It seemed to be the dream that made reality more tolerable. I had hoped Paul's interest would wane, but as the years passed he became more and more preoccupied with his idea.

I belonged to various clubs and served on several committees. I had friends with whom I would have tea or go shopping. I rode my horse every morning. The thought of giving it all up was not something I accepted very readily. There would also be the financial insecurity of not having a fixed income. Yet I knew I had no choice when I thought of Paul coming home at night, mentally and physically exhausted and sometimes too tired to be tolerant of the children's exuberant recounting of their day's activities.

The problem was how to retire at thirty-five with a young family to educate. Paul's early years in the bush gave him the knowledge of wildlife, so we thought of possibly game farming. Breeding the large antelope like Eland and Kudu in captivity was very profitable and wildlife were less susceptible to the diseases cattle were susceptible to. We wrote away for information but finally decided it was too much like ranching. Paul wanted to live in a wilderness area. Gradually, the idea formed of starting a safari lodge in some remote wilderness area. This way we could live in a remote area, enjoy the wilderness he so hankered for, and he could share his knowledge of wildlife with others. A safari lodge would provide the income and the lifestyle he was searching for. Then came the problem of finding a suitable place. We spent weekends in the bush in Swaziland, Mozambique, Rhodesia and the Lowveld of South Africa. We found many beautiful places but each was rejected for one reason or another until I think our friends thought our idea was just a pipe dream.

Then we heard of Malapati in Rhodesia. It was an undeveloped area in the Rhodesian Lowveld, bordering on Gona-re-Zhou, the Place of the Elephants, which was being developed as a future National Park. Gona-re-Zhou itself was at this stage not yet proclaimed a national park. Malapati was thirty-five miles from the Limpopo River, the boundary between South Africa and Rhodesia, and ecologically an extension of the area on the South African side which formed the Kruger National Park. The Nuanetsi River snaked its way through Gona-re-Zhou and continued on to Malapati and then down to the Limpopo. It was very wooded around the site we thought we would build. At that stage of my life, I doubt I knew the names of more than a few trees. I gradually learnt the common names of the various trees and shrubs and, in time, the botanical names too. It opened a whole new area of interest for me. The vegetation close to the river was a heavy canopy of the sycamore fig trees (Ficus Sycomorus). While they were fruiting, the fig trees were very popular with the monkeys and baboons, the lime colored green pigeons, and the raucous Trumpeter Hornbills. Along the river, there was a dense undergrowth and the Combretum Microfillum, a creeper with stems sometimes twelve inches in diameter, winding and twisting its way up the trees. It would spread itself on the top of the canopy in a shower of red. Back from the river grew the towering Nyala Berry trees (Xanthocercis Zambesiaca) which so often seemed to sprout out of a termite mound. There were numerous varieties of acacias, the lush green of the Natal mahogany trees (Trichilia Emetica) and the Sausage trees (Kigelia Africana) with their massive fruits. Dotted around were the giants of the Lowveld, the baobabs (Digitata Adansonia), with their heavy squat grey trunks and undersized branches. These strange trees lived for up to 3,000 years and grew to an enormous size. One we measured had a girth of 48 feet. This vegetation gave way to mopani, both the trees and the scrub, so typical of the African bush.

Malapati was untouched, beautiful and just what we wanted. We approached the Rhodesian Government with our plans, including a scale model of the Lodge, and the projected capital outlay. Rhodesia was desperate for foreign currency any form of tourism would bring. We could not buy Malapati as it was government land but we hoped they would grant us the 99 year lease which we had in mind. It had to be considered by the Minister and in the meantime all we could do was wait. The suspense was almost unbearable until we were told our plans had been approved.

The Ministry wanted us to pinpoint the exact spot

where we would be locating the Lodge. The Secretary of Internal Affairs and the Provincial Commissioner arranged to meet us in Fort Victoria and fly us down to Malapati for the day. We were anxious to have another look at Malapati and we decided to go up a week ahead of time and stay in the National Park tourist camp at Swimuwini in Gona-re-Zhou Game Reserve for a few days and then drive the 200 miles back to Fort Victoria to attend to various business matters. We could then meet the official party and fly down with them.

We checked into the tourist camp and drove down to the Malapati sub-office. This area was administered by the District Commissioner who had his office at Nuanetsi, ninety miles away. Throughout the district were rest houses and sub-offices where the administrative staff could be accommodated while attending to matters affecting the local tribesmen. These visits by the District Commissioner or his staff were usually just for a day or two, but they were comfortably accommodated while they were there. A high level bridge crossed the Nuanetsi River and at this point there was one of the sub-offices and a rest house. At the rest house, Alan Wright, a former Native Commissioner and later District Commissioner, had put up "some notes for officials and others who may use the Sub-Office quarters." It gave details of the tremendous variety of game to be seen from this point and a foot note "A thought that may bring solace to many. The Sub Office faces east and in that direction there is no human habitation for one hundred miles".

It had the usual caretaker/camp attendant and an African District Messenger. At this stage in Rhodesia, a District Messenger was probably as high as a black person could hope to go in government, so it was a highly prestigious one as he represented the District Commissioner in the tribal area. He was in daily contact by radio with the office in Nuanetsi and all requests or complaints by the tribesmen were relayed by him to the D.C. The District Messenger wore a khaki uniform of shorts and shirt which were kept immaculately pressed, khaki socks, and brown boots which were highly polished. His felt hat had a red flash and was pinned up on one side. The current District Messenger was called Titus and he was of the Shangaan tribe. He was slight, light-skinned and stood proud and erect in his uniform. He covered great distances on his bicycle and he was a mine of information, but as with most Africans, one had to know what to ask him and then extract the pertinent facts. They seldom volunteered information to a white person. We talked to Titus about rainfall and game movements. He had a strange habit of prefixing every reply with "Ah." Paul asked him whether the Africans liked game.

"Ah, yes."

"Do they really enjoy it?"

"Ah, yes."

"They like to come like this to look at the game?"

"Ah, no."

"How then do they like the game?"

"Ah, they like to eat the game."

Had Paul not continued to probe, we might have come away with the idea that the tribesmen were keen conservationists.

Some years previously we had a similar near misunderstanding. At the time we were negotiating to buy a ranch in Swaziland. We questioned an old African who had been in the area all his life. We wanted to know whether there had ever been giraffe on the ranch, but I didn't know the Swazi word for giraffe. We showed him a photograph of a giraffe and he shook his head. "No, never." We showed him a photograph of a wildebeest and again he shook his head. It occurred to us that there might be a misunderstanding, so we showed him a photograph of zebra, which were numerous. Again he shook his head "No never." When we pointed out to him that he had been with us that morning when we had seen a large herd of zebra up at the windmill, he beamed and pointed to the photograph. "Yes we did, but not small like this."

While we were in the rest camp at Swimuwini, we met the Warden and some of the rangers. The Warden was a small man with a round, cherubic face and red chubby cheeks which gave him a very youthful appearance. He obviously had a complex about his girlish looks and stature and as if to prove his authority, he generally didn't sit down as everyone else did. He stood with his foot on a low table and leaned forward, resting his elbow on his knee. We were to find this was a favored pose and most of his actions in administering Gona-re-Zhou were obviously motivated by this need to project a macho image. The night before we were to leave, he and two of his staff came to have a drink with us. We questioned them about the area and game movements, and as they were leaving, we said we would see them some time the following day.

"Well we'd better say good-bye now because we're going to be very busy tomorrow. Our regional Warden and a party of VIPs are coming down."

We drove up to Fort Victoria and early the following morning we met at the airport. Mr. Robertson, the Secretary for Internal Affairs, had been flown down from Salisbury in his Ministry's six-seater aircraft. He was large and had a rather rumpled look about him. His hair was cut very short and he ran his hands through it frequently. His careless, disheveled appearance belied his personality. When he spoke, he was very gruff and to the point and his staff was in great awe of him. He introduced us to the Provincial Commissioner, a slight man in his early sixties with a well trimmed gray moustache, an impossibly British accent, and dressed in long baggy khaki shorts and knee-high khaki socks. He looked like a character out of Casablanca. He was totally overshadowed by his superior. Mr. Robertson told us he had arranged for the Regional Warden of National Parks to meet us at Mabalauta where we would be landing in Gona-re-Zhou at the Warden's camp. For us to be meeting with officials so high up in the Ministry of Internal Affairs and for the Regional Warden of Nation Parks to have been summoned to attend made us realize that we were the VIP party the Warden was expecting.

As we taxied down the runway, I could see the District Commissioner from Nuanetsi, the Agricultural Officer, the Regional Warden, the Warden and his rangers, and African game scouts standing stiffly to attention. I don't think the Warden ever forgave us for being the VIPs.

Chapter 2

Back in Johannesburg, our first priority was to sell our house. We arranged to have our furniture stored and found a home for my horse. We bought two Land Rovers and with our aged Siamese cat, MacGregor, and our fox terrier, Piccolo, we headed for Rhodesia in early December of 1969.

We had arranged with National Parks to allow us to use one of their tourist units at Swimuwini while we were building. Due to the summer rains which could make the roads impassable, the Game Reserve was closed to tourists from November until April, so we were the only visitors. The camp was on the Nuanetsi River, and at this point the river bank was an almost sheer drop of fifty feet to the river bed. This gave one the advantage of being able to sit unobserved and watch the game cautiously picking their way across the dry river bed to Buffalo Bend. The Bend was part of Malapati Game Reserve although it was right in the heart of Gona-re-Zhou. About fifteen miles downstream, Malapati straddled the river and then the boundary crossed to the west bank, but at this point in Gona-re-Zhou the river made an enormous loop, forming the Buffalo Bend. Mabalauta, the National Parks base camp, was immediately to the west of the Bend. Across the river and to the east of the bend was the tourist camp we were occupying. One had the impression that the Bend was an island caught between two portions of

Parks' territory, but in fact it was just the meandering of the river which created this. Buffalo Bend was inaccessible from Malapati as the west bank was very broken rhyolite country with numerous ravines which made an access road impractical. The only access was through Gona-re-Zhou, and National Parks had early on agreed to give Internal Affairs access through Gona-re-Zhou and this was extended to us.

The camp in which we were staying was called Swimuweni, which in the Shangaan language meant 'The Collection of Baobabs' after a group of these trees at this spot. The Baobab always seemed to me to be the botanical equivalent of the elephant. A mature tree grows to a height of about 50 feet and the trunk can have a girth of up to 48 feet. The branches taper rapidly giving it the appearance of having its roots in the air. The smooth-skinned swollen trunk has protuberances which resemble a giant candle with wax dripping down. In November, creamy white gardenia-like flowers appear and they are followed by oval fruit about six inches in length.

The thatch roofed units referred to as huts in the tourist camp had each been built near a Baobab tree. Our one consisted of a large bedroom, which Paul and I used, and a veranda where Christopher and Simon slept. An outside barbecue served as the kitchen and we used the communal bathroom, located in the middle of the camp, for showering and doing laundry. As there was no electricity, bathing at night entailed carrying a gas lamp as well as one's clothes and towels from the hut to the bathroom. For me this was quite an ordeal, being new to it all. I felt we should be armed for this nocturnal expedition as we generally heard lions roaring at night and in the morning there were always signs of elephant and buffalo having been around.

Not having a stove, I was not able to use the usual flat irons as they blackened over an open fire. When I finally discovered the Ember Iron, my problems were over. It had a hinged top which one opened and filled with glowing coals. It looked quaint but was very efficient.

We selected the spot at Malapati where we would build our house. It was to be under a large Nyalaberry tree. We paced it out and marked the various rooms. Suddenly the enormity of what we were undertaking dawned on me. Here we were ninety miles from the nearest paved road, two hundred miles from the nearest town, and planning to build a house with no experience whatsoever. We would have to make our own cement bricks and bring in all our building materials. An experienced builder would have thought twice about it. Fortunately we were ignorant of all the pitfalls.

We were filled with enthusiasm and couldn't wait to get started. We had a collection of 'How To Do Your Own...' books. We hired two laborers, both Shangaans; Jeremiah to make a vegetable garden and John as a general laborer. Jeremiah was tall and gaunt and had enormous feet. When he exerted himself in the extreme heat, the perspiration would pour off him, and when he bent down it would look as though his head had sprung a leak. He had, like so many of the Shangaans, worked on the gold mines. He knew Johannesburg well and he loved to reminisce about it. He spoke reasonable English. I spoke Zulu and since the Shangaans were an offshoot from this tribe, the language was very similar to Zulu. In the meantime, Jeremiah interpreted for me until I reached the stage where I could communicate with the locals.

We drove down to Malapati each morning, taking our needs for the day with us. I used to wear ankle boots which I felt would protect my feet from creepy crawlies. One morning as I was making fire for coffee, I felt a violent burning on my foot. I struggled to get the shoelace undone and removed the boot. A small, angry scorpion dropped out. It had obviously fallen into the side of my boot when I had put the wood on the fire. The pain was excruciating. It was one of those pains one wanted to squeeze to alleviate, but it was too painful to touch. Paul reminded me that I had survived the birth of two children; the pain couldn't be that bad. It was to be a very different story a few years later when he was stung by a scorpion. The pain eventually wore off, but I still remember that fierce, fiery sting.

At first I was anxious about Christopher and Simon. Would they be bitten by snakes? Would they run into wild animals? Soon I realized we would just have to lay down some ground rules about safe behavior and I would have to trust to their guardian angels. We gave Christopher and Simon each a fishing rod and a pellet gun to provide them with some form of activity. I had been against the idea of a gun, but Paul convinced me that it was necessary for anyone living in the bush to know how to handle a firearm and to learn gun manners. An air gun was a safe one with which to learn. To ensure that they didn't just blast away at anything that moved, we made the rule that they had to eat everything they shot. I don't think the idea of eating an owl or a hawk appealed to them, so we had very little indiscriminate shooting. Green pigeons and francolin were numerous and Christopher and Simon often provided the meat for dinner. They fit into their new life with ease – it was every boy's dream.

Chapter 3

Graham Millar was the District Officer at Nuanetsi. He was tall and trim, in his early thirties, and had blue eyes and sandy colored, unruly hair that gave him a boyish look. He was very competent and obviously sure of himself. He ranked immediately below the District Commissioner and wielded almost as much power. His wife, Denese, was an attractive girl and her vivacious personality and blond good looks belied her intelligence. She had been a teacher before she married Graham and she was a highly organized person. She had spent most of her life in the bush and one could consult her about almost anything. They were a most hospitable pair, popular and highly thought of in the district. They invited us to join them at a New Year's Eve party to meet some of the locals.

The party was at the Lion and Elephant Motel. For us this entailed a ninety-mile drive to Nuanetsi village and then a further twenty-five miles on the main Fort Victoria/Beit Bridge road. Denese suggested we drive up to Nuanetsi to shower and dress for the party. What remained of the night we would spend with them and return home the next morning. Not having anyone with whom to leave the cat and the dog, she suggested we bring them too. Christopher and Simon and the animals could stay with their nanny who would be babysitting their two sons.

We set off in the Landrover at 4 p.m. in pouring rain. In no time at all we were using four wheel drive and it was soon apparent we were not going to have a pleasant trip sliding from one side of the road to the other. This was a totally new experience to me and I was terrified when we slid uncontrollably. It didn't seem to faze Paul at all. The wheel wells filled with mud and we had to stop several times to clear them. Christopher and Simon leapt out to help and with each stop the cat and the dog managed to jump out into the mud and then back in again, covering everything in mud.

We arrived at Nuanetsi at 9 p.m., all absolutely filthy. The nanny told us Graham and Denese had gone on ahead. We were totally exhausted and disinclined to party but it had taken so much effort to get this far, we wanted to show ourselves. We showered and changed into our party clothes and set off for the Lion and Elephant. The motel was set in beautiful riverine vegetation with luxuriant gardens. They had an open air dance floor and some ancient records. It was swelteringly hot - midsummer in the tropics - and the men had removed their jackets. The ladies mostly looked like fairies off the top of the Christmas tree with plenty of sequins and spangles. One large lady, who was perspiring freely, danced with a handkerchief tied round her neck. Periodically she removed it to mop herself. Graham and Denese pointed out all the colorful characters and introduced us all round. The party was great but short-lived. Just after midnight the rain caught up with us and the party was washed out.

The following morning, after an enormous breakfast with the Millars, we set out for home. It was still raining. We came to the Tshompani River which was normally just a dry gully. Now it was a raging torrent. There was no alternative but to wait for it to subside. This was so different from anything I had ever experienced, but Paul had encountered flash flooding during his childhood growing up in Botswana. In spite of all the water, we had nothing that was drinkable and inevitably we all developed an incredible thirst. I asked Paul if he was familiar with this sort of thing, why he hadn't warned me. He said his mother had always taken care of that. That day I learned never to travel in the bush, even a short distance, without food and water. We had to wait until that afternoon before the water subsided enough to allow us to cross. We arrived home twenty-four hours after we had set out for the party.

As we drove to our campsite the next morning, we saw the Nuanetsi River trickling down. For seven months it was a wide, dry, sandy riverbed. Now, the previous day's rain was being carried down from all the little streams and gullies. At first it was just a trickle of water and came at walking pace, rolling bits of debris before it. It would froth and bubble as the water disappeared into the dry sand, and as the sand became saturated, the water would reappear again. During the night, the floodwater reached Malapati and the following morning, the Nuanetsi River was a muddy, swirling torrent, stretching fifty yards from one bank to the other.

We had to have water on site to make our cement bricks and Graham Millar loaned us the 500 gallon Internal Affairs water tanker that we could hitch behind one of the Land Rovers. We filled it at a bore hole five miles away. On the second trip, one of the wheels broke off. We were unable to repair it and the tanker looked so forlorn, keeled over onto its side, that it stayed a reminder to us to never borrow anything. It stayed that way for several weeks until the government mechanic came down from Nuanetsi to repair it.

We intended to use the 'sand extraction' system for our water supply, but this could only be done after the floods, when the water had once again dropped below the level of the sand, in about April. With the tanker out of commission, we would have to pump straight out of the river for the garden and building. Graham Miller, who was our source of information, explained what we should do. I was totally intimidated and concerned that Paul , whom I had always considered impractical, might not be able to do what Graham suggested. But, as directed, he had Jeremiah and John dig a small pond and concreted it to hold water. On our next trip to Fort Victoria, we bought a pump and motor and Paul installed it. He brought a pipe up from the river to the pond. It seemed nothing short of a miracle when he started the motor and water flowed into the pond. We now had water laid on, undrinkable, but fine for building purposes. We brought drinking water with us each day.

We ordered cement in bulk. It came by rail to Nyala Siding, twenty-five miles away on the main line to Mozambique. There were three hundred and twenty-six bags to a 'short truck', which was left at the siding, and we had ten days in which to unload, after which we were charged demurrage. We decided to spend one day unloading the truck with the help of John and Jerry and cover the stack with a tarpaulin. We could then pick it up at our convenience. Each Land Rover could only take twenty bags at a time and one trip each day was tiring enough. On the third day we realized our mistake. During the night, the elephants had discovered the cement and they had torn several bags open and had a dust bath with it. We were to find that they were naturally curious about anything new.

Now that we had the cement, we needed to bring in sand from the river. We spread the word that we needed laborers and an odd selection showed up each day. Charlie was tall, very dark and wore his hair combed out in an Afro style. Wilson arrived wearing a pair of sunglasses with only one lens. Elliott was the local clown. Samson lived up to his name. He was incredibly strong and he would stop what he was doing to flex his muscles in a body builder's pose, which greatly impressed his fellow workers. He derided them as weaklings and he insisted that it was the beer and tobacco that sapped their strength.

While Paul picked up the cement with Jerry and John, I took the rest of the gang to load river sand. Charlie was a natural athlete and he could shovel sand with the grace of a drum major. He would follow through with the shovel and then twirl it before coming down for the next scoop. He worked very fast and he would periodically put the shovel down and do a handstand. Samson would

respond by doing his Charles Atlas pose. Digging the sand was not easy, as it was still damp and heavy. Also, the Land Rover couldn't hold much because of the weight. It was obvious we needed a truck for the cement, sand, stones, timber and thatch we would ultimately be hauling.

We made the tedious trip to Fort Victoria and bought a two-ton Mazda truck, which was very comfortable to drive, until we got onto the dirt road and then it behaved like a bucking bronco when it had no load on board. It made a great difference having the truck. We were now able to carry fifty bags of cement at a time and much larger loads of sand.

Once we had our water, sand and cement supply on site, we were able to begin making bricks. We had brick forms and the formula for mixing the sand and cement. Paul was totally confident about the process. I was amazed at how easily he had slipped into his new role. We cleared a patch under a large tree and the workers got the hang of it in no time at all and we were turning out perfect cement blocks. The bricks were laid out in neat rows to cure. Graham told us they had to be kept damp for a few days before they could be lifted. The first night the elephants were overcome with curiosity and walked between the rows. Occasionally, a clumsy one would step on a few bricks, but on the whole they carefully avoided them. Several times it rained during the night, dissolving the bricks which hadn't yet cured. Despite all this, brick making was going ahead at a rapid rate and we were able to begin stacking them.

The workers chose a 'gwadza' system where one allocated a certain amount of work agreed on by both parties to be done each day. By choice, they started at first light and worked feverishly until about 2 p.m. when they would retire to the river. It had now stopped running and had formed large, deep pools in which fish, particularly bream, were plentiful. We were busy and enjoying ourselves. The only jarring note was that Christopher and Simon would soon have to leave for boarding school. Christopher was twelve, Simon was nine, and they still seemed very little to me. The only consolation was that they would be together. In accordance with British tradition, most children went to boarding school as adolescents, but for children who lived in a remote area, there was no choice. We felt they needed the companionship of other children and facilities we couldn't provide. They had to go away to boarding school.

We had booked them into the junior school in Fort Victoria, two hundred miles away, and we had been to visit the school so they would not feel too strange when they finally checked in. The day came for them to leave and we set off with their clothes labeled and packed into the required tin trunk, each with their name stenciled on it. I had given them each a haircut and they looked quite civilized again in school uniforms. They were both very quiet, and Paul and I kept up a steady stream of conversation to take their minds off the impending separation. I remembered the feeling so well from my own boarding school days when my mother would chat away lightheartedly, apparently unconcerned with my tears so close to the surface. I now knew how she must have felt.

We met the principal and their housemaster and the boys chose their beds. I could see it wouldn't take much for Simon to cry. I knew I wouldn't be able to leave him if he broke down. Fortunately, a pigeon flew over and deposited his droppings on Paul's shoulder. We all had a good laugh and we were able to part on a cheerful note. I drove away with a heavy heart. We would only be driving up to Fort Victoria every three weeks for supplies. We were not only two hundred miles away but without a telephone. In an emergency, the local police would have to radio the police at Vila Salazar on the Mozambique border and they would have someone drive to Malapati.

The only way we could keep in touch with the boys was by mail. We had a mailbag at the post office, a large canvas bag which was locked. We arranged with the postmistress to leave our mailbag out to be picked up by the African bus which came through Nuanetsi on Wednesdays, and the driver would drop it off at an African store close to us. Sometimes it was a new driver and we would have no mail. Sometimes the driver had no reason to stop at the store to drop off the mailbag. For several years this was our only means of communicating with the outside world. We were a close knit family and as young as Christopher and Simon were, we had always included them in our discussions and plans for the future. I feared this might be lost now, but in fact we found Christopher was very articulate in his letters and gave us graphic descriptions of everything at school. Simon was less forthcoming and his first letter was rather typical... "We like it here. There are lots of things to do, but it rains all the time, so there is no time to do all these things. Love Simon".

We found the separation made us more aware of them as individuals, and they in turn enjoyed and appreciated home as they never had before. I would write a serial letter, adding to it each day, recounting what we had done. On Wednesdays when the African bus came down from Nuanetsi with our mail-bag, we sent off a long letter to the boys. With one of Simon's letters came one for me to address to a friend in Johannesburg. "When are you coming to see us? There are lots of wild animals. Tell your Mom there's nothing to be skird of."

Chapter 4

A charming young American called Lionel Hurd dropped in to see us. He was the doctor in charge of the Chikombedzi Mission Hospital and he did a weekly trip down to Domisa, about ten miles from us. It was really just a name for a place in the bush. There his patients would sit under a tree and wait for him. He would minister to their bodies and souls and then return home at the end of the day. Lionel was a typical American College boy. He must have been about thirty, but he seemed very youthful. He was tall and athletic looking, with a crew cut and twinkling blue eyes, which told the world that he enjoyed life. He was soon going back to the States for a year on 'furlough' and the prospect really appealed to him. Just talking about it would elicit a broad grin as he thought of the States.

Chikombedzi, where he was based, was probably one of the most unattractive places I ever saw in Rhodesia. It was arid and stony with hardly any ground cover at all and no really sizeable trees, just scrub mopani and innumerable goats which stood on their hind legs to reach the leaves, leaving a 'goat line,' the height to which they had cropped the bushes.

Lionel told us that he had once approached the headman about reducing the number of goats, but one only slaughtered livestock to eat and these goats could not be eaten. They had once devoured soiled bandages from the hospital and the headman had explained to Lionel that should they now eat these goats, they would catch all the diseases which had been on the bandages. So the goats proliferated.

The missionaries made their homes very attractive with wallpaper and furnishings brought with them from the States, but about Chikombedzi they could do very little. The village was about half a mile from the Mission, and consisted of a cluster of African stores which never seemed to close and which sold everything from gas to beer. The exterior walls had ancient metal signboards advertising various products. The one which always amused us was one advertising a Raleigh bicycle and which depicted a grinning African leaping onto his bicycle confidently, pursued by a roaring lion. I thought it rather appropriate for this part of the country.

Chikombedzi was the stopping place for the African buses owned by Amon Mpepu who had built himself a small empire. He also owned the leading store, which was run by a very astute woman called Mina. Attached to the main store was what had once been Mpepu's Butchery, and although no longer used, was still referred to as such. The cooling system had broken down one summer, the contents of the butchery had putrefied, and they were never able to get rid of the smell. The cooling system was never repaired and the butchery was now used as a storeroom for bottled drinks and beer that passing government officials bought if they were thirsty enough. One had to be very thirsty because everything stored in the butchery not only smelled, but was tepid. Mina's store also had the only telephone, which was for several years our nearest means of speedy communication.

The African buses disgorged their passengers who then squatted on the veranda among the scrawny chickens, resting in the shade. There they would wait with the patience that only the Africans possess, until the bus was ready to proceed. They seemed to have an unanimated look about them. I often wondered whether they went into a semi-trance. One could go off and do something and return several hours later and find the same people sitting in the same place, not even bothering to swat the flies which settled on their faces.

The Mission was run by the New Methodists, all Americans. They were a breed unto themselves, always kind and utterly selfless. At times they were almost blind to the African's failings. It was difficult to understand how people from such a sophisticated society could be happy in such a remote and unattractive part of Africa, devoid of almost all facilities and amenities. But they were happy. It showed in everything they did. They simply glowed. Life could not have been very exciting for these missionaries. At the best of times, Africans are distrustful of white people and consequently uncommunicative, and these primitive people were doubly so. The rewards were obviously spiritual because if any of the missionaries had been drawn to Africa to learn more about the people and their customs and had come to Chikombedzi, they would have been disappointed. Occasionally, one encountered an individual who was prepared to discuss or explain customs, but on the whole, the Africans preferred not to do so and if one questioned them, they would give the answer they thought one would like to hear, or they said they didn't know.

So I could understand Lionel's boyish anticipation of his furlough back to the States. With a shake of his head he would say "Man oh man...." as though remembering something really tremendous waiting for him to do when he got back to Grand Rapids. His baby daughter had been born at Chikombedzi and she was going back for the first time to meet her grandparents.

Whenever we stopped to pick up fuel, someone wanting a ride would generally approach us. We would agree and he would say he would just be going to get his "katundu," his belongings. Invariably this would include a friend or two, or his wife and children and perhaps his mother with a few scrawny fowls, tied together at the feet and objecting vigorously at being carried upside down. Then would come the sleeping mats and a cardboard box or two. For some reason it annoyed Paul when one person asked for a ride and three or four piled on.

On one occasion, a man asked for a ride, but he wanted to run back for his things. Paul asked where they were and he pointed just ahead. We were in a hurry so we suggested we drive there. Each time we asked how much further, the man would reply "Duzi," close. It turned out to be a detour of almost half a mile. If they were going only part of the way, we would often realize they were past their getting off point, but they just sat mutely on the back. Frequently when they wanted to go down to Malapati, which embraced a wide area in our vicinity, they would ride all the way home with us and then remain sitting in the back when we got out. When we pointed out that this was the end of the line for us, they would reply that they were going another mile or two across the river, as though it was public transport. When they did get out, they seldom thanked one. They saw it simply as 'you are going my way anyway,' but European custom had conditioned us to expect them to acknowledge that we had done them a favor.

As we left Chikombedzi, Mina always said, "I wish you all God's luck," whatever that may have been. If it was good health and happiness, her wish certainly came true for us. We looked forward to each new day and whatever it brought, with enthusiasm.

A wide assortment of people called on us, providing interest and entertainment. They always stopped for tea and frequently stayed for lunch. We had far more callers than we had ever had as city dwellers where most of the men worked in an office in the city. After living a lifetime in a society where there were rigid social barriers and our contact was only with people of our own background, it was interesting to meet such a wide spectrum of individuals, from the road grader to the President of the country. In Johannesburg, one would be glad to make social contact with the President but one would not search out the road grader. Yet when we were thrown together as we were in this little community, it came as such a pleasant surprise to find that the man doing some modest work was sometimes a great deal more interesting than some of one's city friends. They were often more sincere and friendly and they had a lot to contribute from a more practical experience of life.

One man who called on us was wearing what many Rhodesian males wore - a khaki safari suit, knee length socks and dress shoes. He was a smoker, as most people were, and not being smokers ourselves, I would forget to have ashtrays around. As we were chatting, I noticed he was putting the ash from his cigarette into the side of his shoe. He didn't want to bother us for an ashtray!

We were once invited to have tea with a dear,

kind woman who was intent on doing the right thing socially to impress us 'city folk.' She had a new cook who had obviously been trained by someone who knew exactly how to do things. As he walked into the living room with the tray with her best china, she gave him a horrified look and said, "Why have you brought the teapot into the living room? Take it back and pour the tea in the kitchen." I had never seen it done this way, but to her, the new cook had done something tantamount to serving dinner from the pots on the dining room table. The poor cook must have been very confused.

We soon discovered that many Rhodesians spoke their own brand of English which incorporated certain African words. Possibly it started with the domestic help speaking to the children and finding some English words either difficult to say or to remember. Where the parents didn't insist on pure English, this quaint mixture became common usage and one found entire families speaking this way. Cattle were mombies; hills were gomos; belongings were katundu; any metal object was msimbi; meat was nyama; fowls were hukus; near was duzi; mad was penga; anything bad or horrible was mubi; corn meal was sadza, the staple diet of most Africans, so breakfast, lunch or dinner was referred to as sadza time. Small black children were referred to as picannins and an older boy was an umfaan. Then there was guti, a word that is so typically Rhodesian and has no English equivalent. It is more than mist, but not yet rain.

Much later in our lives when Christopher was in the South African army, he was sent to an undisclosed destination and all mail was routed through military headquarters in Pretoria and carefully censored. At the time, there were rumors that the South African forces were in Rhodesia helping their security forces. Both sides vehemently denied this. We had a letter from Christopher telling us it was a guti day and I felt certain he was in Rhodesia. When he went on to say he had seen Method, we knew exactly where he was. Method had been one of our employees. It later transpired he was in fact in Rhodesia. He was in the Parabats, a parachute battalion. They had been issued with Rhodesian army uniforms and even Rhodesian I.D. tags and sent to the Malapati area which was then considered a 'hot spot'.

Chapter 5

Christopher and Simon enjoyed our weekends together but they dearly wanted to spend them at home. We were told that the Mathers had children at school in Fort Victoria. Mr. Mather was the Station Master at Mbizi, about 50 miles from us. We thought we might be able to come to an arrangement whereby we could bring the children down and the Mathers could take them back.

We had to go up to Salisbury to pick up some camping equipment we had bought, so we had to take the two ton Mazda truck. As it was the rainy season, it was possible we could get stuck if it rained as the Mazda didn't have four wheel drive. It seemed sensible to have the Land Rover to haul it out if necessary. We could leave the Land Rover at Nuanetsi, since the road was hard top from there on.

The plan was for me to take the Land Rover up along the railway line to Mbizi to speak to the Mathers. Paul would take the direct route to Nuanetsi and attend to some matters with the District Commissioner and then wait for me there. I had never been along the railway line, but Paul explained that immediately after I crossed over the railway line I should turn left. It seemed a poor road even by bush standards but I pressed on. It was a beautiful sunny day with the early morning dew still on the grass. The vast expanse of mopani in every direction seemed endless. The only thing to remind me of civilization was the railway line. I was reminding myself how lucky I was to be able to experience all this. I was brought down to earth with a thud as the Land Rover lurched. I found that one of the little mopani bushes I had ridden over was in fact a large jagged tree stump that had sprouted again. I had not only punctured two tires but buckled both wheels as well. This was quite a problem as I only had one spare wheel. I was to discover that I was on the railway service road, right next to the railway line. The road I should have taken ran parallel to it, about twenty-five yards away, and was in any case not a much used road. I realized Paul would assume I had stayed to have tea with the Mathers and wouldn't become anxious until lunchtime.

This was the main Bulawayo/Maputo railway line and trains came by at regular intervals. I was dressed for town in a wool suit, panty hose, and my good shoes. I clambered through the fence and tore my hose on the barbed wire. I tried flagging down a couple of trains going in my direction by waving frantically, but the driver just waved back equally frantically until he disappeared round the bend, no doubt glad to have had a diversion.

At lunchtime, an African on a bicycle stopped to commiserate. I gave him a note to anyone who had a telephone, explaining my predicament and asking them to call Paul at the D.C.'s office at Nuanetsi. I gave the man a dollar for his trouble. The hours dragged by and the sun began to set. In the distance, I heard the sound of an engine and a vehicle drew up behind me. Pete Kok, from Mpakati, arrived with two new wheels. He had found the note on his dining room table. The enterprising man I had dispatched with the note had found no one but the cook home. He had left the note for Pete Kok, but he had also taken the precaution of calling the D.C.'s office at Nuanetsi, so a short while later Paul arrived with another two wheels. By this time it was dark and Pete invited us to spend the night at their house at Mpakati. Pete was the government Agricultural Officer who was in charge of development of the three irrigation schemes - Malikanga near Chikombedzi, Chilonga on the Lundi River, and Manjinji, which was down our way. At these irrigation schemes, the tribes people were encouraged, under the expert guidance of African Agricultural Demonstrators, to grow cash crops. Seed and fertilizer had been supplied free initially and each person had been allocated one acre for which they had to pay a nominal rental of one dollar a month. The government transported and marketed their produce for them and hoped in this way to help these primitive people to raise their standard of living and to teach them to be self-supporting. Chilonga and Malikanga were fairly successful but Manjinji was eventually closed. The Shangaans lacked the drive to continue. The authorities were frustrated at every turn. After the first season, the Africans were expected to use part of their profit to contribute towards the cost of the next season's seed and fertilizer. They bought the seed under protest, as they obviously couldn't grow anything without seed, but they were not prepared to pay for fertilizer. Pete explained they had to replenish what they took from the soil and insisted they buy the subsidized fertilizer. He later discovered many of them had dug a hole and buried it rather than take the trouble to spread it.

The Chilonga scheme was a model of its kind. When farmers attained a given crop quota for three successive seasons, they were awarded a Master Farmer's badge. It was an enormous brass medallion and a great status symbol. In African society, it is generally the woman who does the manual labor, so it was quite common to see a woman wearing a Master Farmer's Badge. The Sengwe Africans, near us, were not yet ready for organized agriculture. They were remote and had not been touched by civilization to the same extent as had the Chilonga farmers. They were content with their age-old method of farming. When the soil became exhausted, they abandoned the village and moved to new ground. They set fire to a new area of bush and then cultivated that for a few years. If they had really good rains one season, they wouldn't bother to plant anything the following year. It was a simple outlook and they may have been hungry sometimes, but they didn't get ulcers. They were a tremendous frustration to a government who was trying hard to incorporate them into the twentieth century.

Pete Kok was a thirty-five year old bachelor. He had black hair and a deep tan from being in the sun all day. He was very quiet and had a rather diffident way about him. He had a nervous laugh which hid the real person. When one questioned him on anything about agriculture or the practical mechanics of farming, one realized he was very knowledgeable. He was an incredibly kind and helpful person.

Pete lived with his mother at Mpakati which was close to Chikombedzi and about midway between the two most distant irrigation schemes. Nevertheless, a trip to Manjinji or Chilonga, although it was only 35 miles, still amounted to a minor safari. Mrs. Kok was a widow who had produced eight children, of which Pete was her second youngest. Several years earlier, she had come down to Mpakati to get Pete 'settled in' and she had stayed. She was an amiable extrovert who loved company. When they came down to Manjinji, it was generally for about three days. The vehicle was packed to the hilt, with Pete's African orderly sitting on top of it all. The Land Rover was a vintage model and a quick getaway was impossible as various wires had to be connected to get it working. No one else could have driven it as even the gears had a knack to them, and I'm sure the same applied to the brakes. It was a nondescript gray color which might have been the original color or it might have worn down to the base coat with the passage of time.

On one trip down to Manjinji, coming through Gona-re-Zhou, Pete had rounded a corner and found himself confronted by an elephant. It flapped its ears and raised its trunk and with a spine-chilling trumpet, it came for them. Pete had slammed the Land Rover into reverse and stalled the engine. They watched in horror as the great beast bore down on them and stopped only a few feet from the radiator. Even Pete, who seldom dramatized anything, admitted to having been shaken by the experience. After that, with every elephant that made a rush at them, Mrs. Kok relived their nightmare experience. Elephants were her particular phobia and she refused to travel through the Game Reserve after 4 p.m. when the elephants were likely to be on the move.

Pete and his mother were generally away during the week and returned home on Fridays. Like most country women, Mrs. Kok was an excellent cook and very hospitable. She was plump, friendly and vibrant and she spoke her mind about everything. Her home, although only established since coming to live with Pete, was comfortable and interesting. She had a magpie quality which most people acquire to some degree in the bush. Her veranda was crammed with a fantastic assortment of bric-a-brac of the bush variety - bits of driftwood, gourds, quaint walking sticks, crystal quarts or smooth river stones. Only such a colorful personality could have coped with Pete. He was a very quiet and gentle person. I only knew him to get angry twice.

Chapter 6

On one occasion Pete had an altercation with the Game Warden of Gona-re-Zhou over a trivial incident. The Warden in his offensive way had angered Pete who, in replying, had made his point rather strongly by poking the Warden in his chest with his finger. Three hours later when Pete arrived at Nuanetsi, the Warden had already reported him to the District Commissioner for attempted assault. Pete's anger had subsided by that time and his only comment to the D.C. had been typically terse — "I wish I really had assaulted him sir."

On another occasion some months later Pete was down at the Malapati government rest house across the river from us. Two other government officials, an Animal Health Inspector, and a young policeman were also using the rest house. It was comfortable but had no electricity which precluded most things except going to bed early. The evenings were long and tedious and the three young men had decided to go out and shoot spring hares in the Tribal area, a perfectly legitimate pursuit. Pete always carried a light caliber rifle, as he was occasionally called on by the tribesmen to shoot duiker or other small buck which strayed into the irrigation scheme and damaged their crops.

We had a film crew staying with us at the time, and they were anxious to tape the sound of an elephant trumpeting. We thought if we went to Mankonde Pool we would be sure to find elephants. But for once they were not there and we decided to continue on into Gona-re-Zhou along our access route to Buffalo Bend which was part of the Malapati Game Reserve. We reached the river crossing at the Bend without seeing a single elephant and decided to return home.

The Warden was in Buffalo Bend, which was part of Malapati, shooting impala for rations for his African staff. He should in any case have been shooting in the Game Reserve and not in Malapati, but prior to our arrival, they had had the run of the entire area. When he heard the sound of our vehicle, he sent a young ranger to investigate. He could still see our dust, but we were some distance ahead of him. When we turned off onto our road, he missed us, continued on, and crossed the river. By now he was convinced he was tracking poachers who were trying to evade him. He picked up the sound of Pete's vehicle cruising around and went to the rest camp and asked the attendant whether there were people staying in the camp. He said there were, but they had gone out hunting. When Pete and his party arrived back, the ranger confronted them and accused them of poaching. He asked to see the carcass. When they looked puzzled, he examined the back of Pete's Land Rover where he saw some water from a leaking water bag.

"You have already washed the blood out of your vehicle."

Pete in his mild manner had tried to explain, but the young ranger felt so sure of his facts he would only comment, "The Warden will deal with you. He would like to have the likes of you barred from the area."

By now he had said enough to Pete, to whom the mere mention of the Warden's name was anathema. Pete used a few choice phrases and again used his attempted assault technique. Feeling some doubts in the face of all this, the ranger called in and asked us whether we had been driving round. We told him where we had been, unaware of what had happened. The following morning, an African game scout arrived with a letter from the Warden. It told us that his ranger had been deeply embarrassed as a result of our driving around at night and he would have no hesitation in recommending that we be barred from entering Gona-re-Zhou when it was proclaimed a National Park. He sent a copy to his Regional Warden and a copy to his head office in Salisbury.

We had heard stories of the Warden's ambitious drive and his determination to let nothing stand in his way to the top. We had decided not to let his reputation color our relationship with him. When we had first met him, he had been friendly. He and his wife were educated people who enjoyed music and we had been glad to have people our own age with whom we could make easy contact. Mabalauta, where they were based, was only fifteen miles from us. We had had dinner with them and they with us. Only a week before the 'poaching' incident, the Warden had spent the morning with us and had borrowed several bags of cement to complete their swimming pool. We were naturally taken aback by the tone of his letter, when so much more could have been achieved had he driven over and discussed it in a friendly way. But, of course, had he done that neither the Regional Warden nor his head office would have known about the incident. Apart from everything else, we were perfectly at liberty to drive through the Game Reserve since this was our only access to Buffalo Bend, which was part of Malapti.

At this stage, the Warden decided he wanted a record of people entering the area, and he provided a visitor's book in a little office manned by one of his game scouts. A stone cairn proclaimed "ALL TRAFFIC MUST REPORT TO THE OFFICE." It was not couched as a request and irritated the locals who used this route as an access to some other point. For the most part, they chose to ignore the annoying directive. A Ranger was sent after one District Officer from Internal Affairs. The D.O. did in fact go back and words were exchanged which I am sure the Warden later regretted. Shortly after this incident, the D.O. was appointed District Commissioner which made him the supreme authority in the area and in a position to make things very difficult for this particular Warden had he chosen to do so.

In this vast wilderness, one could hear a vehicle engine from miles away. Had the Warden just made a point of going out when he heard a vehicle and approached each of the regular road users and explained that he wanted a record of traffic to justify his claim for extra funds for road building or extra staff, or whatever his reasons were, I am quite sure everyone would have complied.

This same Warden once found himself out of beer and he drove to the police club at Vila Salazaar, about twenty miles away on the Mozambique border. He joined them for lunch and then asked whether they could sell him a crate of beer. A police orderly was sent to pick up the beer and the Warden strolled after him. Hanging up in the cold room was a goat, skinned and decapitated. The Warden asked what it was and the man replied that it was their rations meat.

Since National Parks always use the available game meat for rations, I suppose it was natural he should assume it was an impala carcass, but he said nothing to his hosts. He took his beer and returned home. He then wrote to John Scott, the Member-in-Charge, saying John was obviously not aware that members of his staff were shooting illegally, etc. with the usual copy to the head office. John was extremely angry, not over the understandable assumption that there had been poaching by the police, but by the fact that he had said nothing about it at the time. For once, the copy to head office backfired and he had to write a formal apology. This individual was an aggravation but he did provide many people with endless hours of conversation topics.

Chapter 7

On one of our trips to pick up cement from the railway siding, we met Mr. and Mrs. Palfrey, an elderly Scottish couple who lived on the Mozambique border. They invited us to tea the following day. They were a tremendous source of information on the area. They owned three trading stores - one at Pafuri on the Limpopo River, one close to us and referred to as the Malapati Store, and another at their homestead about twenty miles from us.

The house was built on a slight rise which gave it a view of the countryside for miles in every direction. It had the usual gauzed in veranda and very spacious rooms. On the outside gable was a drawing of a horse and the words "Palfrey's Camp." It gave the elevation and was signed C. Radio von Radius. It transpired that the artist/sign writer had been a surveyor who had done some work in the district many years before. Mr. Palfrey had a wrinkled face and wispy white hair, giving him a Santa Claus look. His eyes were almost black and seemed to sparkle with suppressed laughter. He could see something funny in most things. The only thing which really irked him was officialdom and he was constantly warring with some government department.

It seemed he had recently had words with the Game Department about the signing of the book. He had sailed through Mabalauta as he had done for fifty years and a ranger was sent after him. When the young man stopped him, he listened patiently and then said, "Sonny, you tell your Warden that I have lived here since before he was born and I'm not going to start signing any book now."

Mr. Palfrey was in his eighties but he still managed his stores and chugged around in an aged Land Rover which always seemed to give him trouble. He had very bad arthritis of the fingers and servicing his vehicle was a case of having his 'spanner boy' undo each bolt under his direction.

Whenever we saw him, he had wounds on his hands. When we asked about it, he would be evasive but Mrs. Palfrey told us it was Burky. It seems Burky was part jackal and part German Shepherd and didn't like bathing, so every time he was bathed, the dog bit his master. Mr. Palfrey insisted Burky was otherwise a trusty companion.

Mr. Palfrey had come out to Rhodesia in the early days and had fascinating stories to tell, some against himself on his brushes with authority. His more interesting stories were about eccentrics who had inhabited these parts. He had at one time been in partnership with Mark Spraggon, at Marumbini, in the labor recruiting business for the South African gold mines - WNLA (Witwatersrand Native Labor Association). When the partnership didn't work out, the Palfreys moved to their present home and set up the three stores. Spraggon had remained and had also set up a trading store. When his cash box was stolen one night, he suspected two Shangaans who were promptly summoned and handcuffed. In this remote corner of the country, he was self-proclaimed judge and jury and was reputed to have meted out the punishment too, on occasion. After interrogation, the two suspects still protested their innocence and he set off with them on a trip he would normally only have undertaken once a year. When he returned a week later he told the families the thieves had been imprisoned and had told the magistrate where they hid the cashbox. He dug at the base of a large nyalaberry tree in the one man's village and recovered his money.

When the men didn't return after several years, a family member made the trip to Nuanetsi and found the police knew nothing about the incident. On being questioned by the police later, Spraggon said they had escaped into Mozambique on the trek to Nuanetsi and he had lied to the families because he thought it would sound suspicious! The police accepted this story. In his broad Scottish accent Mr. Palfrey said, "I think he got carried away with the third degree to make them talk."

Mrs. Palfrey gently countered, "Dad, now you don't know that for sure. You weren't there." But he insisted it was true just the same.

He told us of another colorful character called Blake Thompson who had been well known in the Lowveld. He had studied medicine at the Sorbonne in Paris, although he never graduated. After World War I, he had emigrated to Rhodesia. The WNLA recruiting depot had closed down at Marumbini and a Rhodesian group took over, recruiting for their mines. At this stage, Blake Thompson was appointed Manager of the Marumbini Labor Recruiting Depot where Spraggon had once ruled. Thompson was fondly referred to by all as Marumbini Thompson. He was a great extrovert with a vivid imagination. He seldom left Marumbini, but was exhilarated by having visitors. He used his salary to provide medicines for the local Africans. The Palfreys had once called on him and, as was customary in the bush, they had been invited to stay for lunch. The old man regaled them with wild tales. Eventually at 3 p.m. he announced lunch was ready - it was too hot to eat any earlier, he said. "This is lunch and dinner, then my chaps can go." They had an enormous meal at the end of which the old man clapped his hands and the domestic staff filed in, led by the cook. On signal from the boss they began to sing:

"Bye-bye, Sir! Good-bye. Bye-bye, Sir, bye-bye."

To which old Marumbini responded with his own version of the old song. "Bye-bye, Blackbirds. Bye-bye Blackbirds". Then the trio withdrew.

Mrs. Palfrey was a kind and gentle person. She was a stocky little Scot with deep blue eyes and thick white hair. She saw only the good in life and had a childlike quality in her enjoyment of everything. They had a charming home full of beautiful furniture which had been handmade for them many years before out of local woods. Each piece had that special bloom of age from being lovingly cared for over the years.

Mr. Palfrey warned us of the danger of having a gap between the ceiling and the roof when we got to building our house. A large monitor lizard weighing about ten pounds had once crawled into their roof during the cold weather and settled itself on the ceiling. In urinating, it had softened the ceiling boards and one day it had come hurtling down onto the dining room table.

While we were having tea, two Customs officers from Vila Salazar border post called in. We were to find this 'calling in' of passers-by a regular feature of bush life. Mrs. Palfrey fussed over them in her motherly way. Shortly after tea, they left. On our way home, we encountered them walking back to the Palfreys. Their vehicle had broken down and they wanted to use the Palfreys telephone. We felt quite sure they didn't have a telephone but the Customs men felt equally sure they did.

Sure enough, the Palfreys didn't have any means of communication, except by mail which was sent to Nyala Siding twice a week. The canvas mailbag would be left in a little hut by the side of the railway line. Outgoing mail would be put into the bag and picked up by the train going the other way again. The Palfreys also had their provisions and supplies for the store railed down. It was hard to think of these two old people having lived in this remote spot for most of their lives.

Their three children had been sent to boarding school from here when the present roads were just tracks in the bush. The children were driven down to the Limpopo River and from there they were taken across to South Africa in a small row boat. They were then taken by the WNLA truck ferrying recruits (known as blackbirds) to work on the gold mines. At Soekmekaar, the WNLA depot, the children were put on the train by a recruiting officer and the school met the train in Johannesburg. Mrs. Palfrey wasn't able to drive and I asked her what would happen should her husband become ill. She replied with a serene smile that she would send their houseboy on a bicycle with a note to the police camp at Vila Salazaar.

We offered to take the two young men back to Vila Salazaar. They showed us a 'short cut' along the Mozambique border fence. It was a precipitous track and I feared we might cut our tires on the jagged rocks. We were able to recognize landmarks Mr. Palfrey had told us about. The early surveyor Radio von Radius had pointed out this area as being, in his opinion, the end of the Great Rift Valley. It was an interesting drive, but it would have been quicker to have gone back along the Gona-re-Zhou fence and through the Game Reserve on relatively flat dirt roads. We did an extra 40 miles playing the Good Samaritan, but we were to find that in the bush one was very dependent on one's fellow man. City dwellers did not jeopardize their survival if they remained aloof from their neighbors. In the bush, no matter how well organized or self-contained one was, once in a while there would be a mishap and one would need help, always readily given, with the friendly assurance that it was 'no trouble at all.'

Vila Salazar turned out to be a little border post on the Rhodesian side, and it consisted of a police camp, two Customs officials, two Immigration officials, and the Animal Health Inspector. It was dreary, set in sandy mopani scrub which grew only a few feet high. The personnel, all bachelors, were generally only posted there for three months at a time. The police numbered about eleven whites and about twice that many Africans and they had made themselves very comfortable. They had a quaint little clubhouse called the Gona-Stagga-Inn. It would perhaps have been more aptly named the Gona-Stagga-Out.

John Scott was the senior officer at Vila Salazar and as such was the Member-in-Charge. He was a thick set, ruddy faced, young Englishman who had come out to Rhodesia to join the British South African Police, a name the Rhodesian police had retained since the days of the Chartered Company which had founded Rhodesia. John had an easy manner with his staff, but he managed to retain strict discipline, not an easy matter when one lived in such close proximity to one's subordinates.

The Rhodesians had named their border post after Dr. Salazar, then President of Portugal, and the Portuguese had reciprocated by naming theirs Malvernia, after the first Federal Prime Minister, Lord Malvern. Fortunately for the Portuguese, Sir Godfrey Huggins had been given a peerage in 1955 and became Lord Malvern, or their settlement might have had the bizarre name of Hugginsia!

A number of political detainees, including Joshua Nkomo, were held in the detention camp close by, which accounted for the relatively large number of policemen. The camp was not visible from the road but several large notices warned that this was a restricted area.

John Scott invited us over for a barbecue and a movie the following Saturday evening. These Saturday night barbecues were a regular thing and it was their way of repaying hospitality extended to the police while they were out on patrol. Each Monday a Patrol Officer was sent out, followed later in the week by a Section Officer, to check on possible problems in the area. They always called in to see us and stayed for tea or a meal.

Vila Salazar was about twenty miles from us, through the Gona-re-Zhou Game Reserve, along an appalling road which the elephants made worse by pushing trees across it at frequent intervals. The road was a series of detours into the bush around these obstructions. This road was not open to tourist traffic, but although the Warden allowed local traffic to use it, it was not maintained. It was used by us on our trips to Nyala Siding, by the Animal Health Inspector on his trips into the Sengwe Tribal Trust Lands, and by the police on their rounds. John Scott once offered to send the police five-ton truck into Gona-re-Zhou along this road to remove the fallen trees, on condition that the police camp could utilize the firewood. For people living in the area, wood was the only form of fuel for cooking or heating. The Warden refused the offer. He felt it would disturb the balance of Nature. The termites would in time remove the trees.

We were to encounter this pettiness on more than one occasion and one had to learn to laugh it off. It was very easy, living in the bush in comparative isolation, to lose one's sense of perspective and over-react to these things.

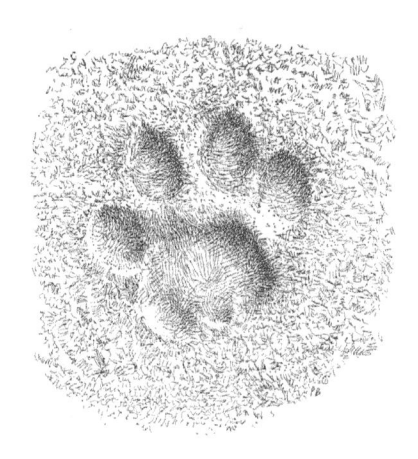

Chapter 8

On our daily trips between the rest camp and Malapati we would encounter a wide assortment of game. An entry in my journal shows that one morning as we were leaving the rest camp, we almost collided with a buffalo. A short distance further, we came across a herd of zebra and later, three different herds of elephants, totaling thirty-six in all.

We came to know where we could find the beautiful nyala, a rare antelope which inhabits the riverine vegetation. We discovered the 'hog spot' where a family of warthogs would invariably emerge from the ground and take off with their tails characteristically erect like little antennas. They would run for some distance and then stop to look at us.

Four young Bat Eared Foxes must have had their lair near the road because we frequently saw them, their soft coats reflecting the last of the sunlight and their enormous ears erect to catch the slightest sound. They were always at the same place as we drove back to the camp at night. One evening, we found a pack of wild dogs devouring an impala. They barely paused as we drew up to watch them then resumed their hurried feeding. As we rounded a corner one night, we almost collided with a male lion. We stopped and he crossed the road ahead of us and then lay down and watched us in an irritated manner. A little further on, we came across a large herd of buffalo crossing the road. They jostled each other like cattle as they made way for us in their dusty confusion. It seemed we had disturbed the lion that was following the buffalo. We estimated their number at about two hundred and fifty.

One of the Land Rovers needed attention and we decided to go up to Fort Victoria for the day and do some shopping at the same time. Our Siamese cat MacGregor spent most of his day sleeping, so we always left him at the camp while we were working at Malapati. He would hear our vehicle approaching at night, come to life, and rush out to greet us lovingly. I thought we might possibly be back from Fort Victoria late, so I asked the camp attendant to feed MacGregor that evening. Piccolo, our Fox Terrier, always travelled with us so she was no problem.

Unfortunately, the garage couldn't attend to the vehicle until the following day and we had to spend the night in town. When we arrived back at Swimuweni the following afternoon, MacGregor didn't rush out to meet us. The camp attendant told us the cat had eaten the previous evening but he was gone the following morning. When there was still no sign of him the next morning, we became anxious. His hearing and eyesight were no longer very good and he had never fended for himself. We scoured the camp and surroundings all day. The following day, we picked up five of the laborers from Malapati and brought them to the camp. We offered a substantial reward for the one who found him, dead or alive.

The disturbing thought was that he might be lying injured somewhere, or caught on a branch by the collar I had so foolishly left on him when we left the city. The temperature had reached 98 one day, followed by heavy rain that night. Had he survived that, there were still the predators. Wild dogs had been round the camp for two nights in a row. On the third day, we accepted that he was gone for good. I realized that after twelve years we didn't even have a picture of him. I packed away his food and water bowls. It seemed such an unsatisfactory ending for an old friend who had shared the greater part of our married life.

That evening MacGregor limped in, bedraggled, disheveled, and with very sore paws. He had obviously covered a great distance looking for us. I removed the collar and the next morning, MacGregor was photographed for the record. I have often wondered what stories he would have to tell if he could talk.

We were finding the daily drive from the rest camp to Malapati interesting, but we were adding unnecessary mileage to the Land Rover. We had bought eight tents from a safari company and we now set five of these up at Malapati. We had a large double tent for ourselves, a smaller one for the boys, a dining tent, and two which served as storerooms. Our tent housed our two beds, a dressing table, a book stand, a desk and typewriter as well as a treadle sewing machine. The tents had come with collapsible zip-up cupboards and we used one of these for our clothes, but as they were waterproof, and the tent was somewhat crowded, we stood it just outside the entrance where it also acted as a windbreak.

A little below out tent, we leveled an area for an outdoor kitchen. The sink, intended for the new house, was propped on bricks and it made a satisfactory scullery. A sheet of corrugated iron on bricks held the utensils and provisions. I cooked over an open fire and it wasn't always easy. One had to remember to keep adding firewood, utensils became blackened with soot which rubbed off on everything, pots toppled over, and working by lamplight at night, one had to lift the lid of a pot very carefully to prevent moths from fluttering in. In the perverse way smoke does, it would follow me around the fire as I dodged for a clear spot, with eyes streaming.

I baked in a termite mound which Christopher and Simon had hollowed out for me. We had to make a substantial fire inside the hollow and keep it going for several hours until the 'oven' had heated sufficiently. We then removed the embers and placed whatever was to be baked into the oven. The aperture was then closed and sealed with mud to retain the heat. This oven was a great success and produced some delicious casseroles and bread.

The water level in the river had now dropped sufficiently for us to install a temporary well point. This entailed cutting slits into a 2" diameter metal pipe for about twelve inches from the end and hammering the end closed. This 10' long pipe was then driven into the sandy river bed. The piping was attached to this rod and to the pump which sucked the water up through the slits with the sand acting as a filter. The water came out clear and sweet. The subterranean water in the area was heavily impregnated with mineral salts and had such a strong taste that one could detect it even in tea or coffee. Now our water was well filtered, and it was a joy to have clear, fresh water of our own.

We built a rustic open-air shower and an equally rustic long drop toilet, some distance away. We were now living at Malapati in comparative comfort. We had our share of dramas while we were living in our tented camp. We were woken one night with an enormous crash of pots and pans. My first thought was that the elephants had walked through my 'kitchen'. It had been raining and the newly leveled kitchen area had subsided and everything had collapsed into a heap at the bottom the slope.

We frequently heard elephants browsing in the bush around us and I sometimes had the fearful vision of a curious elephant lifting the tent, leaving us exposed and cowering in our beds.

One night, we were sitting outside having coffee when we heard the impala blowing the way they do when they're alarmed. Piccolo, who was very much a city bred dog and afraid of the dark anyway, retreated into the tent. We shone a flashlight around and picked up the eyes of an enormous herd of impala circling our camp. The following morning we discovered what had alarmed them. We found the spoor of two lionesses and a lion. They had passed not twenty yards from our tent. We tracked the spoor down to the soft river sand where we could see a clear imprint of their pads. The male had the biggest paws we were ever to see at Malapati. It was larger than my hand with the fingers extended. Paul took a plaster cast which we later hung in the pub.

Another night, we were woken by a lion roaring so close that we could feel the vibrations. I was suddenly very aware that there was only canvas between him and us. Paul assured me there was nothing to fear, but he later admitted that he too had been worried. On the whole, it was pleasant lying in bed with the sounds of the night all around us. It was fun trying to identify the various noises and to think of all the activity which took place in the bush each night.

One evening before going to bed, we walked up to the long drop - our version of an outhouse. We were accompanied as usual by Piccolo, who wouldn't be left for a minute in these wilds. An equally anxious MacGregor brought up the rear with the loud protests that only a Siamese cat can make. As we were about to retrace our steps, our old cat decided to investigate the structure, jumped up, missed his footing, and plummeted into the depths. Since it was a fairly new long drop, there was no immediate danger to MacGregor but he was unhappy and we had to get him out somehow. Paul peered down the hole and hastily withdrew. After much persuasion, he hoisted himself down into the depths and handed up a very bedraggled old cat and Paul and MacGregor spent most of the night washing themselves.

On one of our trips to town, we bought a 2,000 gallon water tank which we loaded onto the back of the Mazda. We also had a quantity of white plastic plumbing pipes which were difficult to strap on. Whichever way we tied them, they worked loose and we had to make frequent stops. This made us very late returning home and driving through the Game Reserve after dark meant that one would inevitably be charged by elephants. With the tank on the back and the white pipes protruding, we looked like a caricature of an elephant. Perhaps we were sufficiently formidable, because that night we didn't even see an elephant.

We discovered that living in the bush produced 'experts' in every field. Whatever one wanted to do, there was always someone who knew all about it and each person's advice was quite contrary to the last person's. There were also the people who didn't know how to do it but knew how not to do it. They would cite a case of someone who had done this very thing the wrong way, always with disastrous consequences. Trying to decide on a support for our water tank was one of these instances. One person would suggest a metal framework. "Much too costly," the next one would say, "You can't utilize the storage space below. Build a storeroom underneath."

"The roof would collapse under that weight of water," the next one would say.

"Use one inch reinforcing rods in your concrete slab."

"Play safe and put a supporting pillar in the middle."

Finally we decided to build a storeroom. We used corrugated iron as shuttering for the concrete slab which we reinforced with half inch rods. It not only held the weight of one full tank, but we later put up another 3,000 gallon tank. While we were building this storeroom, Paul used John, one of our laborers, as his assistant to mix cement and pass the bricks. Thinking that John might enjoy his job more if he knew what they were making, Paul tried to explain to him. Paul had always been short on any language but English and he knew only about two words of Shangaan which served him. Lo "this"

and lapa "there" were his favorite words. Gesticulating, Paul pointed to the water tank and said, "I want to take "lo" and put it "lapa." John looked at the rising walls and then at the enormous tank and thinking he was being asked to lift the tank onto the top of the tower, he grinned and with the cheerful willingness of an African, he said "Me try." This is an endearing quality Africans have. No matter how crazy a white man's request they will always try to comply.

Chapter 9

We were now ready to start work on our house and we contacted an African called Roger Ntuli. He had some experience in building cattle dips and he agreed to supervise the building of the house for us. With him came Juta and Edson who were bricklayers. Edson was the son of a chief who had for some reason given up his chieftainship and now worked for the D.C. in Nuanetsi. Edson was quiet with a dignity which distinguished him from the others. He spoke good English and was the smartest of our employees. Perhaps he had been allowed to remain at school longer than the others had, but we had the feeling that some of our labor force could have stayed in school forever without noticeable improvement.

We took on Shadrek, Julius, and Renos as general assistants to the bricklayers. Renos had the distinction of being able to bend his tongue so as to whistle out of both sides of his mouth at the same time which greatly impressed Christopher and Simon. We pegged out the foundations for the house. We wanted to pour the slab in one operation and Graham Millar lent us the government's cement mixer. The laborers loved it. It symbolized the white man's ability to avoid sweat and toil. They ran back and forth with their wheelbarrows, chanting and joking. We were not quite finished when the light faded, so we parked the vehicles and turned on the headlights until we had finished.

We designed the house around a central patio with the living room and kitchen on one side, the dining room across the top, and the two bedrooms with a bathroom between them along the other side. The bathroom had two doors so it could be accessed from either room. The front of the house was open and looked down onto the thick riverine vegetation with the river beyond. All the rooms had French doors leading onto the patio. The outer walls had large openings about four feet by seven feet with brick piers, and would have screens instead of glass to allow maximum air flow during the summer and to keep the insects out. Off the main kitchen we had a smaller "hot kitchen." This would house the wood burning stove which became very hot in summer. There seemed to be no reason to have an outside door leading into the hot kitchen, so we just made an archway. We later found that bats were attracted by the warmth at night, but by this time all the building activity was centered on the Lodge and domestic alterations were low on the list of priorities. I asked Renos to make what we called a 'bat curtain' of strings of threaded reeds, each piece separated by a 1" ring of PVC pipe, and hanging parallel to each other, suspended from a rod at the top. As it was only used at night, it was tucked away onto the outside windowsill during the day to allow easy access during the day. We had so enjoyed our shower under the stars that we added a shower leading off the bathroom. It had a screen wall about seven feet high and room for a small shade garden in the corner, so we were still able to shower under the stars.

Juta was assigned to making the brick piers in the dining room. He was small and very dark with a very serious expression. He worked slowly and was very proud of his bricklaying. The gap between the columns was 4" wide and he had reached a height of about five feet. He was standing back admiring his handiwork when Wilson, wearing his one-lensed sunglasses, swung a scaffold plank and knocked the whole lot down. I thought Juta would cry. In true African tradition, the entire labor force crowded around to view the tragedy with many expressions of regret. Then they turned their attention to Wilson and now the laughter broke out. Perhaps it was the fault of the glasses. Possibly the lens he had couldn't see. With an air of great resignation, Juta cleaned up the debris and started again with instructions to Wilson to stay away.

The District Commissioner decided to build a new rest house near the high level bridge. Alongside it, they built a house for Roy and Anne Borlase. Roy was the new Field Assistant and was presently housed at Mpakati near Chikombedzi. Roy's duties were to supervise the dipping of the tribesmen's cattle, road construction and maintenance, and to keep an eye on matters in the district. He had to submit a weekly report and once a month he had to attend a meeting at the D.C.'s office at Nuanetsi. He was in daily contact with Head Office by two-way radio which was operated by the District Messenger. Manuel had replaced Titus as District Messenger. Manuel was tall and with almost Arabic features. He had served with the Rhodesian troops in Burma and his bearing was very military. His khaki uniform was always immaculate and he wore his service decorations very proudly. In the course of the month, complaints and reports would be recorded and dealt with at the monthly meeting in Nuanetsi. At one of these meetings, a Field Assistant whose spelling was rather poor, had recorded in his report that he needed "two more munts" to complete a job. The D.C. had been horrified at the use of the word 'munt.' It was an abbreviation of the word 'muntu' which in several African languages meant a person, but abbreviated it was sometimes used by whites to refer to Africans and had taken on a derogatory connotation. It was naturally frowned upon in official circles, especially in this Ministry which handled tribal affairs. The D.C. pointed to the offending word and asked what he meant by it. The Field Assistant looked at the report and replied "Sorry Sir, it just means it's going to take longer. I left the H out. That should have been "two more munths."

We had our doorframes railed down and we bought our roofing timbers from a firm in Chiredzi. There we met Chris Sparrow, a well-known rancher in the area. He would come down periodically to visit and he always remembered to bring us newspapers and bread. Everyone who came to Malapati enthused about our homemade bread, but to us, bought bread tasted like cake. Chris had grown up on a ranch and he knew this. Newspapers were a luxury, especially when they were hot off the press. My sister Edna sent us the Sunday newspapers from Johannesburg and they arrived two weeks later via the African bus. We read them avidly and then passed them on to the staff who couldn't appreciate the contents but they were highly prized. They used them for wrapping things and for starting their cooking fires. Those newspapers certainly were used to the maximum.

I was working in my new vegetable garden and as I dug I felt resistance, rather like rubber. I dug again and out jumped a very large and angry frog, which growled at me aggressively. Allowing for the fact that a frog is the one creature I am terrified of, I was still not prepared for my family's reaction to this story. Some time later, I read a newspaper article which described these frogs. They are Pyxicephalus Adsperses, which not only have teeth and are carnivorous, but they can 'bark' and growl aggressively. They quoted a Mr. Gary Gray of the Zoology Department of the University of Capetown, a venerable institution. He told of these frogs stopping a soccer match in Bulawayo when they swarmed onto the field and bit the ankles of the players. How I wished I had had access to all that information at the time when my family fell about laughing at my encounter with the frog that 'growled.'

One morning, Jerry came to me in his doleful way and said a porcupine had dug up some of the potatoes. This was bad news, as we had to have fresh vegetables. We spent the day fencing but that night the porcupine dug under the fence. The following day, we dug a trench under the fence and filled it with stones, but again he burrowed through. By now he had unearthed all the potatoes and was digging up the onions, which he didn't eat. It seemed he would systematically destroy the whole vegetable garden. We waited up for him that night and as he trotted up the path in the moonlight, Paul shot him. He quivered for an instant, rattling his quills, and then he dropped.

When we came up to his lifeless body, he looked so defenseless and I felt a horrible remorse at having initiated this. We were the intruders and he had only been doing what he had always done, foraging for food at night. I resolved then never again to destroy anything like that. If I couldn't keep them out, I would accept it as one of the hazards of living in a wilderness area and plant a little more for us all. The duiker and monkeys jumped over the fence, francolin flew over, and on one occasion the elephants stepped over the fence, but somehow there was always some left for us. Buffalo also proved trying during the dry spells. On more than one occasion they chomped our banana plants down to the ground.

The walls of the house were up and the roof was on. I had always wanted to have brick floors, so Paul decided he would try to make them. We were to learn that one could improvise successfully for most commodities when one has to. He made 3" x 4" x 8" standard bricks in a brick mold and when they were just beginning to set, he sprinkled a mixture of pure cement and brown pigment on the top and then smoothed it with a metal trowel. It was a slow process but very successful and we soon had Renos trained to do them. We did all our floors this way and the finished effect was most attractive.

We were given a set of pipe dyes and with the help of the "How to do Your Own plumbing" Paul was able to do this tedious job. We decided to let a carpenter from Chikombedzi do the various cupboards. His name was Philamon and he spoke good English. He was a large, very dark Karanga with a disconcerting way of staring at one before replying. When he was doing the kitchen cupboards, I frequently had occasion to be in there for long spells with him and we conversed about different topics. It always interested me to hear the black people's views on some topics. We had been warned that he was "a political trouble-maker" but his views didn't seem radical to me. One day he startled me by asking, "Do you favor rape?" I was taken aback but managed to blurt out, "No, I don't think I do."

His next question baffled me. "Have you ever tried it?" I assured him I hadn't and left the kitchen, rather shaken. The next day Philamon presented me with a bunch of what looked like cauliflower leaves. "This is rape. Would you like to try it?" It turned out to be kale. I felt so foolish but somehow the mission educated Africans always used certain words and phrases in a quaint way. It always amused me when I asked a rather mundane question like, "Have you fed the chickens?" to have the pontifical reply, "I have failed to do so." Another peculiarity of speech many of them had was to repeat things after one. They might ask if they could have the day off on Friday. If I replied with a simple yes or no, that would be fine, but if I elaborated by saying I wanted them back on time the next morning after their day off, they would repeat "Day off?" as though it was I who had first mentioned it and they didn't know what I was talking about. I concluded they needed time to formulate a reply and they used the process of repeating a word or phrase to allow themselves time to think.

Roy and Ann Borlase moved into their house at about the same time as we moved into ours. By city standards they were a long way from us, about four miles, but in the bush they were our neighbors. Ann was small, gentle and soft-spoken. She was an extremely kind person and very shy. Roy was a great extrovert and knowledgeable on a wide range of subjects. He did all the vehicle maintenance with the help of his 'spanner boy,' Phineas, and he could turn his hand to almost anything. He had taught himself to paint and to play the guitar and, with a little more opportunity, I think Roy could have excelled in one of many fields. His job as Field Assistant necessitated traveling throughout the district. He was in touch with what was going on and he was a useful source of information.

Our house proved to be the most functional we ever had. It was ideally suited to the climate and our needs. We did discover though that the cement mixture Roger had used to build our house was the same as he used in making the cattle dips which have to withstand the impact of a beast plunging into the water. It seemed our house was not just functional - it would probably stand forever!

Roger bought a store which he now wanted to manage. We felt we had gained enough experience with the building of the house to be able to undertake the building of the tourist accommodation without him. At any rate, we would try.

Chapter 10

We had just moved into our house when Ronnie and Colleen Wilson, old friends from Johannesburg, wrote to say they would like to visit. As they were a family of five, we decided to let them have the house and we moved back into the tents. Christopher and Simon were due home for the school holidays and they were coming by train to Nyala Siding. They were due at 9 p.m. and as the train just stopped to let them off in the vast, dark expanse of bush, we had to be sure of being there when they arrived. I stayed home with our guests and Paul set off to meet the train.

The elephants had pushed trees across the road, but one was usually able to find a way around through the surrounding bush. Paul made several attempts to get past, but large fallen trees blocked his way in every direction. He tried to move the tree blocking his way, but he found it too heavy for one person to lift. An elephant trumpeted close behind him and with that spurt of adrenaline that comes in times of crisis, he picked up the fallen tree and pulled it out of the way. He arrived at the siding just as the boys were getting off the train.

That night we had three lions roaring from different directions around the house and we realized the wisdom of having put the Wilsons in the house. After dinner the following evening, Simon took the gas lamp and set off for the tents. Christopher had a bad cold and we thought sleeping in the tent was not a good idea, so we had put up a camp bed for him in the kitchen. As Simon stepped off the patio, Ronnie asked him whether he was not afraid of going off on his own. Simon assured him he wasn't. When we went to bed, we could hear Simon singing very loudly in his tent. He was still fully clothed, sitting on his bed. He told us the elephants had been pulling branches off the surrounding trees and he had been too shy to come back and admit to being nervous.

Without electricity, our laundry had to be done by hand. I asked Jerry whether he knew of anyone who would do the laundry. His number one wife was Esther. The other was Nandi whom he had inherited from his dead brother. He thought Esther could do it because she was "more clever than Nandi."

Esther was overwhelmed by everything, including me. I left her with the clothes and the soap powder. When I returned ten minutes later Esther was still standing as I had left her. I called Jerry in to see what the problem was. She didn't know how to make the water come! I measured out the soap powder, put the plug in, and turned the water on. With an enormous smile she attacked the washing.

Suddenly I heard shrieks coming from Esther. I ran in to find the water about to overflow and still running. She didn't know how to make it stop. I realized I was going to have to start from scratch with her. So much that I took for granted was totally new to her. She had always done her laundry at the river and the fact that hot water could come out of a faucet was quite wonderful to her. She never did get used to the idea of using hot water for the laundry, but she managed to get the clothes clean just the same.

Esther found it difficult to understand my accent and she would stare at me wide-eyed. Jerry had taught her to say, "Good Morning Madam," and she said this to me whenever she saw me, regardless of the time of day. She never quite mastered Madam - it always came out as Mother.

Jerry told us of an African called James who could make furniture. We sent word that we would like to see him. He arrived on an ancient bicycle which had a wooden seat, and one pedal also made of wood. He was a light colored Ndebele with a roguish smile and a lovely sense of humor. He told us he had mahogany trees felled and maturing and would be happy to make the Lodge furniture for us. It seems he dug a pit in the forest under a selected, fallen tree. Then, he stood in the pit with a helper at the other end of a two-handled saw to cut the planks and plane them smooth. From these he made up the various pieces. He eventually made the dining room tables and chairs, furniture for the guest huts and all the doors. But James could be trying. He worked feverishly just before cattle sales which were held at Sengwe every six weeks and overseen by the District Commissioner's Office. People came from all the surrounding districts and the day before the sale was like a fair. Hawkers sold sugar cane and beer flowed freely. This was what attracted James. Just before the sales, he would come for an advance and then we wouldn't see him again for weeks. Fortunately for us, his father took tremendous pride in his work assisted James. Left to himself, James might have given us three-legged chairs. This was strange because the Ndebele were known to be industrious and enthusiastic about handcrafts.

When we needed extra labor, we would mention it to our staff who would provide a suitable person of their choice. We found this worked well because the person was either a relative or friend and there was a greater camaraderie and rapport among them. On one occasion, we employed a laborer who had appeared at the door and asked for work. The first day all went well, but halfway through the next day, someone commented that the new man was not around. Instantly, everyone stopped work and a search party set off at a trot for the compound where they all lived. It then transpired that the man had a reputation for being a thief and was shunned by everyone. They now suspected he had decided what he wanted to take from the compound and had slipped away to do so while they were all at work. The remaining workers may as well have joined the search party because they did no work. They stood around recounting similar incidents. It seemed their fears were justified because they found the man at the compound. They dealt with him and sent him on his way, and the rest of the day was written off because it was spent re-enacting the scene and recounting the dialogue. We asked why, if they knew the man was dishonest, had they not said anything when we employed him. Because we hadn't asked them!

At this stage we employed William Chauke. I planned to train him as the cook for the Lodge when we had guests. He was Jerry's brother but he was the antithesis of Jerry who was extremely tall, thin, and melancholy. William was short, rotund and jolly. He was very industrious and he never forgot anything I told him. He could neither read nor write so he had to memorize all the recipes we worked from. He took his job very seriously and sometimes it was difficult not to laugh when William came out with his interpretation of what I said. Spaghetti was forgetti, phone number was number phone, sheets were sheet beds, fly screens were fly screams and steel wool was stainless steel wool.

The first time I showed him how to prepare a Chinese dinner, he looked dubious when I told him we would use chopsticks instead of cutlery. He queried me twice to make sure he was not misunderstanding me. William no doubt found many European customs odd. I was reminded of the much-told Rhodesian story of the woman who employed a new cook just before Christmas. She asked him whether he knew how to do a roast suckling pig and he assured her he did. She went on to explain that she wanted it served with parsley in the ears and an apple in the mouth. He queried this and she repeated "parsley in the ears and apple in the mouth" which she mimed for him, to which the cook responded, "Oh yes." When the cook announced that he was ready to serve dinner, the hostess seated her guests and the cook walked into the room bearing the roast pig on a platter and in the cook's ears were sprigs of parsley and in his mouth an apple!

William would be most distressed if he broke anything. He would greet me with, "Madam I mak mistake," and it would be a broken plastic cup or something equally insignificant. We had a beautiful silver coffee set with two large coffeepots. They were very elegant and stood on four legs about three inches long. I planned to use them once the Lodge was built as they were too large for us. When William came to me one morning with "I mak mistake," I didn't worry too much, but I found he had decided for some reason to use one of the coffee pots and had stood it on the stove while he filled it and the legs had melted. My heart almost stopped when I saw the coffeepot standing at a crazy angle, two legs shorter than the rest. This was an heirloom, which had been in the family for generations. Fortunately only the legs had been damaged and Paul filed them all to the same length. It didn't look too bad unless one stood it next to its elegant, long-legged mate. Then it took on a Toulouse-Lautrec quality.

One of the tribesmen arrived and offered to supply us with milk. I really didn't want it, but I didn't want to offend him. He had come a long way to see us. I asked the price. He thought for a while, scratching his head and looking into the distance. Finally he indicated a half-gallon tin. "One and sikkies." One and six was the old sterling monetary system - one shilling and sixpence or fifteen cents. Fifteen cents was ridiculously cheap, but I didn't relish the thought of drinking milk that was not only unpasteurized but which had probably been milked by one of the man's young sons, to whom our ideas of hygiene meant nothing. I thanked him for coming and explained that we preferred to use powdered milk.

As he turned to go, he asked how much I wanted for Piccolo. I told him I didn't want to sell her. He said something to Jerry and they both laughed. Jerry translated. I must have a great deal of money if I don't even trouble to ask how much he was willing to pay for the dog. He added that she was a beautiful dog and would be excellent for hunting. He was right. Piccolo would have been a good hunting dog. Now that she had grown used to the bush, she loved nothing more than to go out with the boys and we constantly had to reprimand her for chasing monkeys or squirrels. But she was only beautiful because she was well fed and confident. At an African village, the dogs only eat what they can find and are constantly shooed away so they tend to cringe. We once had a bag of raw corn meal eaten at the laborers' compound by scavenging dogs.

Piccolo had many lessons to learn. She loved to ride in the Land Rover with us, and at first her greatest joy had been to hang out of the window barking at anything that moved. Reprimanding her seemed to have no effect. Frequently, driving along the narrow dirt roads, the bushes would brush against the sides of the vehicle, and on one occasion she was hanging out of the window barking at an impala. Paul reprimanded her and at that very moment a thorn branch caught her on the snout. She suddenly got the message and never again barked at the game. She still hung out of the window, but she now made funny little barking sounds with her mouth closed, rather like a dog barking in its sleep.

Jerry had to go home for a awhile. A relation of Esther's had died and he had to "go and cry," but he brought a nephew called Mishek to stand in. I needed another gardener so it seemed a good time to take him on. Mishek was just a teenager and very exuberant. He would frequently borrow William's bicycle, which he rode with complete abandon. I would encounter him on the road with his hands clasped behind his back, zigzagging across the road and I would narrowly avoid hitting him.

When William announced one morning that Mishek was away because he had had an accident, I naturally assumed it was on the bicycle. I asked him how it had happened and he said with a girl. Still thinking Mishek had been on the bicycle, I asked whether he had been giving her a ride on the bicycle. William smiled and said, "No Madam, he have an accident with a gal in the bushes." It seemed Mishek had to have the day off to discuss the matter of damages. The girl was pregnant. This was a custom I found so sensible. If the girl became pregnant there was no obligation to marry her, but the man had to provide a specified number of cattle, varying with the girl's standing in the community. These cattle were added to her father's herd and acted as a sort of trust fund for the grandchild.

Our gas lamps were cumbersome to carry around so we bought some Aladdin lamps. They had the elegance of the Victorian kerosene ones and gave off a brilliant light. Unlike the pressure lamps, they were silent. The only snag was that the glass funnel acted as a magnet to moths. They would flutter down and batter the fragile mantle. The size of the flame was also critical.

Turned just slightly too high and it would make the mantle turn black. It then had to be turned very low for some minutes until the carbon had burnt away. So it was a great joy when we heard of a young cadet who was being transferred from Nuanetsi who was selling his battery operated fluorescent light, complete with battery and motor to charge it. It was wonderful having a good strong light without any of the attendant problems of lamps but it didn't last long. First the battery gave out. We replaced it and then the light fizzled out. Then we heard the story from various people who came down from Nuanetsi. It seemed our light/battery/motor was about fourth hand, but no one had told us that before we bought it. Now everyone had ideas about lighting arrangements. Someone told us about a very cheap generator that had been for sale the week before, but we had missed that… and so it went on. We got the impression that all of these "good buys" we had missed were large enough to light up a village.

On our next trip to Johannesburg, we decided to replace our fluorescent light. It turned out to be so inexpensive that we bought several for the various rooms in the house. In the dining room we hung one over a picture. Soon, a small white tree frog ensconced himself on the top of the picture frame. Unlike an ordinary frog with its slimy skin, which looks as though one touch would give one warts, the tree frog had enormous eyes and a smooth fine grained, leathery skin which made one want to stroke it. From his perch he had his choice of insects every night. He only had to open his mouth as the food came flitting by. He blended well with the picture frame and sat so still he was almost invisible. During the day, he would tuck his legs in and flatten himself so that he had to be pointed out to people. In spite of the abundance of food, he never seemed to fatten up. His bones protruded and the skin was tightly stretched over them. He lived with us for more than a year and when we took a trip to Europe, he was the one creature we didn't have to think about — he could take care of himself. We were gone for six weeks and when we returned, our tree frog was dead. He may have died of old age or perhaps he had got out of the way of foraging for food and with the light not being turned on while we were away his food supply had stopped. He was totally desiccated and perfectly preserved.

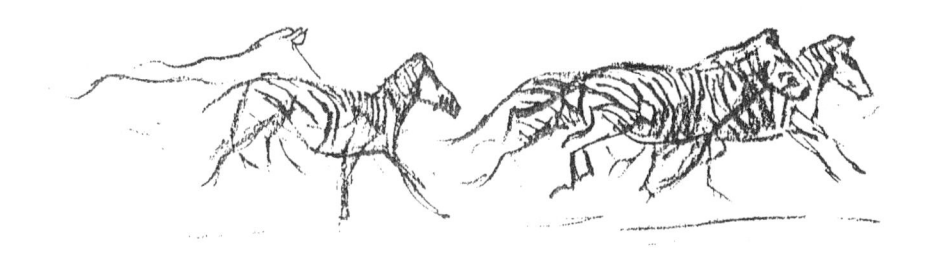

Chapter 11

If ever we happened to be passing when cattle sales were in progress, we would look in. These sales, controlled by the government, were introduced to protect the African stockowners from unscrupulous cattle traders, who in earlier days would barter cattle for some trifling object or for an insignificant amount. They would then fatten up the beast and sell it for a profit. Many fortunes were made this way.

The Sengwe cattle bore traces of the blood lines of the stud bulls from Nuanetsi Ranch which in former times had used Sengwe as winter grazing for many of its 125,000 head of cattle. Now it was illegal for a European to buy cattle from an African, except at a cattle sale, where the minimum price was fixed for a particular grade of animal. At the sale, the slaughter grade animals were brought in first. The grades were G.A.Q. (good average quality), F.A.Q. (fair average quality), Compound (not quite as good as fair), Inferior, and finally Reject, which meant the beast was not fit to travel and had to be bought by a local buyer. The first three grades were good meat and were bought by Imperial Cold Storage and butchers who attended the sales. After the slaughter stock came the young stock, which were selected according to the number of teeth they had. Those with a full mouth fetched less than the younger ones. The remaining young animals were then graded into Selected and Unselected. The Selected were the ones the European ranchers came down to buy. They were considered good breeding stock or they would fill out well as slaughter stock.

It was all done at great speed and to the uninitiated it was as mysterious as a visit to the stock exchange. The cattle grader sang out the grade and weight as the animal was prodded onto the scale. The auctioneer then put up the price. If this was more than the seller expected he would say, "Ndinobvuma!" (I agree), but if he refused he would say "Ndaramba!" (I refuse). The sale assistant would sing out, "Waramba!" (He refused), the cry would be taken up by the gate attendant, and the beast would be released to its owner, who may just have wanted an assessment of its worth. After an animal was sold, it was entered on the owner's stock card, but this card was seldom a true reflection of his worth because all animals listed on the card had to be brought for the weekly, compulsory dipping against ticks. Should the number of animals not tally with the stock card, the tribesman had to have a good reason for the Animal Health Inspector or a fine would be levied. This was to control the animal borne diseases. The A.H.I. used the weekly dipping to check for foot and mouth disease. If not caught early, this scourge of ranchers could affect the entire cattle industry. However, it was an impossible task because it was well known that most tribesmen kept a 'ghost herd' in the bush to avoid having to pay the paltry sum levied annually, 30 cents on each animal. After the animal was sold and entered on the stock card, it went into another cattle race where it was branded for the new owner and herded into a holding pen.

Cattle sales were dusty, noisy and exciting and the high spot of the month for locals. They were decked out in all their finery, and dogs and children darted in every direction. Women squatted in the dust under the trees selling sugarcane, peanuts, or sadza, their boiled corn meal. But the most popular of all was the beer, brewed from millet. The drinking would start the night before and they would sit up all night playing their drums and reveling. I think I must have seen too many movies because the muffled sound of the drums wafting on the night air always had an ominous sound to me, no matter how much I told myself that it was just a natural accompaniment to their merrymaking.

The lions were invariably attracted by the large gathering of cattle. We could always hear them roaring down near the sale pens, but I think the raucous mob and the drumming kept them at bay because we never heard of any being taken by lions at the cattle sales.

Jostling through the crowd, we would sometimes be greeted warmly by an ex-employee, hardly recognizable in his glad rags, generally with sunglasses and a cane. The teenage boys displayed their skill at wielding the long cattle whip with deadly accuracy. Once on the way to cattle sales, we saw three youngsters in a stationary, two-wheeled cart, known as a Scotch cart, to which two donkeys were harnessed. The driver satisfied himself that we were watching and stood up to crack his whip. The donkeys, perhaps anticipating what was coming, took off, throwing the young driver backwards. His feet hooked on the back of the cart and then he dropped onto his behind in the dust. He leapt up and ran after the rapidly disappearing scotch cart. This time he didn't look at us.

The Shangaan women were mostly still very primitive and few of them had much contact with white people. They went barefoot and they still wore the gaily-colored cloth under one arm and knotted on the opposite shoulder. They were extremely shy and were expected to kneel when talking to their men. I thought this could make quarrelling very difficult, but I suppose when one is that subservient, one doesn't quarrel. The women seemed to have very little status. Their prime objective was to bear children, preferably female children who would bring in the lobola, bride price, when they were given in marriage. The lobola was the parents' insurance for their old age. It was hardly surprising that birth control seemed an insane idea to them.

The women tilled the fields with hoes and they would work in the blazing sun, without any head covering, bent to their task of removing the weeds. During the growing season, they would go off to the fields in the morning, often with a nursing infant strapped to their backs and a small clay pot of drinking water balanced on their heads. They would return at sunset to prepare the evening meal. The men did the plowing which was done with a hand held plow and pulled by a team of donkeys. The building of the huts was a joint effort. The men cut the timber, mostly mopani. They would plant the poles in a circle, leaving an aperture for the door. The women then plastered these with anthill mud to a thickness of about 12". This would harden as it dried. The men then assembled the roofing timbers and thatched the roof with the grass the women had cut. Their thatch was very roughly done and had the look of a bad haircut. The Shangaan huts had a very wide roof overhang to protect the mud walls from the heavy summer rains. The women made the grain storage bins, which were on stilts, with the floor made of poles and then mud plastered.

If a family went anywhere, the wife would often have an infant strapped to her back, hold the next youngest by the hand, and carry the sleeping mats and any other baggage on her head, while her husband strode on ahead. The men seemed to have very little consideration for their women. At William's village, I saw his wife Lydia kneeling on the ground with a flat basket in front of her. She was holding another similar basket with ground corn in it which she was gently shaking and rotating. The fine powdered corn settled in the second basket leaving the husks behind. It seemed a desperately slow process and I asked William what she was doing. He thought for awhile and then said she was doing what I would do with my sieve. I was astounded, as it would obviously take her most of the day to collect enough of the powdered corn for a single meal. I asked him why he didn't buy her a sieve to do the same job in a few minutes. He thought this very funny and told me she had all day to do it, so she didn't need a sieve. The Shangaans seemed to live only to survive. They had no handcrafts at all. They were notoriously unmotivated but honest.

The Ndebele women were on the whole more talkative and approachable. The outsides of their huts were painted in an attractive design and they were neatly thatched and their villages had an orderly look about them. They made attractive clay pots which they used for water and beer. They also combed the leaves of the sisal on a plank with nails which exposed the fibers. These were then washed and worked into rough twine by being rolled between the hands. They used natural pigments from the bark or fruit of local trees to dye this twine which they made into little mats. I commissioned several sets to use as place mats for the Lodge dining room. Beadwork was another of their crafts and they made the most intricate designs. They also made attractive hats from the fronds of the mlala palm and interesting baskets and sleeping mats from reeds.

The mlala palm was plentiful in Sengwe. In summer, the Africans tapped the sap of the plant by cutting a slit in the stem and inserting a skewer. This had to be expertly done or it could destroy the plant. A clay pot was then placed in position to catch the sap. It was all covered with palm fronds to keep out the numerous insects which buzzed around any form of moisture.

It would seem that it ferments as it collects in the pot, because I once went with William to buy some. I had taken a plastic container with a clip-on lid. William offered to hold it for me on the way home but I assured him it was not necessary as the lid clipped on securely. Unlike a white who can't wait to air their superior knowledge, an African will not contradict one, but will leave one to find out for one's self. The 'securely' clipped lid shot off three times on the way and William ended up holding the lid down. The mlala wine, as it was called, had a pleasant fermented taste, more like beer than wine, and it had the kick of a mule as we discovered when we had two glasses each one night.

We brought Christopher and Simon home for the long weekend at Easter. Paul was not feeling well and had stayed in bed. We were building the living room for the Lodge and with Paul out of commission I had to supervise the work. As I stepped through the newly installed door frame I almost sliced the bottom off my big toe. It bled profusely, and as with any injury, it seemed that was the most used part of my anatomy. Walking was almost impossible but I cut the toe out of a pair of tennis shoes which allowed me to hobble around. With Paul ill and the boys home only a few days I couldn't sit around.

By that evening Paul was worse. It didn't seem to be malaria although I had taken the precaution of giving him an extra dose of Chloroquin. His temperature was 102° and I realized we would have to get him to the hospital. We put a mattress into the back of the Land Rover and made a bed for him. Christopher and Simon were in their pajamas as we expected to be home very late. My foot made driving very painful.

Floyd Hicks had replaced Lionel Hurd as the doctor at the mission. He and his wife were already asleep when we arrived at the hospital at Chikombedzi. He immediately diagnosed blood poisoning from a mosquito bite on Paul's hand. He gave him a shot but insisted we spend the night in their guest cottage so he could check on Paul's condition in the morning. In our haste to get Paul to a doctor, we hadn't considered the possibility of having to spend the night. I had brought nothing with me, not even a comb, and the boys were wearing pajamas.

Floyd told us that Mina who ran Amon Mpepu's Super Store at Chikombedzi had almost died. She was in her forties and had discovered she was pregnant. When her feet swelled up, she accepted this as one of the discomforts of pregnancy and she had developed toxemia. Fortunately, they were able to help her at the hospital and she had just produced a robust little boy. The Hicks' were returning to the States as their daughter, who had allergies to almost everything, was not well. I'm sure the hot dusty surroundings of Chikombedzi didn't help. We were sorry to hear this, as they were a kind and charming family. Lionel Hurd was coming back for a second tour of duty.

Floyd told us of acquaintances of ours who had paid us a surprise visit some months before. They had left Malapati and a few miles beyond Chikombedzi they had developed engine trouble. They sent a message with a passing African, asking for help. The message was relayed to Floyd at the Mission and he had gone to help them. He found a mechanical fault which could only be rectified by replacing the part. The nearest garage was 50 miles away on an unpaved road. He took the wife and children back to his home while he and our friend set off in Floyd's vehicle for the garage. By the time they had repaired the vehicle it was too late to leave, so they spent the night as the Hicks' guests.

Early the next morning, there seemed to be heavy rain clouds over the Nuanetsi area, but they decided to leave. Floyd warned them that there were areas of basalt, which became impassable with just a little rain. They didn't have a four-wheel drive vehicle, and even in dry weather, this was not a road for a car. Floyd was worried they might get stuck. He asked them to telephone him from Nuanetsi post office to let him know they had got through safely. If they hadn't phoned within three hours, he would go out and look for them. Three hours later he set off, certain he would find them along the way. He drove the entire 45 miles to Nuanetsi and then realized they had just not bothered to phone. I asked Floyd whether they had written to thank him for his kindness and with true charity he said he was sure they had, but the letter must have gone astray. They had spent two weeks with us and hadn't bothered to write, so I felt certain, with total lack of charity, that they just hadn't written to thank the Hicks.

After breakfast, Floyd pronounced Paul well enough to go home although he was still not well. On the way, we were flagged down by a group of Africans from our area. I knew them by sight and didn't want to seem to be driving back with an apparently empty vehicle, but with Paul lying the back, there was no room for them. I stopped to explain that I had no room, but they took my stopping as an invitation to jump in, clambering all over Paul who was asleep. He was obviously on the mend, because with some well-chosen words, he had them standing on the side of the road again in no time.

Chapter 12

Osric and Joyce Bristow were friends we had met before coming to Rhodesia. Joyce was what I had imagined a rancher's wife to be. She wore no makeup and had a deep tan with very blue eyes, a round cherubic face, and her waist length hair pulled back in a French knot. "If you're going to live in the bush, you've got to grow your hair so long you don't need to worry about it or cut it so short it doesn't need attention," was one of Joyce's many bits of wisdom.

Osric was a good-looking man of about middle age. His hair was thinning and this caused him great concern. He also had very fair skin which couldn't tolerate the tropical sun, so he always wore a long sleeved shirt and blue cloth hat. The only part of his body which seemed imperious to the ravages of the sun were his legs and he always wore shorts. This in spite of having legs which were less than straight, giving him a sort of rolling gait. His distinctive walk and blue hat made him easily recognizable at a distance. He was a born showman with an incredible ability for story telling. Listening to him relate some episode where one had been present to witness what had seemed a rather mundane incident, made one realize how much the average person missed in the most ordinary encounter. He was a natural raconteur and could hold people spellbound as he recounted a simple incident. He never stopped talking, and his stories were so vivid one almost felt one had experienced it oneself.

Osric and Joyce had ranched near the Limpopo River for many years and they were now living on a beautiful ranch called Le Rhone, adjoining the Zimbabwe Ruins, near Fort Victoria, about 200 miles from us. Many of the problems we were encountering, they had experienced during their days in the Lowveld and they were able to give us valuable advice. They had three sons. Norman and his wife Lena ranched near Chiredzi; Roland and Marinda had built tourist accommodation on Lake Kyle a few miles from Le Rhone; and Viv and Carol helped Osric and Joyce on the ranch.

Joyce had started with a few cheetah cubs which had been brought to her by the locals and which she had hand reared. They were later used for film work. In time, people began bringing them orphaned animals, which, being hand reared, could be used in films. Osric did the training. He had a way with animals and was able to establish a rapport with them. He would pick up some little idiosyncrasy an animal had and then develop it into a trick. If a lion club flopped onto its side, he would say, "Die" each time it did so until it associated the command with the action.

Joyce had endless patience with animals and she did all the feeding of the young animals. At times her house was like a zoo. One would arrive to find six young crocodiles swimming in the bath, or it might be hyraxes, the rock rabbits which lie around on warm rocks, being reared by Joyce, each one now lying on its own hot water bottle in the living room. They had a wide range of animals - cheetahs, lions, elephants, wild dogs, baboons, monkeys, hyenas and many others which were in various enclosures on the ranch. Osric loved animals and he loved an audience. Their nucleus of lions bred well in captivity and with each litter, Joyce would remove one cub to train, so there was invariably a lion cub wandering around the house. At one stage, they were given a baby elephant that they called Shapi. Elephants are gregarious creatures and in Nature there is always a mother or an aunt to hold onto. This is one of the problems of rearing a single young elephant. Osric and Joyce solved this by taking turns sleeping next to Shapi on a camp bed. When he grew older, they gave him a donkey stallion as a stable mate. All went well until the night the donkey kicked the stable door down and went courting. When Shapi found himself alone, he wandered up to the house in search of Joyce. They were woken by the crash as Shapi pushed the kitchen door down.

We spent many happy weekends with Joyce and Osric at Le Rhone when we went to Fort Victoria. Up until this time, the Mathers had alternated with us in bringing the children home. We would pick the children up in Fort Victoria and drop their children off on our way home, and they would in turn put our boys on the train at Mbizi and we would meet them at Nyala Siding. The Mathers had been transferred, so now we would go up to Fort Victoria every three weeks and do our shopping at the same time. We spent the weekends with the Bristows. Sometimes we would stay at the Lodges down on the Lake with Roland and Marinda and at other times we would bring one of our tents and camp somewhere on Le Rhone.

When we heard an aircraft buzz the house one morning, we went out and recognized Osric's airplane. He circled several times and then dropped something out. It had a string attached to it and a piece of red cloth which helped us locate where it landed in the bush, only a few hundred yards from the house. It was note asking us to drive to Mabalauta, the Parks office, where he would be landing as he had business to discuss with us.

We raced over and Osric told us he had a film unit of thirteen people at Le Rhone and they needed certain wildlife sequences. He asked whether we could accommodate them. It was tempting. We had the tents we had lived in while we were building and the camping equipment, so we agreed. It would be tremendous to have money coming in again for a change. I gave Osric a long shopping list for provisions which they would buy in Fort Victoria and the film unit would bring with them.

We worked feverishly setting up the tents in a large semi circle on our front lawn. Two camp beds, chairs, clothes cupboard and a table with gas lamp went with each tent. They looked attractive and comfortable. We turned our patio into a dining room using the new chairs and tables James had made.

By 6 p.m. when they arrived, it was all set up and ready for them. Jack Hawkins was to play the lead but he would only be flying out later. In the meantime, they used a stand-in who was also the make-up artist. Physically, he could not have been more different from Jack Hawkins who had a robust build. The stand-in was slender and lithe with the graceful movements of a ballet dancer. When it was necessary for Jack Hawkins to appear in a sequence, the stand-in would wear a heavily quilted jacket under his safari outfit. He wore a brown wig and hat with a leopard skin band, the standard dress for the Hollywood bwana and never worn by people who lived in the bush. The stand-in was only used when he was sitting in the vehicle and he always looked the other way when they were shooting.

The leading lady had brought her two pre-school sons with her as she didn't like to go away without them, so I had to take care of them. I was terrified they might be attracted to the river or wander off into the bush. This was my first experience with movie making and at times I wished I had a camera to film a film being made. It would have been hilarious. An aspect we had not considered when we agreed to accommodate thirteen extra people was that we had only one bathroom! One of the cameramen would closet himself in our bathroom for the longest time. Fifteen of us had to share the one bathroom and we stood round rather like the cartoon drawings of a long line of dogs waiting at a tree in various stages of discomfort.

We had some hair-raising moments when they wanted close-up shots of elephants charging and we had to wait at a water hole until an aggressive animal decided to give chase. With guests, we always took off at the first sign of danger, but now Paul was asked to slow down and the cameraman, who was right at the back of the vehicle, calmly filmed the charging elephant as though it was no more than a suburban dog giving chase.

They generally came back for lunch, but one morning Paul came back mid-morning and asked whether they could have a sandwich lunch as they didn't want to interrupt filming. William and I prepared sandwiches and coffee and Paul sped off with their lunch. As I was sitting down to my own lunch, I heard the vehicle return. They had got their shots sooner than they had expected and decided to come home. The forgotten box of sandwiches in the back of the Land Rover was now just a jumble of bread and lettuce after several hours of jolting round in the bush and William had to make omelets for the hoard.

They needed several sequences, one of which was a herd of buffalo with backlighting. Fortunately, we were able to provide everything they wanted, including the buffalo which came over the top of a hill early one morning with the light behind them. It was great fun having a crowd with the constant activity but I was not sorry to see them go. It was a lot of work under difficult circumstances.

One of the missionaries called in to see us as they generally did when they were passing. He had been down to Chief Sengwe who was a Shangaan and who was notoriously unprogressive. He did little to encourage the people to send their children to school or to change their unproductive life style. This missionary felt it was his Christian duty to see the chief and to point out the error of his ways. When he asked to see the Chief, the women told him that the chief was in his fields watching his corn grow. The missionary made his way to the field and found the Chief sitting under a shady tree. It is customary, in conversation, not to launch straight into the business at hand, so he made small talk for awhile. He was offered some palm wine. As he sat there in the shade of the tree listening to the birds, he was struck by the fact that this primitive man had not yet lost the art of relaxation. The missionary eventually came away having just paid the

Chief a social call. "I couldn't bring myself to tell him this was not the way to live his life."

I was often struck by this very fact. These people were so relaxed and their whole life style encouraged it. They were patient and tolerant and they simply accepted what came their way. Young children ran around naked and the bush was their playground. Their families were large and there were always playmates. The house was made of mud and grass and there was nothing that could be dirtied or broken. Living the way they do, they have few problems. They have no rent to pay, no car to break down, no plumbing to go wrong, no shrilling telephone, no radio to tell them of impending disasters. Yet we were always trying to foist our Western way of life on them while we constantly strived to recapture their art of relaxation, to breathe unpolluted air, to eat unprocessed foods - in fact to get closer to what more primitive societies still had. The people who were really caught in the middle were the ones who left the protection of their tribal way of life. They went to live in the white man's cities where they were somehow always attracted to all of the worst aspects of white society.

Chapter 13

Our guest accommodations were to be some distance from the house and the plans were for a dining room, living room, bar, office and six double huts with private bathrooms. We wanted to use the design of the Shangaan mud huts with the wide overhang of thatch supported by pillars all around. The walls would be made of brick and rough-plastered and painted to simulate mud. The construction of the huts was simple and we were able to do the bricklaying on several at once with Paul overseeing the work.

One morning Edson, who was always very punctual, didn't arrive for work. Charlie told us his belongings were still at the compound, but Edson hadn't returned after the weekend. A few days later we received this letter.

Dear Sir:

I am sorry about this. One of my brothers was told by other people that I took his wife, yet this is not true. So he hurt me very much. He think to kill hisself or to kill me. I am afraid to come and work. I can't work in pleasure because I will be looking side by side to see who is coming to destroy me. I told Charlie to collect all my tools and send them here. I am sorry to lose my work at you. I remain here, your servant, Edson Chauke.

We once again marveled at the quaint 'mission English' many of the educated Africans used. With Edson gone, I think Charlie hoped for the job, but although he was capable of laying bricks, he would do the most unexpected things. When he found we were running low on cement, he told the laborers to change the cement mixture: double the sand and halve the cement. This used considerably less cement but it would just have crumbled away and it had to be redone, so we had to find a replacement for Edson.

We were having thatching grass cut at Domisa Mission, about ten miles away, and we picked up the cleaned bundles every second or third day. The Shangaan women who were cutting the grass infuriated us. They would settle on a price for each bundle of grass and then raise the price when we came to pick it up, or the price would remain the same but the bundles would be half the size. Sometimes we would drive all the way down to find they hadn't cut any grass at all. We had an enormous stockpile of thatch, but when we started thatching, we found that what we had thought was enough for all six huts was only enough for two.

We located a good thatcher called Amon from Chikombedzi. John was promoted to act as his assistant, passing the bundles up to him. John worked with a will because Amon would let him wear his watch while he was thatching. A watch was a great status symbol. Graham Millar had once had trouble with the winder of his watch catching on things. After having it replaced several times, he had taken to wearing his watch upside down so the winder would be on the other side. He quickly learned to tell the time upside down. Pretty soon Titus, who was now the District Commissioner's messenger at Nuanetsi, was also wearing his watch the same way. He hadn't learned to tell the time upside down and it was most amusing to ask Titus the time because he almost had to put his arm around his neck to get the watch right way up.

One of the game rangers told us of an African game scout who had bought a watch which he would check constantly with an ostentatious flick of the wrist. Suspecting that the man couldn't tell the time, the ranger had one day asked him the time. He had looked at his watch for a long time, then up at the sun and said, "Morning time."

Simon had been badgering us to learn to drive, and since we had private roads, he started and in no time he was able to handle the vehicles. He was only nine and had to perch on the very edge of the seat to reach the controls.

Christopher was not particularly interested in driving. His major interest was birds and weavers in particular. He longed for them to nest near our house. He could identify a breeding nest from a bachelor's experimental structure and he would pick these and festoon our trees with them in the hope of attracting the birds to establish a colony, but he never had success. He always had to view them where they chose to nest.

In early December, we were running low on cement and we ordered a short truckload. The delay was usually a month or more before delivery, but I think we must have been the only people in Rhodesia building around Christmas time because the cement order was processed immediately. Paul had gone down to Johannesburg on business and the day after he left, I had notification that the railway truck load of cement was waiting at Nyala Siding to be unloaded. This meant I had to transport 326 bags of cement on my own. I did two trips each day leaving at 6 a.m. and taking 40 bags each trip. It was a grueling drive on a very bad road. One was seldom able to change into top gear. The Mazda was a fantastic vehicle mechanically and, despite rough treatment, it never gave any trouble, but it had been designed for paved roads. If one hit a pothole, the nose would go down and then whip up, flinging one up against the roof with a force proportionate to the speed at which one was traveling. So one didn't travel too fast. In places, the road was so badly washed that one had to go into low gear and ease down into the gully and up the other side. On one of the trips, we were exhausted after the loading and finished off the drinking water we had brought with us.

I noticed a new road and I decided to try it. We had been told of this proposed road which would make a tremendous difference in miles and wear and tear on our vehicles. It started off as a beautiful road and then I realized it was narrowing down until it was just wide enough for the vehicle. Sand was piled high on each side of the road. The surface was very soft and I could feel we were about to get stuck. I ground on in low gear hoping to find a place to turn. Finally, the engine gave an unpleasant whine and I realized it had overheated. I had Jerry, John, Christopher and Simon with me. We opened the engine and stood looking at it but it was all foreign to me. John slid into the cab and undid the radiator cap which was under the driver's seat, scalding himself and spewing what remained of our water all over the inside of the cab. At times like this I wished they would not use their initiative.

This was a new and unused road and we could wait for days without anyone finding us. It was 9 a.m. and I asked Jerry to walk to the police at Vila Salazaar to ask for help. I really wanted another opinion on whether I had seized the engine. We were about four miles from Nyala siding and V.S. was another five miles from there. I suggested Jerry try to borrow a bicycle from someone at Nyala siding because I knew there were a few African huts near the railway line. John set off with the empty canister to look for water in the vicinity.

The boys and I sat in the shade of a tree, and in that vast expanse of wilderness, I felt very helpless. Whatever happened, we would at some stage have to turn the truck around, so Christopher and Simon took turns with the spade we always carried to dig away the bank of sand on the one side. This would eventually allow me enough room to turn the truck and go back the way we had come. John arrived back about midday with water from a water hole. I was not thirsty enough to drink it but I was grateful to have it for the vehicle. The engine still heated up and Christopher discovered the problem. The radiator looked like a grass mat. It was absolutely choked with grass seeds and couldn't draw air. We cleaned it away and set off gingerly for Vila Salazaar to find Jerry. If he hadn't been able to borrow a bicycle and had to walk, he would have been pretty close to the police camp by now. At Nyala Siding we saw Jerry sitting under a tree. No one at Nyala had a bicycle to lend him he told us. Just walking instead of sitting down hadn't occurred to him. This is what could happen when they didn't use their initiative.

We arrived home just before sunset to find William about to go for help. He felt we had been away too long and had decided to walk over to Roy Borlase and ask him to look for us. I thanked him for his concern and quietly told myself I would never again be irritated with anyone who used their initiative, whatever the outcome.

The laborers had worked the whole day unsupervised and Charlie had decided to put in the door frames in number four and number five huts. He had put them in the wrong way so that they both opened outward and had to be removed again.

During the night it had rained, but I thought not enough to make driving the truck a problem. Christopher and Simon chose not to go with me after the previous day's debacle. They wanted to spend the day in the bush, so I set off with Jerry and John. About ten miles from home, I got stuck in the mud. The only thing was to walk back and bring the gang of laborers to help push. It was no use sending either Jerry or John because with Christopher and Simon out for the day, there would be no one to drive the other vehicle. I took a shortcut through the bush and came out almost opposite the house. I was relieved, because stories were legion of old hands having walked around in circles in the bush.

I found the boys still at home and this rescue operation appealed to them, together with all the laborers who squeezed into the back of the Land Rover. We drove to where the Mazda was standing up to the axles in mud. With the Land Rover pulling and all the hands pushing, we got the Mazda out amid a great deal of cheering. We now had two vehicles and only myself to drive. Simon had never driven without one of us beside him. He begged to be allowed to do his solo. The laborers were all in the back of the Mazda, but when they realized Simon was going to be driving the Land Rover, they shouted for me to stop. They all squeezed onto the back of the Land Rover, shouting encouragement to their little driver. Seeing Simon handle the vehicle with such apparent ease, we had a string of applications from our labor force to have driving lessons.

Christopher and Simon decided to clean out the duck pond which was so murky that the ducks wouldn't use it. I defrosted the kerosene refrigerator while William made bread. When it came to re-lighting the refrigerator, a chore Paul always attended to, the burner burnt with a wild orange flame that sent smoke belching out the top. I now wished that I had watched how Paul did it. But when we had first arrived, Mrs. Rabe from Nuanetsi had warned me never to light a kerosene refrigerator or deep freeze by myself. One woman in the district had been killed instantly when she lit her freezer. The drum they had used for kerosene had previously been used for gasoline. When she struck the match, the gas fumes had ignited and the freezer had exploded. Several ranchers' wives had been luckier and had survived explosions but had

had their faces and arms disfigured. Mrs. Rabe's advice was, "Always leave it to your husband to do."

I was glad to abandon the refrigerator when John came with the news that we were out of water. It seemed impossible. We had filled both tanks a few days before, but it proved possible. The boys had put the hose in the duck pond to fill it and they had forgotten about it. The water had been cascading down the bank for hours.

William told me the stove wasn't burning properly. He thought the 'shimney' was blocked. I tried poking a long reed down the chimney without success. Paul had built a very attractive chimney with six little pillars on top. They supported a cement slab covering the chimney top. It occurred to me to use the hose which was the only flexible thing I could think of to push down the chimney. While I was considering whether to leave the nozzle on the end for extra weight, Esther, who had never done a thing without being told to do it, saw me standing with the hose in my hand and turned the water on. I was standing about a foot from the wall and I was totally drenched.

We got the hose onto the roof, by which time Christopher and Simon had joined William up there. Simon sat on some plumbing which Christopher didn't think would hold his weight and told him so, reinforced with a punch. Next thing they were wrestling all over the roof, leaning backwards over the edge at times. My calls to stop were to no avail and they were out of reach. I grabbed the discarded reed intending to prod the next one to appear over the edge, but instead I caught the end of the reed in the string 'bat curtain' hanging over the kitchen door and it enveloped me like a cobweb.

This diversion ended the wrestling. The hose was wiggled around and the soot dislodged. William told me it was fast. I didn't think it had been. It seemed to have taken an eternity. The third time he told me, I realized the nozzle of the hose was stuck 'fast' in the plumbing pipes Paul had concealed in the chimney. It needed four laborers up on the kitchen roof to lift off the slab so we could extricate the hose. I expected at any moment to have the lot of them come crashing through into the kitchen.

I went to have a shower and found the drain blocked. I tried pushing a piece of wire down the drain but it had a U bend and would go no further.

I went to the outside outlet and found a frog wedged into the outlet pipe. I was reluctant to poke him out with the wire as I felt sure I would injure him. I was wondering what to do when Roy Borlase came by and he just poked him out with his finger. The frog was enormous and I was surprised that he could have squeezed into such a small pipe. Roy had tea with us and chatted for a while. When he left I went back to my delayed shower and again found the drain blocked. The fat fool had again wedged himself into the pipe. I called Charlie to come and poke him out. The rest of the gang gathered around. I explained that he should just poke him out with his finger. Being squeamish about frogs, I stood back and Charlie interpreted this as danger. He crept forward, poked it with his finger, and then leapt back. I was furious with him but I could not bring myself to touch it. Not one of the spectators was prepared to remove it. I sent them back to work and decided I would make the pipe too uncomfortable for the frog. I gave him a good dose of hot water and that dislodged him.

Christopher and Simon arrived back from a walk and it was difficult to believe that with their hair cut and combed, they could be put into school uniforms and look like young gentlemen. They wore motorcar tire sandals, their shirts hung out, and their shorts hung almost down to the knees, weighed down by the mass of vital equipment they carried... skinning knife, pellets, pebbles and slingshot. Christopher wore a camouflage cloth hat that flopped over his eyes so that he had to tilt his head back when he spoke. Simon wore a peaked cap with a flap at the back to shade his neck.

A few days later, John came to tell me there was a snake in the fowl run. It was a sizeable python which had gone into the roosting house. The fowls stood about foolishly, walking a few steps and then standing with their heads to one side, wide-eyed. Then they would dart off as though pursued. I had to get the snake out. Judging by the distance John stood from the fowl run, he was not about to remove it. As always, the workers gathered around. Charlie had a lot of stories to tell and a lot of advice to offer, including the suggestion that I give him the shotgun with which to shoot the snake. He had made the same suggestion with regard to the frog, but I felt sure he didn't know the butt from the barrel. In any case, a python was Royal Game, a protected species. I did not want to destroy it if possible. I thought getting it into a sack would be the best way to go but I realized I would have to do it myself.

Charlie stood around telling all the stories he had ever heard of pythons fastening their tails around some object, "like this gatepost," to act as an anchor while they squeezed their victim to death. He was very put out when I suggested he tell his stories elsewhere, or at some other time. The snake was coiled up in one corner and I used a long stick to prod it and it gradually uncoiled. With careful prodding, I managed to get it into the sack and we tied the top. Now there was no shortage of helpers who carried the sack and drove with me to the river crossing where we released the python.

Things didn't seem to be going too well. These dramas didn't seem to happen when Paul was home, or if they did, he said nothing about them to me. I was once again impressed by how well my apparent city slicker husband had adapted to life in the bush. I was very relieved when he returned from Johannesburg.

Chapter 14

We asked around for an experienced bricklayer and Joseph presented himself. He spoke good English and was a mild and inoffensive man. He was not a Shangaan and in fact not even a Rhodesian but a Tswana married to a Shangaan woman. He got on well with all the staff except for Charlie who no doubt resented him. Joseph was a good bricklayer and we found him a great help too with doing the roofing timbers and overseeing the work of the others.

Paul went up to Fort Victoria to pick up some building supplies. He left at dawn and planned to be back late that afternoon. As it grew dark, I became anxious. I thought of all the things that could have happened to him. It was with tremendous relief that I heard the sound of the Land Rover in the distance. As it drew up at the house, I went out to meet him and found a young policeman from Vila Salazar. "John Scott sent me over to tell you...." Suddenly it seemed all my fears were justified.

"Is he hurt?"

"Yes, but not seriously. They need your permission to operate if they need to."

"How did it happen?"

"He broke his elbow falling out of a tree."

It seemed such a bizarre accident for Paul to have had on the way to town.

I asked him what he had been doing up in a tree and he said they had had a radio message from the police in Fort Victoria who had been telephoned by the Principal of the school. It was only then that I realized it was one of the children. Paul arrived as we were talking and we invited the young policeman to stay for dinner. He was unable to tell us which of the boys it was.

Fortunately, before we were able to leave for Fort Victoria the following morning, my brother-in-law Ted arrived with his two sons. My sister Daphne was away in Europe and they had decided to visit. They had called in at the school and were told about Simon's accident. They visited him in the hospital and he was comfortable and cheerful. Ted was able to give us first hand news. An orthopedic surgeon was flying down from Salisbury, and if he considered it necessary to operate, they wanted our permission to do so. The principal had been most emphatic that we shouldn't worry. They would keep us informed of developments via the police at Vila Salazaar. Simon had broken his arm in the elbow joint, but when the surgeon saw him, he decided to immobilize the arm initially and then evaluate the situation. If Simon had less than 70% mobility when the cast came off, they would consider operating. Fortunately, with therapy, he eventually regained full use of the arm without surgery.

Henrik Groenewald, was the owner of the garage at Rutenga and a kingpin in the district. He was the only mechanic in the area, the agent for the most popular make of water pump and the local agent for PVC piping and all the fittings used for doing one's own plumbing. As a result, anyone who had anything to sell contacted Henrik who invariably found a buyer. We had now bought a new, highly efficient water pump from him and he and his brother were coming down to install it for us. We invited them for the weekend and suggested they bring their wives.

We had built a concrete platform onto which the pump and motor were to be bolted. In no time at all, we were connected up. It was exciting to know that this was the best system available. Paul had removed his boots while he was helping them, because they were sloshing around in the water while testing the capacity of the pump. They walked back to the house with Paul carrying his boots. Suddenly, he felt a searing pain on the side of his foot. By the time they reached the house, he was in agony. There was just a single red pinprick, obviously a scorpion sting. We tried everything to ease the pain. We soaked his foot in iced water which had as little effect as hot water had. I kept coming back to ice water because I remember Osric had told of being stung on his finger by a scorpion and of having found relief by immersing it in ice. When Osric arrived at the hospital, the doctor told him that having had his finger on ice for so long could have given him frostbite or gangrene which could have cost him the finger. He had removed his finger from its ice pack only to have the searing pain return. At that stage he would have welcomed the loss of the finger and he had stuck it back into the ice until the antivenin shot had taken effect. He hadn't lost the finger and he swore by ice as the only palliative for scorpion sting.

Paul spent a horrible night pacing up and down; standing; sitting; hot water; cold water. Nothing made any difference. It was rather a dampener to our weekend guests, but being country people, they were most understanding. The following morning, they insisted I take Paul to the hospital. William could make breakfast for them and they would visit again some other weekend. We drove to the Mission hospital at Chikombedzi, but we found Lionel was away for the day. Sister Straight, who was in charge in his absence, had spent the greater part of her life doing mission work in Africa and probably knew as much about scorpion stings as anyone. She felt that having survived twelve hours without anti-venin, it would be pointless administering it at that stage. She gave Paul some powerful pain killers and lots of sympathy. I couldn't help but think of his flippant reaction to my scorpion sting. To this day, he insists a more venomous type of scorpion stung him. By the next day, the venom had worked itself out of his system and he was fine, but he never again walked barefoot.

We were given two sheep, but as my deep freezes were all full, I thought I would keep them for a while. They grazed around during the day and that night I thought I would put them into the chicken run for safety. I had a large enclosure for the fowls, but at night they roosted in a Shangaan-type fowl house inside the enclosure. This was a thatched hut on stilts to protect them from genets, who seemed to get through any fence to eat the hens. I waited until they had roosted for the night before I brought the sheep into the run. The sheep made rather a lot of noise and the poor old 'hukus' closed up in their coop, heard the bleating and stomping, but couldn't see what was happening. They set up the most dreadful cackling which startled the ducks who spread their wings and took off down the river. I didn't know domestic ducks could, or would, fly. They landed on the river where they paddled around happily in the twilight. Paul went after them and waded into the river up to his waist, but the ducks had now discovered the vast expanse of the river. As he approached them, they took off and landed further down the river. Paul had only one idea in mind - to get the ducks back, dead or alive. He was irritated by the thought of our duck population swimming up and down the river now that they had discovered it and gradually being taken by crocs. The fact that he was risking his own life by going after two dozen ducks didn't seem to enter his mind. He vowed to go out early the next morning and shoot them all and put them in the freezer. Apart from the fact that the whole debacle had only taken place because my freezers were already full, I wanted my ducks alive. I planned to beat Paul to it the next morning and coax them back with food. When I went out the following morning, they were back in their duck pond the tame domesticated ducks I had always known, waiting to be fed. I took the precaution of clipping their wing feathers to foil any further escapades.

The furniture James was making for us had to be oiled and Mr. Palfrey told us they had used old engine oil from their vehicle. It not only oiled the new wood but it gave it an attractive dark stain and seemed to act as a deterrent to borers and termites. We had several drums of sump oil. Each item needed several applications and it was a slow and tedious process. Christopher suggested we use the small pond we had originally made to hold water when we were making bricks. It was rather like a deep fishpond and it could hold several chairs at a time. We emptied the oil into it and submerged the furniture and left each item there for several days. They came up beautifully without any real effort.

It was time to go back to school again. Christopher had completed primary school and was starting high school near Gwelo. They had a sensible system of having the new boys arrive the day before school started, for orientation, so they could settle in before the rest of the school arrived. New parents would be entertained to lunch and meet the staff. We woke at 4:30 that morning to pelting rain and it seemed we wouldn't be able to get out. At 5:30 we decided to attempt the trip. Every stream was a rushing torrent. We slithered and slid all of the 90 miles to the main road. We had no hope of arriving at the school in time for lunch, but at this stage we just wanted to arrive some time that day. It took us ten hours to drive the 300 miles from Malapati to Gwelo. A few miles from the school, we stopped for Christopher to change into his uniform. He looked so grown up in his grey long pants, blazer and straw boater. We barely had time to meet his housemaster and look at his dormitory. As we were leaving, I expected the usual hug from Christopher, but now he stood smiling nonchalantly with his hands in his pockets. He gave us the thumbs up sign of a big boy who was fairly indifferent to his family's departure.

We spent the night in town and Simon was quite tearful that evening. It was the first time they had been parted and we had given Christopher's new school a tremendous build-up. Simon would dearly have loved to be joining Christopher at his high school where they had so many interesting clubs and facilities. They had squash, golf, shooting, a natural history society, explorers' club, mechanics' club and a host of others. We reminded him that he would be a senior at his school, whereas Christopher was just a humble new boy and he seemed happier by the time we dropped him off at his familiar old school the next day, one of the old boys. Our trip home was much easier than going up had been, but the mud had dried into deep ruts which made driving very bumpy. We stopped off at the post office at Nuanetsi to pick up our mail. We mentioned to the new postmistress that we had just taken Christopher to school at Gwelo and she told us there had been rioting in Gwelo that morning, but she hastened to reassure us that should a boys high school be attacked, they would give as good as they got! I felt distinctly uncomfortable. Until she mentioned, it I hadn't thought of Christopher's school being attacked. It turned out to be a very local disturbance in one of the African townships and, as so often happened, the rioters had destroyed facilities that had been provided for them. Among other things they had destroyed the local beer hall. The Gwelo Town Council later voted funds destined for African amenities to make good the damage they had caused. It seemed self-defeating and senseless. The Pearce Commission had been sent out by Britain to evaluate the situation in Rhodesia and these 'disturbances' were created to give the impression of unrest. The disturbances suddenly became more widespread and it was a worrying time. Our laborers had been given leaflets outlining the terms of the settlement which the British government proposed but it was couched in such sophisticated terms, I can't imagine how anyone thought the majority of rural Africans would understand it. Jerry as a village elder had been summoned to Nuanetsi to have it explained to him so that he could in turn explain it to his people. But even in simple terms it was incomprehensible to him. When I asked him about it, he said, "England wants to be friends with us now and then we can get gasoline again." This was a reference to fuel rationing, but since the majority of Africans didn't even have cars, it didn't seem to be a strong incentive for a settlement with Britain. With sanctions had come fuel rationing. We had to complete a questionnaire stating our residential and business address, among other things. Each vehicle was then issued with a monthly quota of coupons which had to be presented when buying fuel. When our allocation arrived we found we had been given four gallons, presumably on the basis that we didn't have to travel to work. We wrote and explained that our nearest gas station was 35 miles away and we would use half our month's allocation just getting home again. We applied for a bulk fuel permit in view of the amount of traveling we had to do to get building supplies, provisions, etc. as well as at a later stage ferrying tourists around. I think the fact that our business had the potential of bringing in much needed foreign currency helped because we were granted a bulk fuel permit. The gas company provided us with a five hundred-gallon tank which stood on a seven-foot metal stand. The fuel tanker would come periodically and fill our tank. It was an offense to travel with a gas can in one's vehicle, so we had to have coupons when we went to town to allow us to get back again.

On one occasion when I went for our coupons from the Fuel Rationing Office in Fort Victoria, a missionary from an outlying district was in the office. He had run out of coupons and he needed just enough to pick up his children from boarding school. The official was adamant. Such requests had to be made through Bulawayo. I asked the man how many coupons he needed and he said he needed five. I offered to lend him five if he would mail them back to me as soon as he got his next allocation or we would run short. He agreed to do this, took my name and address, and thanked me profusely with "that is a very Christian gesture." We certainly didn't have coupons to spare but it must have looked like an impressive amount for a city dweller who had very little traveling to do, because two weeks later a note arrived from the missionary saying that since our allocation was so much larger than his, we could no doubt spare five units, but they would like to repay us. Would Paul and I like to drive up to Fort Victoria to hear their mission choir sing some Saturday afternoon… 200 miles away!

The District Commissioner told us they would be bringing the members of the Pearce Commission down to Malapati to address the local tribesmen. He asked whether we would entertain them. We agreed enthusiastically, feeling we would have an opportunity to talk to people who had an objective view of the situation in Rhodesia.

There were three commissioners headed by a former Kenyan judge. Britain had sent them out after the terms of the proposed settlement had been drawn up and leaflets had been distributed to the Africans. The government explained these terms as best they could to a very unsophisticated rural population. This Commission was now doing the rounds to ensure that the Rhodesian government had not misled the people. We asked the Commissioners how long it would take and we were told it took just a few minutes. They no longer got around to explaining the terms. The Africans were asked whether they understood the terms of the settlement and they always said they did.

They were then asked whether they agreed to the terms of the settlement and they always said NO. I wish I could think this had been true. The political agitators had had too much time to get around the country and intimidate the rural people.

To impartial observers like ourselves, it seemed logical to accept the terms. It offered millions in educational aid from Britain matched by the same amount from Rhodesia, and a qualified franchise. This was the stumbling block, yet the qualified franchise seemed the answer. Many white people living in Africa must have shared our feelings - the conflict between conscience and common sense. Experience had shown that in an independent African state, democracy was generally short lived and a new form of oppression soon took its place …dictatorship, corruption and erosion of the economy.

Ian Smith, the Prime Minister of Rhodesia, was leading a country with a white population of 375,000 people and defying the entire world by resisting the granting of full political rights to predominantly tribal people who did not understand the concept of voting. I was very glad I did not have to make the decisions he was called on to make. He had aged visibly in a few years. We had met him once and had been most impressed with him as a person. He had a tremendous charisma which unfortunately didn't project itself on television.

Chapter 15

We were using Androstachys wood for our Lodge roofing timbers. The Africans knew it as nsimbiti or ironwood and it was impervious to borers and termites. This was invaluable in an area where a piece of fabric or timber left on the ground for 24 hours would be attacked by termites. The Veterinary Department was felling some of these trees on the Mozambique border, near Vila Salazar, and we were told we could use this timber. On one of these trips, we drove through several herds of elephants. While we were loading, it began to rain. The road ran through an area of basalt and on the way home we didn't see a single elephant. At the first sign of rain, they move out of the basalt into the lighter sand veld. Presumably, it's the fear of being stuck in the mud. Several years previously, in the Matetsi area near Victoria Falls, an extensive basalt area, we had seen elephant foot prints eighteen inches deep. It must be quite a harrowing experience for such a large animal to sink into the mud.

Joseph, who was normally very reticent, began to behave strangely. He became talkative and was making the most elementary mistakes. Early one evening, Charlie arrived at our house, breathless and agitated. Joseph had announced that he was going to kill someone that night. He said he would write the man's name in the sand and they had all gathered round to see. When Joseph wrote Charlie's name, the intended victim took off and ran all the way to our house. Charlie said Joseph was mad; he had seen it coming for days. Paul told Charlie to wait at our house and drove to the compound where he found Joseph quite calm but incoherent. He gave Paul a letter from Lionel Hurd, the Chikombedzi doctor, dated several years back stating that Joseph was a schizophrenic and had to be on regular medication to maintain his equilibrium. Joseph said he had stopped taking his medicine.

Paul persuaded Joseph to spend the night with Manuel, the Internal Affairs messenger at the Sub Office, where he could be confined for his own safety. Joseph agreed and Paul drove him there. Manuel said he would put him in the 'stocks,' which I thought a rather medieval arrangement, but it turned out to be the name for the overnight lock up for offenders pending transfer to Nuanetsi. In the morning, we drove Joseph to Chikombedzi and Lionel decided to hospitalize him.

We arrived home to find the river was rising again. A young man from Nuanetsi arrived to say the D.C. had asked him to warn us that the river was in flood at Nuanetsi and the Sosonye River had washed the bridge away. As all this would be coming down our way within hours, we had to remove our water pump to avoid having it washed away. Before the floodwaters reached us, we filled both the water tanks and then removed the pump.

The following morning, the river had risen to just below our house and spread to a width of 100 yards. The massive wild fig trees along the riverbanks were submerged up to their branches. The bridge at the Sub Office was totally submerged with five huge uprooted trees stuck on it. The force of the water was awesome.

The young man who had come down from Nuanetsi was returning the following morning, so we drove over to the Sub Office that evening with our mail for him to take back to Nuanetsi. We found the rest house full of people all stranded on the wrong side of the river waiting for the floodwater to subside. On the way home, we used a short cut and suddenly we sank into the mud up to the axles. Roy Borlase had a tractor, so Paul walked back to ask for help. Unfortunately, Roy had already broken the axle of the tractor pulling out one of the Land Rovers whose owner was now ensconced at the rest camp which had taken on a convivial air. One of the other young men offered to use his four wheel drive vehicle to pull us out. Paul warned him it was not just mud but a real quagmire, but he came too close to the soggy patch and his vehicle also bogged down. The rest house was overflowing with people and Roy and Anne were now accommodating some of them at their house. They offered to find a place for us to sleep.

We were only four miles from home and the prospect of going to sleep quietly in our own beds had more appeal, so we set off on foot along a very rocky road. I had worn sandals for the visit and I soon found they were not ideal for walking on a rough road. We stumbled along in the dark. In places, the road was a steady stream of water. Occasionally, impala would snort in agitation and I was uncertain as to whether they were afraid of us or whether there was a predator in the vicinity. We arrived home after midnight, very wet and very tired. The following morning we took the other Land Rover down to extricate the first two, and that also got stuck. Finally, we walked home and brought all the laborers to push and lift the vehicles out of the mud. From then on we avoided that short cut during the rains.

Some enormous mushrooms sprouted out of the termite mound in front of the house. Elliott, who was an authority on these matters, said they were edible and promptly ate one. I decided to wait until the next day to see if he had been wrong. He showed up for work and obviously the mushrooms were edible, so I cooked some and they were the nicest mushrooms I had ever tasted. All during the rains, they sprouted from the termite mounds and we had a continuous supply of these delicacies.

The shrub mopani was the dominating feature of our area once one got away from the river. There were occasional mopani trees but they didn't grow in dense forests as they did in parts of Gona-re-Zhou and along the road to Nuanetsi. Some people insisted the shrub was just a stunted version of the tree, due to unfavorable growing conditions, while others insisted it was a sub-species of the tree. The leaves are split like the wings of a butterfly and they give off a pungent, turpentine-like smell when crushed, yet animals eat it. During the hot weather, the leaves fold back on each other, possibly to reduce evaporation. The mopani trees grew up to fifty feet in height and the leaves were identical to that of the shrub but the stem grew to a sizeable girth. The bark was gray and heavily striated. The wood burnt well and provided most of our firewood. The wood was heavy and it was able to withstand the weather and termites. When the Africans use it for building purposes, they lie the timber in a fire for a short while to ant proof it. It seems heating it had a chemical reaction on the resin which made it impervious or unpalatable to termites. The tree has the unusual quality of being able to withstand incredible injuries to the stem. A tree fractured at right angles to the main stem by elephants would heal and continue to grow and then turn upright again, producing the most interesting sigmoid growth. On trips to Fort Victoria in summer, we would notice the appearance of the mopani worms. They looked like multi-colored, overfed silkworms. They spurned the shrub mopani in favor of the trees and we would often see them crossing the road in enormous numbers, all going in the same direction. Further along, others would be crossing to the opposite side. It made one wonder what it was that made these caterpillars undertake the slow and arduous crossing of the hot and dusty road when there were perfectly good trees where they came from. They were capable of defoliating trees completely, so that it looked like winter, but the trees soon came out in new growth again.

The Africans gathered the caterpillars, squeezed the innards out, and then dried them in the sun so they could then be stored. They were such a delicacy to people who were used to them that they had to be exported to the laborers on the gold mines in South Africa. Christopher and Simon tried them and pronounced them 'nice' but I noticed they didn't eat any more. I was never able to overcome my revulsion at their appearance, but I suppose it's all in the mind. When I eat escargot I don't relate them to the snails that slime their way round my garden.

We started work on the landing strip. The government had agreed to share the cost with us, as they sometimes needed to land an aircraft when they flew officials down to the Tribal Trust Lands. We selected a site about a mile east of our house. It had good drainage and not too many really large trees to remove. One always felt reluctant to chop down a tree that had taken hundreds of years to grow. For the most part, the trees were Acacia Robusta, a pioneer species, so called because they grew fast and provided cover for grasses and seedlings of slower-growing and more permanent trees.

The acacias would look perfectly healthy, but a beetle that looked like an enormous roach often infiltrated them. They would bore their way into the softwood and lay their eggs in large hollowed out chambers. During one of the stages of their life cycle, they are enormous white grubs curled up in the cavity in the softwood. Christopher and Simon called them Malapati prawns. They were a great delicacy among the Africans who roasted them and they were no doubt a good source of protein. The Acacia Robusta frequently grew at an artistic angle, and since a tree that had been invaded by the beetle would be riddled with little excavations, the structure of the tree would naturally be weakened. They would topple without warning. On more than one occasion, we drove under the attractive canopy formed by the spreading branches only to have the tree drop with a crash of splintering wood behind us, activated no doubt by the vibrations of the passing vehicle. The Africans would pounce on the tree to remove the grubs.

The trees we really didn't like to remove were the large old Nyalaberry trees. They were a slow growing hardwood and the ones at the airstrip must have been hundreds of years old. These trees which always grew out of a termite mound unless they grew on the riverbank fascinated me, but even there they sometimes had a termite mound for a base. Did the tree attract the termites or did the termites burrow down and carry up to the surface some substance which promoted germination of the seed? Only much later, I discovered that the termite mound does come first and, being particularly fertile, it assists germination. But the key to it lay in the fact that the seeds of the Nyala berry are animal dispersed and many animals will look for a perch from which to defecate. Frequently, a termite mound would be the highest point. At the river, the bank itself would constitute a perch, or the riverine canopy would be used by the birds and baboons that ate the seeds of the Nyalaberry and then deposited them in the rich alluvial soil. The fruit of the Nyalaberry looked rather like dates and they were prolific. One of the old missionaries told us that during severe droughts, in former times, the tribesmen used to boil the fruit with animal hides, which eventually broke down into some sort of curd, providing a protein which sustained them. Now during drought periods, the government arranged for famine relief. I imagine this use of the Nyalaberry will gradually be forgotten. The wood of the tree caused severe irritation to the nose and eyes while being worked, and whether for this reason or for the fact that it is an extremely hard wood, the laborers chose to burn the trees out on the site of the new landing strip. They built a fire around the base of the tree and kept it going until the tree caught alight. It then burnt for a week or more, smoldering down into the ground until the very roots had burnt away.

The remaining trees were Acacia Robusta and the Loncocarpus Capassa, both softwoods, which we chopped down easily. Once the area was cleared of vegetation, we had to contend with the termite mounds. When they were chopped open, they revealed the most intricate structure of spiraling honeycomb pattern to aerate the structure. When one sees the height to which the termite mounds rise, at times as much as ten feet above the ground, one has to marvel at the endurance of those tiny creatures, burrowing out the sand and moving it a grain at a time. We were never able to establish how far down the subterranean structure went, but I had the feeling it was at least as deep as it was tall. When we were still living in the tents and using our termite mound oven, we were able to see the speed with which the termites worked. If we were ever away for a few days we would return to find reconstruction work under way. In two weeks, they were almost able to seal up the aperture we had made. When we were opening it up again, the boys once dug too deep and broke through into a large central chamber. The upper cone that we were using was solid. They dropped a stone down the hole and it dropped a considerable distance.

The termite mounds couldn't be removed by hand and we had to use a bulldozer. It took three days to flatten them all. The D.C. agreed to let his grader do the final leveling. Their workshop at Nuanetsi also made the metal mast for the windsock. This was a great help as it had to be hinged about three feet from the ground so that it could be lowered to adjust the windsock, which occasionally wound itself round the pole. The mast itself was set into a concrete base and, with the help of several of the laborers, we hoisted it. We had been given specifications by the Department of Civil Aviation for the various requirements, in order to have the strip registered and licensed. Having it licensed entailed considerably more work and consequent expense, but insurance regulations allowed a chartered aircraft to land only on a licensed strip. The runway was 850 yards long and we had to have an overrun of 70 yards at either end. We had to make concrete markers, each 10ft. x 3ft., and they were placed at specific intervals down the side of the runway. The name MALAPATI had to be made out of enormous concrete letters surrounded by a large white circle. The name and markers were painted white and it looked most impressive. We were also required to keep two fire extinguishers at the strip. We made a parking bay for the aircraft and dug a six-foot trench around it with a causeway where the aircraft could be pushed across and parked. These elaborate precautions were to deter elephants. We planned to replace the causeway with a drawbridge if necessary, but we never had an elephant enter the parking area. The trench scared them off. The elephants were always curious about something new, and in feeling around an aircraft, they might have dislodged something. In one corner of the parking bay we built a box with a glass front to house the fire extinguishers. The door was locked and the glass had to be broken in an emergency.

It took us three months to complete our airstrip. The day after we first hoisted our bright orange wind sock, we drove up to admire our handiwork and we found an elephant standing beneath the mast trying to reach the windsock, fluttering in the breeze. He ran his trunk up the supporting wires and down the mast and we fervently prayed he wouldn't wiggle it. He was obviously satisfied because after surveying it for a while, he walked off.

When the Department of Civil Aviation came down to inspect our airstrip, they remarked on the high standard. It was in fact considerably better than the strip at Beit Bridge where all light aircraft from South Africa had to clear Customs. The inspector explained that the strip would have to be maintained at all times with regular checks for antbear holes or any other damage to the surface. It would be inspected by them without prior warning and if at any time it did not conform to specifications, we would have our license revoked. The airstrip proved to be a popular gathering place for game. At night, we would sometimes drive up after dinner and in the headlights we would pick up the eyes of hundreds of impala, twinkling like stars in the black night. The males would square up to each other, sometimes so engrossed in the squabble that we could drive almost up to them before they moved off to resume their aggressive posturing some distance away. Sometimes the headlights would blind them and they would bounce around, almost on the spot and then suddenly take off. In the mornings we sometimes saw lion footprints and the obvious signs of a chase, but I don't think they had much success on the strip. It was too exposed which was perhaps why the antelope and the zebra favored it.

Chapter 16

Our cook, William, had fields some distance from his village. His wife and daughters had harvested the corn that was piled into stacks at the edge of the field. The women carried the bundles to the village, but as this was a slow process, the elephants inevitably discovered the stockpile and began to eat it. William spent the greater part of his nights beating a drum next to a fire in his field to keep the marauders away, but as soon as he went to bed the elephants would raid his corn again.

We gave him several thunder flashes - enormous firecrackers that had a striker attached to the base, rather like a built in match. One ignited it and then had about ten seconds to hurl the cracker which went off with a thunderous explosion and a blinding flash. The District Commissioner had given us some when the elephants were troubling us while we were making bricks. The D.C. issued these to the tribesmen on request and as we had some on hand we offered them to William. He assured us he knew how to use them but at about nine p.m. we heard several go off in quick succession. I think he must have been tired of waiting and decided to let them off as a precautionary measure, because the following morning he reported that the elephants had been back at the corn. We decided to transport it to his village in our truck.

The thunder flashes were very successful in our experience with elephants. Usually the elephants were not destructive, but one evening we heard one tearing up the garden. I had some precious Cycads that were difficult to acquire and I didn't want them uprooted. I definitely wanted to discourage this elephant. We walked very quietly over to the sound and stood in the doorway of the camp living room which was only about thirty feet from where the elephant was tearing up the plants. He was so engrossed in his noisy browsing that he was totally unaware of us. Paul tossed off the thunder flash that landed next to one of his hind legs. He noticed the fizzling object and turned round to inspect it, but fortunately he turned away again just as it went off. In the brilliant flash of light, we saw him lift off the ground in fright and then take off through the undergrowth. The following morning, we saw that the imprint of his feet where he had landed was actually several inches deep. On the whole, the elephants were curious rather than destructive. One night, one of them stepped onto a newly completed septic tank and smashed the top, but fortunately he didn't fall into it. They would investigate anything new and they loved to come to the birdbath at night and eat the shoots of the sprouting birdseed. Their feet would leave huge indentations in the lawn, like a giant necklace strung across it. We just filled these in with sand again. It was a small price to pay for the excitement of having elephants on our front lawn.

We were woken one night with the berries dropping onto the roof and we thought it might be baboons in the Nyalaberry tree. Paul went out to drive them off and, as he stepped out through the front doorway, he almost walked into the back end of an elephant that was pulling down branches to get the berries. Both he and Paul took off in opposite directions.

The dry season always attracted a variety of animals to our gardens where everything was lush and green from constant watering. The Kudu came onto the lawn at night and they would browse the tops off the young mahogany trees we had planted. We had to protect each tree with a circle of mopani poles. Early on, we had discovered that we couldn't have garden taps as the elephants could smell the water and they would uproot the tap, draining the tanks overnight. Our water points were gate valves sunk into small cement squares in the garden. When we built a fish pond in the camp area, we attracted a wide assortment of birds and smaller game, including the ever-present baboons. They came in large numbers, leaning into the pond with their rear ends in the air. If we approached, they would lope off, ridiculously like humans on all fours, looking back at us. At a safe distance, they would begin to walk leisurely, still glancing back. They would seldom move at speed unless they were caught unawares and then they would screech and bark hysterically. Once when the water level in the fish pond had become too low for comfort, they had figured out how to open the gate valve and left it running, only to overflow and cascade down the bank. This was quite a feat, as the handle was quite difficult for me to turn. We then had to place a heavy rock over the top.

On a weekend visit to see Simon, we stayed with the Bristows. The Umtali museum had just sent down a newborn vervet monkey. A dog had mauled the mother and the baby had been removed by Caesarian section. He was pink and only partially covered in hair and he looked very small and helpless. Just then, the Bristows didn't have the time it would take to rear him, so I offered to take him. We bought a doll's feeding bottle and formula for him. We called him Tamba, 'one who has become urbanized.' He loved his bottle and would hold it with hands and feet. As with all primates, he had a need to cling which had one major disadvantage. I never knew when he would mess on my clothes. Every time he wet me, I would involuntarily call out, until the poor little fellow got the rather distorted message - his bodily functions were accompanied by a rather shrill screech. As he grew older, we would take him for walks with us and he would hop down and explore and then leap back onto me again. It was interesting to see how a harmless ibis or other large bird could fly over and he would ignore it completely, but a bird of prey would send him scuttling back to me, chattering.

He did not care for Paul. He would open his mouth and wiggle his scalp and jump up and down on the spot. This was a really threatening gesture. Needless to say, this didn't endear him to Paul. Doing my hair was impossible with Tamba around as the brightly colored rollers fascinated him and he would undo them as fast as I rolled them up. One day, I put him outside the bedroom door, which lead onto the patio. He sat at the window screeching to be let in and suddenly I noticed a full-grown male vervet monkey approaching, seemingly attracted by Tamba's apparent distress. Tamba was leading an unnatural life and I thought perhaps it would be a good idea for him to join the troop, but when he caught sight of the old male, he was terrified. When I went out, the monkey backed away, but for days afterwards he would wait around in the trees and come down and behave in a threatening manner towards me. This would make Tamba shriek in fear, which in turn encouraged the monkey to try to rescue him.

As he grew older, Tamba became destructive and he would unroll the toilet paper or bite holes in a tube of toothpaste. He was a menace in the kitchen, as he knew where all the snacks were kept. He once took a reel of exposed film on to the roof and sat up there unwinding it. Eventually, we built a large cage for him with a swing and a ladder that kept him amused. When I was working in the garden in the mornings, I would let him out and he would play around me. He delighted in jumping into the duck run and rushing around after the staid old ducks and making them run, and occasionally removing a tail feather. When he was in his cage, he would entice the guinea fowl by pushing bits of food through the wire and then rushing up and down his ladder, apparently showing off to the little gaggle of surprised looking guinea fowl. If ever he saw me eat anything, he would pry my mouth open, at the same time himself going through the motion of eating, in anticipation of sharing the treat. He dearly wanted to play with Piccolo and he would grab at her as she walked by. She was very confused as she sensed he was young and part of the family, but at the same time monkeys were to be chased. He would come up behind MacGregor, sedately walking in the garden, and push him from behind as though to speed him on his way. MacGregor left Tamba in no doubt as to how he felt about that.

When the water level in the Nuanetsi River dropped, the river would form pools that were good for fishing. One afternoon, we went down with the boys and they spotted two adult Egyptian geese with a young one. The adults flew off a little way, hoping to distract us from the chick, I suppose. As we watched, a crocodile surfaced and took the chick in one snap of the jaws. It was a sobering sight. We regarded the river as an extension of our garden, a recreation area, and we never thought of death lurking there. Only a few days earlier, a policeman at Chiredzi had been walking along a river with his dog when a crocodile had taken the pup. Reacting instinctively, the young man had grabbed and retrieved the bruised dog, but he lost a few fingers in the process. We had mentioned this to Christopher and Simon and warned them about standing too near the edge when they were fishing, but actually seeing a crocodile in action really brought the danger home to them.

We had heard an incredible story of a crocodile's aggressiveness. A fisherman who was sitting on a rock some feet above water level was taken by the foot by a crocodile and pulled into the water. The man managed to beat the croc off and stumbled ashore and was surveying the damage when the crocodile came out after him and dragged him back into the water. He again managed to beat it off, but this time he dragged himself clear of the danger.

One often hears that crocodiles will not take Waterbuck because the meat is unpalatable. This is not so. We were watching a herd of Waterbuck coming down to drink at a pool in the river one afternoon. They were upwind so they were not aware of us, but they behaved nervously, circling the pool and retreating. Eventually, one came down to drink and a huge crocodile lunged at it. The buck rushed off and the crocodile came out of the water and ran after it for some distance before returning to the water.

One afternoon, Paul was walking up the river with Piccolo. During the floods, the river had split, flowing on either side of an island of sand, leaving a high sand dune in the middle of the river. The dune had a great many small stones on the one side and clambering around on this, Paul dislodged some of them. A crocodile must have been sunning himself on the bank furthest from the water and, hearing the noise, but not sure of its source, the croc rushed for the safety of water. Paul heard the crashing of stones and suddenly the crocodile clattered over the top of the dune, passing within feet of him and Piccolo before it plunged into the water.

We wanted to visit an interesting looking island we had seen from the bridge at the D.C.'s restcamp. We left the vehicle and walked down the dry river bed. It looked as though the river had once flowed in a straight line to the left of the island. With the passage of time, some enormous boulders had been exposed and the sand had built up against them, detouring the river to the right in an enormous loop and rejoining the old course further down, leaving an island of about 1/4 mile long. We climbed around and found the skull of a crocodile wedged between two rocks. It still had remnants of skin attached and had probably been washed into these rocks during the previous heavy floods. Paul wanted to take the skull home to add to his collection. A dead crocodile's smell is something indescribable but Paul needed help. I was carrying several aloe plants and Simon had filled his pockets with interesting river stones. He needed both hands to hold up his trousers. Paul put a stick through the eye sockets of the skull but needed someone to hold the other side. Christopher was the only one with free hands and as he plodded along beside Paul he complained all the way. If only he had caught a swarm of bees instead of just looking at them, he would also have been able to walk ahead of us. Paul's urge to have the skull seemed to have dulled his sense of smell. Christopher held his nose and breathed through his mouth but he said he could taste it. Simon and I jogged ahead of the smell until we reached the vehicle.

Paul put his smelly prize into the back of the open Land Rover and I imagined we could outride the smell. I was never able to understand why we couldn't, but it seemed it had something to do with air being sucked in from the back. We sped home and Paul hung the skull in a tree by the river where it could slowly weather and lose its tang. Unfortunately, it was so pungent that it served as bait to the local hyenas and, despite the height at which he had wedged it, they managed to dislodge it and eat it. They did leave some of the teeth which Paul rescued. Some time later when it became fashionable to wear teeth and claws as necklaces, Christopher proudly wrote from school to say he had sold a croc-tooth necklace to someone at school for $10.75. He had set a loop in the top and bought a chain for $10.00 so he had made $.75. Paul rushed to his box of croc teeth and sure enough, the biggest and best tooth had found its way onto that necklace.

Chapter 17

When we went to pick up the boys for the summer vacation, we found Christopher had four stitches in his nose, three on the outside and one on the inside. The school doctor had said we should have our doctor remove the stitches in five days. It transpired that one of the seniors had accidentally shot Christopher with a slingshot, splitting one nostril. Christopher was still very much in awe of all seniors, and knowing there would be serious repercussions if the true facts emerged, he had concocted a story as to how it had happened to avoid making an issue of it. Five days later, none of us fancied the long drive to the doctor, so I had to remove the stitches.

One of the Section Officers at Vila Salazar gave us some cartridges for our shotgun. The Springhares were digging up the camp lawn each night and we decided to see whether shooting a few would deter them. Simon held the flashlight for Christopher to shoot. He shot one and as it fell, Piccolo dashed off to dispatch it and it fastened on to her neck. She had never been a brave dog and she now began a tremendous howling. Simon ran to help the dog, taking the flashlight with him. There was a great deal of shouting. "Finish it off. It's killing Piccolo," and "I'm standing in thorns and I've lost my shoe." When we finally got light onto the scene, the Springhare had succumbed and the yelping hound had no more than a negligible bite on her neck.

Christopher was very proud of his prize, and he announced that he would shoot every Springhare that ventured onto the lawn until he had enough skins to make a blanket. He asked Simon to gut and skin his trophy for him. Simon, no doubt thinking of the skin blanket and seeing this as the first of many such requests, decided not to set a precedent and wisely refused. He did lend Christopher his special skinning knife and sat around offering advice on the gutting which had to be done immediately as William was to be given the meat. Having gutted it, Christopher decided to skin it in daylight and hung it up in a tree. During the night, a jackal came and ate it and that, fortunately, was the end of the skin blanket.

On a trip to Fort Victoria, we had met Pat and Peter Wright. Peter was the National Parks Warden at the Zimbabwe Ruins. They had previously been stationed at Wankie but they now had two young daughters and Peter had opted out of bush stations for their next posting. He obviously missed the bush tremendously, but Pat enjoyed the advantages of comparative civilization. Pat was pretty and petite with long dark hair. Their daughters were like two little dolls. Peter had that gentle quality that characterizes so many people involved with Nature. He was extremely kind and helpful and was most competent at making or building almost anything. They were a charming family.

Peter had asked Christopher and Simon to collect specimens of bats for him. They had to be shot and then injected with formalin to preserve them. He gave them the syringe and formalin and this opened up new avenues for them. They shot a hornbill and filled it with formalin, eliminating the messy business of gutting, they jubilantly told us. They could now taxidermy anything. We put a stop to that as the formalin was intended for Peter's museum specimens, but the old hornbill was suspended from the ceiling of their bedroom by a piece of fishing line. He swung in the breeze with a Nyalaberry clutched in his beak.

When the road from the airstrip needed leveling, Paul wired three tractor tires together and fastened them behind the Land Rover. Christopher and Simon perched on the tires and they were soon caked in dust and beside themselves with excitement. Now they wanted to do nothing else. When the leveling of the road was done, they negotiated with William for the hire of two donkeys for the following day to pull just one of the tires. The donkeys arrived with two boys from William's village to drive them. Neither they nor the donkeys showed much enthusiasm. These boys had not had much contact with white children and they were intrigued by the rather strange behavior of the two white boys squatting on the tire, waiting for the donkeys to take off at the speed of the Land Rover. However, the reluctant donkeys just plodded. Christopher and Simon were becoming quite frustrated until William came out and took stock. Perhaps feeling guilty for having over charged them for the use of the donkeys, he stepped out with a torrent of words. He snatched a stick from one of the boys, gave each of them a hard shot on the behind and the same to the donkeys, and they all disappeared in a cloud of dust.

Vacations were a wonderful time of endless exploring for Christopher and Simon. They would leave straight after breakfast and would always indicate the rough direction they would be going. Some days they would take a picnic lunch. If they shot pigeons or a Francolin, they would make a fire and cook it for lunch and we wouldn't see them till late afternoon. It was a time of learning about Nature and a time of unbridled pleasure at living in a wilderness area and they were never bored.

They discovered a clutch of guinea fowl eggs. There were seventeen in all and we agreed to let them remove twelve. It was just as well we did, because a predator steadily removed the rest, one at a time. We put the eggs under a broody hen. Their incubation period was 28 days as opposed to the domestic eggs that hatch in 21 days. After a week, we added two hen's eggs to the clutch so as to be able to compare the behavior of the chicks. We were curious to see whether the hen would remain sitting after three weeks, but she did and hatched them all. It was interesting to see the difference between the chickens and the baby guinea fowl. The chicks remained under their mother for the first day and then emerged on wobbly legs, while the little guinea fowl darted about as soon as they were dry. They were little brown and black striped creatures and, like so many of the game birds, perfectly camouflaged while they were young. At the slightest sign of danger, the mother hen would alert her brood and spread her wings for them to take cover. The domestic chicks would rush in and hide under her while the little guinea fowl would take cover under the nearest bush and remain quite immobile. Even knowing they were there, it was often difficult to spot them.

The hen would scratch for them and then cluck as she unearthed some tasty morsel. While they were eating, she would scratch again, sending one or two of them rolling, but they seemed to thrive. As they grew older, we started imitating the guinea fowl call whenever we wanted to feed them and in no time we could whistle for them and they would come running. The two little fowls, a hen and a cockerel, responded to the same call. Once they wanted to start roosting, the mother hen abandoned them. We planned to have them return to the wild if they chose, so we didn't want to cage them at night, but we also didn't want to have them taken by predators. The solution seemed to be to get them to roost in the big tree above the house where they would be safe. I found that by leaning a ladder against the wall of the house and putting food on each rung as I backed up, they would climb up after me until they were on the roof. I did this for several nights and then they began to fly up on their own.

We had met a Mrs. Mac William who knew all there was to know about fowls and birds and she had given me sulphamethazine in case any of my fowls should ever suffer from 'the droops.' She described it as 'walking round with their hands in their pockets.' When one of the young guineafowl began to droop, I was able to recognize it immediately. I dosed them all via the drinking water and in a few days he was fine.

Christopher's interest in bees now became serious. We bought him a beehive and all the literature and gear that went with it. He would walk for miles through the bush looking for bees. He not only wanted company, but he needed a helper and he would implore Simon to go with him. Simon always went very reluctantly, and when I offered to go with him one day, I realized why. He spent most of the time up a tree and had to have things passed up to him at the end of a rope. I was reluctant to desert him, but once he became engrossed in his bees it was almost impossible to communicate with him and I was left standing below while he puffed away with his smoker. Periodically, the smoker would come sailing down on the rope to be recharged with burning rags or dried elephant dung. He told us he had found a swarm of bees in an old acacia tree near the fowl run and he wanted to chop the tree down as the bees were inaccessible. We were quite definite in saying no to that. With the aid of six-inch nails and a rope, he finally managed to scale the tree. He puffed away all day and only came down that evening when he could no longer see. He was quite despondent about his lack of success and our lack of co-operation. First thing next morning he was at our bedside. The tree was gone! We went out to have a look and sure enough it was no longer there. The smoker must have given off a spark which had set the inside of the old tree alight, and during the night it burnt to just a heap of ash. The bees had settled in a more accessible tree and he was able to get them into the hive.

Christopher walked for miles through the bush looking for bees and it took a lot of effort. He had always had the knack of finding an easier way to do things, sometimes with disastrous results. Once when he was trying to dislodge a swarm of bees from a very old Nyalaberry tree, he had spent several hours with his smoker with no success. Then he hit on the idea of making a fire in the bole of the tree, just a small fire, he later assured us. The tree began to smolder, the bees took off, and we were left with a smoldering tree. It took the entire labor force several hours, running with buckets of water, to extinguish the fire. With all the time Christopher spent on his bees, one would have thought we lived on honey, but he seemed to have very bad luck with his bees. Once when he had in ignorance used string to tie the waxes onto the frames, the bees had removed the string. In the process, they had fluffed it up like cotton and dropped it onto the floor of the hive. It eventually formed such a dense mat that it had stopped the airflow and the bees had moved out. Several times ants attacked the hive. He then stood each leg of the hive in a pot of oil, but a vine fell onto the hive and the ants walked down the vine. Added to this, Christopher could not resist looking at his bees and they would become upset and move out. One day he spotted a swarm overhead and he yelled excitedly as he took off after them. Unfortunately, he lost them and came back dejectedly. To console himself, he peered into his hive, only to find it was his swarm that had taken off.

He soon found another swarm which had settled in a tree near the airstrip and he thought they would be easy to remove, but he needed help early next morning, preferably two people. Simon was adamant he was not going. My little gardener, Mishek, and I went with him. Christopher and Mishek were dressed up in overalls and hats with the bee veils fitting over the hats. I was hot wearing a light summer dress and I guessed the two of them must have been extremely uncomfortable. Christopher at least was motivated but Mishek was just lending a hand. They scrambled up the tree and Christopher expertly coaxed the main swarm into a bag. He was tying it closed with the remaining bees swarming round them angrily when Mishek was suddenly overcome by prickly heat on his scalp. He plucked off his hat to scratch his head and the angry bees settled on his head. He had several stings before leaping out of the tree. I made it clear to Christopher that from now on his bee keeping, which gave no one but himself pleasure, would have to be done on his own. When Mishek told me he had to go home for a while, I suspected the bees might have had something to do with his decision.

One night when we went to bed, we noticed the glow of the gas lamp Christopher had left out when he had gone to check on his hive. The bees had been attracted to the light and they had completely covered the lamp. Unaware of this Paul, went out and picked up the lamp and was severely stung. He was most upset and muttered late into the night, alternately wishing a plague on all ill-tempered African bees and wishing Christopher would develop a normal boy's interests.

Lindsay Bell, a school friend who had started Christopher on bee keeping, came down to stay with us for two weeks. Lindsay had a sizeable bank account from the sale of his honey. He had one swarm that had moved into a clay pot. This prompted Christopher to put a large clay pot, which the Shangaans use for making beer, into the fork of a tree near the fowl run. The bees were not attracted to it, probably because there were so many available trees. Everyone forgot about the pot, fifteen feet above the fowl run, until one afternoon when I was collecting the eggs. The pot fell out of the tree and landed right next to me and it was my turn to wish Christopher had other interests.

Chapter 18

One afternoon the boys told us they had found a dead Nyala bull quite close to our house. We went to have a look at it and found it had been shot with a primitive arrow that was deeply imbedded in the carcass. The animal had been wounded and had gone into a thicket to die. Many tribesmen still hunted with bow and arrow and when they were caught poaching their hunting tools were confiscated. One of the policemen from Vila Salazar gave us a beautiful specimen that we hung in our pub. This started Simon on a bow and arrow phase and he eventually graduated to a crossbow. Each one he made was larger than the previous one. He was amazingly accurate but they were potentially lethal and we had to call a halt to the shooting with a crossbow.

One of the ranchers brought us a young Duiker, a small antelope, whose mother had been savaged by dogs. She was quite tame and followed me around. We went for long walks and she would stop to nibble at her particular delicacies. For safety, I locked her in the fowl run at night. In the morning, she would be waiting for me with several bold fowls perched on her back When she saw me, she would shake them off and trot to the gate to be let out and spend the day wandering around the garden. She was with us for about a year, and she eventually moved further from the house each day until she only came back for snacks in the morning and evening. She eventually found a mate and would bring him with her, but he kept his distance if we were around.

We didn't encourage the keeping of wild animals. With rare exceptions, one was not able to re-introduce them into the wild and they ended having to be caged. Christopher and Simon once brought home a tiny lemur, the charming 'bush baby' with enormous eyes and huge bushy tail. They admitted having robbed a nest in the bole of a tree and we insisted they return it to its nest. Occasionally they would ask for a second dog, but in the bush, once one has a pair, they often don't stay around the homestead and are tempted to go off hunting. Roy and Ann Borlase had a pair of German Shepherds who were constantly killing animals, including a number of the beautiful and harmless Civets. Eventually a crocodile took the one dog. The second dog had an extremely unpleasant experience one night when he barked at lions walking through their garden. Roy and Ann heard the lions and when the dog began to bark, Roy went to call him in, but the dog didn't respond. In the morning, the dog was missing and they found lion spoor and dog prints and obvious signs of a struggle with a considerable amount of blood. Both the dog's prints and the lion's led up the road. Ann followed the trail. The dog had gone two sides of a triangle, pursued by the lion. After about eight miles, the lion had given up the chase and the dog headed for home. About three miles from their house, Ann found him, badly mauled, resting under a bush. She had to give him penicillin shots and stitch a gaping hole in his side. Although the wound healed, the dog lost condition and died several months later.

The boys found a yellow billed kite's nest in the top of a tall Nyalaberry tree. The bird had four chicks. Christopher was very anxious to have two of the young birds to train to do falconry. Normally we wouldn't have agreed to this, but we did feel that they were deprived of many of the entertainments that city children had to fill their days and we hoped they could both learn something from this experience. As it turned out, I was the only one to learn anything. The chicks wouldn't be old enough to remove for another two weeks, by which time Christopher would be back at school. He asked me to get them for him so they would be ready to start training when he came home.

On the appointed day I climbed the tree with a pillowcase tied to my waist. This was on Christopher's instructions so that I could carry the young birds safely when I climbed down. I struggled up through the dense foliage and saw the large nest above me. As I heaved myself up, I looked into the fierce face of the adult bird. She looked formidable so I lowered myself hastily. The following day I waited for her to fly off before attempting the climb. I removed two of the fledglings and dropped them into the pillowcase. The descent proved difficult with the birds dragging at my belt.

I made them comfortable in a box in the kitchen where it would be warm and safe. In the morning, I was horrified at what they had done to the walls. They had a most efficient ejection system which no doubt had kept their mother's nest clean. They would turn around, lean over the edge of the box, and project fully three feet. The obvious place to put them seemed to be the fowl run where their toilet manners wouldn't matter. The fowls were by now so accustomed to strange bedfellows that a pair of young potential predators didn't faze them one bit.

I took them out daily and walked with them perched on a finger, but quite soon I had to wear gloves. The slightest noise would make them grip with their claws and close on my finger. I now began to get frantic instructions from Christopher on how to start their training, which had not been part of the arrangement. I could see his point though. It seemed a shame to have got this far and to miss out on this valuable training period.

I had to tie a bit of meat, fairly loosely in case they took it, to the end of a string. I then had to show them the meat on the string and swing it around slowly. My attempts at training were a disaster. The more dominant, and possibly the more intelligent, of the birds obviously thought I had taken leave of my senses. He would fly up into a tree. From there he would watch us and only come down after the training session was over. The other bird and I persevered for a while but every time the string passed over his head he would duck. The meat also frequently came unstuck. Finally, a letter came from Christopher telling me not to bother. He had been told that they were untrainable. The second bird eventually established his territory in our garden and he always responded to my whistle by cocking his head.

Sitting down at the river one afternoon we spotted two Nyala bulls facing one another. Through binoculars, we were able to see they were squaring up to each other. Their movements were so slow as to be barely discernible. One was an old male who had only one horn and whom we had often seen around. The very deliberate, slow motion movements continued for some time. This must have been a threatening gesture, because without doing anything further, the old bull had the younger one backing away. We were pleased that he had been able to maintain his dominance. A short while later, we went up to Fort Victoria for a long weekend and when we got back we found vultures circling about a mile from the camp. We found our old one-horned Nyala dead under a bush. At first we thought he had been injured in the fight we witnessed, but he had been shot twice through the body. It is difficult to understand why anyone would want to shoot a Nyala which is so rare and Royal Game (protected). It was not the type of bullet an African generally used and an African would certainly not have wasted a second bullet and then not followed the wounded animal. One feels a certain sympathy for a meat-hungry African, but there's no justification for the wanton killing of such a rare creature, just for the sport of shooting.

It was some time since poachers of any kind had troubled us. When we had first arrived, the Africans would drive their cattle into the Game Reserve and use the opportunity to set or check their snares. If they were caught, they always had the excuse of retrieving their cattle that had strayed. In the first few months, we had found wire snares almost every time we went for a walk.

Cow bells had always had pleasant associations of yodeling Swiss shepherds. Now as we started the 'Battle of the Cattle,' the 'clonk, clonk' became very unmusical. Our requests to the tribesmen to keep their cattle out had no effect, so we built a rough stockade of thorn branches, and the next herd to appear were driven into the stockade. They settled down for the night and we intended to send for the owners in the morning. During the night, we heard a lion roar quite close by and suddenly the cattle stampeded. They crashed through the enclosure and we heard them pound off in the direction of the Mozambique border. We listened with distinct glee to the cowbells growing fainter. The owners must have spent days rounding up the cattle and we had no further trouble with them.

During the Impala lambing season, we sometimes heard poachers' dogs barking. On one occasion when we went after them by Land Rover we found a band of young boys running down the young Impala with their dogs. I think they got the fright of their lives because we were never troubled by them again either.

When the river was in full spate, I heard a dog barking one day and found it was a tribesman's dog. It was barking at a large Waterbuck that was slowly backing into the water. The dog eventually plunged into the raging floodwater and began to swim across the river after the Waterbuck. The staying power of these mongrels is quite incredible, but I suppose they were motivated by hunger. The dog proved not nearly as strong a swimmer as the Waterbuck. He eventually reached the opposite bank but had been washed downstream a good distance and he had lost his quarry. Another time, we found two large dogs that had cornered a Kudu bull that was by now utterly exhausted. We drove them off and spread the word that we would shoot any dog found trespassing.

Chapter 19

We were told that the Game Department was going to cull in Gona-re-Zhou. As part of the program, the District Commissioner gave permission for various ranchers, on payment of a fee, to come into the Sengwe Tribal Trust Lands and shoot elephants. When the first of these was shot, our laborers wanted to pick up some of the meat. We drove them down and came on the most incredible sight. Men, stripped to the waist, covered in blood, and hacking off bits of meat overran the carcass. They would disappear into the abdominal cavity to retrieve prized bits. This reminded me of a story we heard of just this happening, and in the darkness of the elephant's interior, one had accidentally cut off a vital bit of another's anatomy!

The surrounding bush was festooned with bits of intestine and special delicacies. Everyone seemed to be calling instructions and the women were shrieking with the excitement of 'meat fever.' They filled flat baskets which they carried off on their heads. Some of them asked for a ride, and seeing the heavy, messy loads they were carrying, we agreed, as many of them as would fit squeezed into the back of the truck. After about five miles, we asked John where the women wanted to get off. He laughed and told us their village was where the elephant had been shot. They had come with us for the ride.

The Gona-re-Zhou elephants were notoriously aggressive, and for some time, the Game Department had been shooting any animal charging a vehicle of theirs. The idea was to eliminate ill-tempered individuals. However, shooting one animal in a herd seemed to make the others who witnessed it associate vehicles with danger. We found that the sound of an engine seemed to agitate them. If they were close to the road, they would rush out threateningly. Several times when we were at Makonde Pool, game viewing by moonlight, we would hear Mackenzie, the Internal Affairs truck driver, approaching. As he drew level with the pool, the elephants would trumpet and mill about angrily, but the instances of serious intent were few.

Once, MacKenzie's truck, with a load of passengers on the back, was charged. The passengers were frequently noisy and MacKenzie took no notice of the shouting as the elephant caught up with them and grabbed the tailgate of the truck and completely removed it. On another occasion, Mike Bromwich, one of the Park Rangers, parked his vehicle at a water hole while he was doing a survey of destruction of the vegetation by elephants. When he returned to his vehicle, he found it had been attacked and badly gouged.

There were endless stories of close encounters people had had with these giants of the bush. One young Ranger had gone out with his girlfriend and his dog. They got out of the vehicle to watch a herd of elephants and the dog wandered too close to the herd. One of the elephants charged the dog which ran back to its master who was then knocked down. The elephant put its tusk through the man's abdomen. However the tusk must have been very blunt and penetrated so slowly that it allowed the intestines to part and avoid a much more serious injury. Within a few

SQUARING UP

months, the Ranger was back on duty again. I would call this a provoked attack. A ranger once explained the difference between a mock charge and the real thing. In the mock charge, the ears are extended but the head is kept down, whereas with the real thing, the head is thrown back with the tusks pointing forward. When a towering gray shape bore down on us with shrill trumpeting, I could never recall afterwards whether his head had been up or down. Just their threats were terrifying. They can charge at up to 25 m.p.h.

Alan Wright, a former D.C. at Nuanetsi, had walked many hundreds of miles in the area and he had often been charged, but he always stood his ground and the elephant always veered off. On one occasion, he had a visiting official in his vehicle with him and he waited in the face of a charge and the animal kept coming until it was within a few feet of them before it stopped. It was so close that its trunk struck the radiator. We were never prepared to test his theory, and when an elephant came at us, we gave way at high speed. Once when we were coming home after dark, we encountered a herd of elephants as we came over a rise. Paul slammed the Land Rover into reverse, only to find them crossing behind us too. It is terrifying to have these huge animals looming over one. On another occasion, we were coming home at dusk through the Tribal Trust Lands on the newly opened Pahlela road. Paul was ahead of me in the half ton Mazda truck we had just bought. I noticed what appeared to be dense smoke from a bushfire, but as I drew up to where Paul had stopped, I realized it was dust from a herd of elephants. They had come crashing out of the bush onto the dirt road and they had pounded along beside the little Mazda, which stood no more than five feet from the ground. He had slammed on the brakes and the elephants had passed in front of him.

People tend to anthropomorphize a great deal about animals, attributing to them human emotions and reactions. This was particularly true of elephants that have a certain mystique about them. We have all heard stories about an elephant burial ground. In an otherwise excellent film we saw on elephants, it was implied that they would carry away the bones of dead companions to some final resting-place. We came across an instance which might have been construed this way. Some years previously, an elephant had been shot in Malapati and the remains had been covered with earth. On one of our trips to Nyala Siding we saw the elephants had dug up the bones and scattered them around. I think it was just their insatiable curiosity which prompted them to do this. They probably smelled a familiar scent and unearthed the bones. When I decided to use elephant dung for compost, we made a neat heap and covered it with earth. A few nights later, the elephants took it apart and scattered the droppings far and wide. On another occasion, Peter Wright, who was doing research into small mammals, asked the boys to trap a sun squirrel for him. He gave them some small wooden box traps, which were painted a bright yellow for easy recognition. They had to be checked twice a day. One morning one of the traps was missing and we found elephant footprints all around and a clear drag mark as the trap had been picked up in an elephant's trunk. It was dropped some distance away and there we found lion prints and the trap itself with two tooth marks where the lion had chewed the trap. The bright color must have attracted them. This playful curiosity seemed to be a characteristic of lions, too. On one of their frequent walks through the camp at night, they found the garden hose neatly coiled up. They chewed it into small sections, one of which we hung in the pub as proof of our story. The lions also uprooted and chewed some of the little aluminum nameplates we had placed to identify the various trees and shrubs.

I think humans frequently misinterpret animal behavior. I feel irritated when I hear the gentle cheetah described as a coward. It is just by nature less aggressive than other cats and it will abandon its food if challenged. The fact that cheetah mothers will abandon their cubs if there is danger is to me not a cowardly action. The human mother will endanger herself and her children by facing any threat, but possibly the cheetah runs away to distract the predator, as do so many ground birds whose young are well camouflaged and more likely to escape detection than if the mother stayed and pinpointed their hiding place. I have also heard the coucal, a ground dwelling member of the cuckoo family, described as 'skulking in the undergrowth.' I prefer to think of him as a recluse. His beautiful liquid call, like water running out of a bottle, makes up for every negative characteristic he may have.

National Parks were now going to cull elephants on a large scale. They planned to take off 2,000 animals because they were 'destroying the habitat!' Proof of this was the destruction around the artificial water holes, strategically placed throughout the Game Reserve to draw the animals away from the riverine vegetation where they might otherwise damage trees hundreds of years old. Many people who knew the area before Gona-re-Zhou was fenced stated that they had seen between 200 and 300 elephants a night watering at Manjinji Pan, yet they appeared to have done little damage to the riverine vegetation there. Around Manjinji were some of the largest trees of every species, but the water was unlimited and accessible and the elephants did not have to wait their turn to drink.

The artificial water holes, on the other hand, were not large - about half the size of a small farm reservoir - and sunk into the ground. Several herds of elephants arriving at the same time would have to wait while one herd at a time drank. The elephants damaged the surrounding vegetation while they waited in much the same way urban humans might turn to graffiti to while away the time. Around these water holes there were now just mopani stumps, and coming on it out of the dense surrounding bush, one had the feeling it must have been hit by an atomic bomb. However, this had been the intention in placing the water holes in the scrub mopani. It covered thousands of acres in Gona-re-Zhou, and since it regenerated very quickly, we found it difficult to understand such extensive culling to preserve the mopani.

Shooting crop raiders who left the safety of the Game Reserve and went into the Tribal Trust Lands would have caused less disturbance. However, when culling in the Tribal areas, the meat had to be given to the local Africans. The danger in any culling program lies in the motive for deciding on it. One couldn't help but wonder whether the decision was not influenced by the economics of the operation. Done commercially like this, the valuable ivory, skins, tails and meat brought in considerable revenue. Obviously once Man interfered with Nature by putting up fences, feeding areas become restricted and the natural cycle was destroyed. Man then has to intervene to control and preserve what Nature would otherwise have done. We understood all that, but we felt that too many elephants were being taken off.

An aerial count revealed 1,200 elephants at the Lundi River end of the Game Reserve. It was decided to take off half this number. After culling, another aerial count revealed 1,200 elephants. Fortunately they hadn't erred in the other direction or they might have taken them all off. Their method of establishing the game population was obviously not reliable. Whatever method they used to establish the numbers at our end of the Game Reserve, I feel certain they misjudged and took off too many. After the culling, one could frequently drive around Gona-re-Zhou - the Place of the Elephant - and not see one for days.

The culling program was highly organized. A team of selected rangers did the shooting using either F.N.s or their personal rifles, as some of them felt more comfortable with a rifle they knew well. The snag about using their own 450 or 500 was that in the normal course of events, a ranger might shoot one or two elephants at a time. Now a team of five was having to shoot as many as fifty animals in one day, and the recoil from such a heavy caliber rifle left them bruised and injured after a day's shooting.

A firm of contractors worked with them. They utilized the skins and the tails that were made into curios and the meat was dried. At a clearing at the crossing into Buffalo Bend, the contractors dried the meat. Poles were set into the ground and chicken wire was stretched across them to form rough tables on which the meat was laid out to dry. Overhead, wires protected the meat from raptors. The carcasses had to be disposed of as soon as possible as there was foot and mouth disease in the Lowveld at the time and it was thought carrion eaters could spread the disease. Bulldozers were brought in to dig enormous pits into which the remains were shoveled and the soil was then smoothed over. The bulldozers left raw tracks into the bush, but fortunately Nature soon healed the scars.

The culling was done over a period of weeks with the rangers letting up periodically to allow the contractors to catch up. We were close enough to the Gona-re-Zhou boundary for us to hear the spotter plane. It would circle a few times and then we would hear a volley of shots. I wrote in my diary at the time, "I can't help thinking of the fear and consternation of the young ones as the adults go down. One must be a very hard person to be able to undertake a mass killing like this. The fact that it is necessary doesn't lessen the horror or it. I hope it is necessary. We have been told that the research officer who recommended the culling is only twenty-four. It seems an enormous decision for such a young person."

The culling of elephants is always an emotional issue. In fairness to National Parks, I must add we were not in possession of all the facts. The whole culling operation was shrouded in secrecy which made one feel there was something to hide. An entire herd was eliminated at a time. The adults were shot first, then the baby males. The young females could be sold to zoos, but the males became difficult at adolescence so there was not much market for them. Females standing less than 36" from the shoulder were also shot. Experience had proved that they could not survive in captivity.

The remaining females were then taken to a stockade to give them time to settle down. After a few days they were let out, one at a time. These little creatures, some no more than three feet tall, would come rushing out into the stockade with ears extended and trunk raised, trumpeting shrilly, with all the confidence of an animal that knows no predator. An attendant would repulse it with a stick. After three or four rushes, it would accept that Man now had the upper hand. It was rather sad but I suppose a sign of intelligence.

Once this stage was reached, they were allowed out for a daily walk. It was touching to see the long line of little elephants walking behind the attendant, with the littlest one at the lead holding the man's hand with its trunk. The really little ones would suck the tip of their trunk, rather like an infant sucking its thumb.

The elephants were sold for $500 each and they were sent to zoos all over the world. I often wonder whether, standing in the snow in Canada, or in a field of English buttercups, those elephants think back longingly, as I do, to the endless expanse of bush; to the secure feeling of being at one with creation; to the strident sound of the cicada beetles or the liquid cadence of the woodland kingfisher; the sharp bark of the baboon; the ethereal call of the fisheagle; the sound and smell of the African bush. I hope they don't remember.

Chapter 20

At about this time, Jack Mudd joined us. He was a friend of the family and lived in Johannesburg, but he was a keen naturalist and hankered to live in the bush. He was young and enthusiastic and got on well with people. He had a delightful sense of humor and kept us in fits of laughter as he recounted the most trivial incident that he managed to imbue with drama. It was a relief having someone to help with picking up the thatching grass, timber, sand etc. We found the Shangaan women cutting our thatch most exasperating. They were being paid for the bundles they had cut. This was sometimes more than a load, and if we left any, they would put them back to resell to us. We then paid only as Jack loaded onto the truck, but in no time they were onto something new. They were cleaning only the outside grass and wrapping it round the bundles of grass that still had the seed heads on. When we remonstrated with them, they would put their hand to their mouth, swivel round on one foot, and giggle. The bundles became smaller and smaller until Jack gave them a wire hoop with which to measure each bundle. Sometimes we would drive all the way down to pick up thatch and find there had been a beer drink and no grass had been cut for several days. This was the other side to living and working in the bush with unsophisticated people.

James' brother, Method, came to work for us. Amon, the thatcher, had to go home for awhile, which generally meant he had enough money and wanted to get back to his family. Tafi took his place. Method and Tafi lived too far away to go home each evening. We hadn't yet built accommodation for our staff who were housed in tents, so Method and Tafi joined them. After the lions had been around the house one night, Paul asked whether they were not afraid of lions, but it seemed they weren't concerned about them. I think the truth was that once they were asleep, they were oblivious of what went on round them. If one ever had to wake them, it was like trying to rouse a corpse.

Method and Tafi were particularly boastful about what they would do to a lion. That evening as they sat around the fire outside their tents, Jack crept up behind the tents and played a recording of lions roaring. In a wink they all leapt into their tents, zipped up the fronts, and sat as quiet as mice. When we called to them and they realized it was a practical joke, they were convulsed with laughter, demonstrating how this one or that one had leapt over the fire and they re-told the story for days.

In this little society, the District Commissioner ruled supreme. He was the top government official in the district and his underlings treated him with the reverence accorded to doctors and ministers. Various D.C.s reacted differently to this attitude from their little community. On the one extreme, Alan Wright had isolated himself completely in his attempt to remain aloof and maintain authority.

The District Commissioner had his own rest houses at various points throughout the district. They were comfortably furnished and they each had a resident camp attendant to cook, wash, and see to the smooth running of the cottage when it was occupied. Before and after this particular D.C., it was common practice for anyone from the Nuanetsi office to use the D.C.'s resthouse. A paymaster, who worked in the D.C.'s office in Nuanetsi, was doing his rounds which took about a week. He decided to spend the night in the D.C.'s resthouse rather than the more austere accommodation intended for cattle buyers, the police, and visiting geologists. Unbeknownst to him, the D.C. was also in the district. The paymaster had his dinner and had retired to bed for the night when he heard a vehicle arrive. He felt no inclination to get up. There were several bedrooms and he would see the other occupant at breakfast. Presently, there was a knock at his door. It was the D.C.'s messenger. Would the paymaster please go elsewhere for the night? The D.C. wanted to use the rest house. He dressed and went out to find Alan Wright waiting in his vehicle for the paymaster to vacate the premises.

A most amusing ritual always took place at the D.C.'s office in Nuanetsi every morning. The African sergeant would parade the African staff, who were all smartly uniformed. The D.C. would get into his car within sight of the office and slowly drive down. As he emerged, the African staff stood rigidly to attention and saluted. When Graham Millar became District Commissioner, he thought it foolish to drive his car down to the office, so he came the few hundred yards on a motorcycle while his staff stood rigidly to attention in time honored colonial tradition.

Graham typified the new generation of district administrator. His dress was neat but casual. His manner was friendly and helpful and in no way lessened one's regard for him as an able administrator. He proved that he and his family did not have to live in isolation to be respected and maintain discipline.

The fact that Gona-re-Zhou and Malapati Game Reserves existed at all was due largely to the efforts of Alan Wright who had spent ten years in the area. This vast chunk of wilderness, topographically unsuited for agriculture, with a habitat which was ideal for game, had been earmarked to be cut up into African Purchase Area farms, and it was due to his ceaseless campaigning that these two Game Reserves came into being.

Alan Wright typified the old school colonial administrator. He knew the Africans as well as any white person could and he spoke their language fluently. He insisted on a certain standard of dress for his staff, explaining that if a tribesman came to see the representative of the government, he wore his best clothes and he expected to see the official smartly attired. He was very correct in his dealings with both Europeans and Africans. He was courteous but aloof, and his wife didn't mix with the wives of the local officials. He was inflexible in his decisions, and this earned him the African name of Chibgwe, which means 'heart of stone.' As with any strong personality, he had his detractors. They referred to him as 'Always Wright,' but I think even these people had a grudging admiration for him. He developed an extensive underground network that kept him informed of the mood of the people in his area. In 1965, it was largely due to his efforts that large-scale bloodshed was averted in this district.

For some time previously, he had been sending reports to Salisbury of subversion of well-known African politicians who were planning a massacre of all the whites in this area. It fell on deaf ears. An African nurse warned her supervisor that a massacre was imminent. Dr. Embree, who was then the doctor in charge at Chikombedzi Mission, immediately drove his family and the rest of the American staff to Nuanetsi. With confirmation from an independent source, Alan Wright was able to persuade the government to act immediately. The leaders were rounded up and arms and ammunition confiscated. A state of emergency was declared and the ringleaders were incarcerated, most of them at the Vila Salazar police camp.

Alan Wright's obsession with his work in the Nuanetsi district brought him into conflict with many people, but there is no doubt that he did a great deal for the district, its people, and the country. At a time when British Prime Ministers' chauffeurs were being awarded the Order of the British Empire, one can't help thinking of the injustice of a man like Alan Wright not receiving official recognition for his efforts. But people like him leave such an indelible mark where they have been that they are never really forgotten. He had already left the area some years before we arrived, but he was still being referred to, scoffed at, and quoted. I am sure the personal satisfaction he experienced in having Gona-re-Zhou and Malapati established for future generations was greater than any decoration would have been.

John Scott, the Member-in-Charge of the police camp at Vila Salazar, was due for transfer and we were invited to the farewell party. It was a long and tedious trip on a very bad road but we wanted to say goodbye to John. They had invited the Station Master from Malvernia and his wife, John Hicks the Police Chief from Nuanetsi and his wife Pam, and ourselves. They had taped music for dancing, but as there was a distinct shortage of women, the men soon took to the bar, leaving the three of us women to discuss domestic matters.

A very impressive looking person arrived. I was told he was the Portuguese Administrator from Malvernia. He had the suave good looks of Latino men. His hair was carefully smoothed down and he wore an enormous diamond ring on his little finger that also had the longest fingernail I had ever seen. He made constant use of it to scratch what seemed to be an incurable itch in his ear. He had a dazzling smile that revealed several gold teeth. The Administrator fascinated me. When I was introduced to him I offered my hand, expecting him to shake it. Instead, he clutched it and bent over it with such a broad smile that for an insane second I thought he would bite my hand. He sipped his whiskey with his little finger elegantly raised, and he didn't stay long.

Beer flowed freely, and soon the Station Master sank into a chair on the veranda with a glazed look on his face. Just above his head, a spray of pink bougainvillea nodded gaily. Someone suggested putting a flower in his hair. Someone else misunderstood and came back with flour that was duly rubbed into the unconscious man's hair. I felt sorry for these young men who were isolated in this remote corner for months at a time. It was a dreary setting for anyone but more so for a young bachelor. They had very little to do in their spare time. The more industrious of them worked on improving amenities and in this way they had eventually built themselves a pool, a miniature golf course, and a clubhouse which was constantly being added to and embellished since it was the hub of their existence.

By way of a change, they could go to Malvernia on the Portuguese side. Not that it had much more to offer. It consisted of a very wide unpaved main street with the railway line on the left and houses on the right. All the houses were identical - fenced in with hibiscus hedge and the whole garden seemingly taken up with growing kale. This was where the Portuguese Customs, Immigration, Police and Railway officials lived. About five Rhodesia Railways families also lived there as Malvernia was on the main Bulawayo/Lourenco Marques line and I supposed well placed from which to operate in either direction. I doubt there were many private citizens. I shouldn't think anyone who hadn't been sent there would choose to live in Malvernia.

The station was a grand affair of true Portuguese colonial architecture, with marble steps and ceramic tiles. The upper story had a large balcony intended no doubt to be used on ceremonial occasions, but in this little outpost, the upper floor was home to someone and the balcony was generally festooned with laundry on a wash line. Further down the street were the shops, a collection of trading stores that were almost identical. The veranda in each case was crowded with plow shears, bales of wire, fuel drums, and cooking pots. The stores were virtually windowless so the interiors were quite dark with the most incredible assortment of merchandise and smells. Portuguese wines with exotic looking bottles stood next to plump black olives, salted macadamia nuts rubbed shoulders with the more mundane tinned goods, kerosene lamps, and strong smelling dried fish. Lengths of brightly colored materials were strung from the ceiling. In huge wooden boxes were the delicious little oval loaves of Portuguese bread, freshly baked every day. On the other side of the railway station was the Club which was the place to go for prawns. They were sent up from Lourenco Marques by train twice a week and the local cook made prawns peri peri that one dreamed about until the next trip to Malvernia.

The Cassurina tree was very popular in Mozambique and almost the only tree planted in Malvernia. They were planted the length of the dusty street and by their very nature they had a scrawny look. The stems were painted white and a ring of white stones, which didn't enhance the overall effect, surrounded each one. Malvernia was bleak and unattractive.

Going through to Malvernia was something we only did if we happened to be in Vila Salazar and short of wine, sardines, cashews, or olives. The Rhodesians would wave us through, but at the Portuguese barrier, a rather languid African would saunter out, donning his cap and sunglasses and get into the vehicle with us to escort us to the station where we were motioned into the Immigration office. The official always seemed to have something urgent to attend to just as we arrived. He would finally put down his pen and let forth a torrent of words. My limited Portuguese always failed me under this pressure, and with a weary sigh, he would turn and bellow for Julio or Augustino, who would turn out to be a Shangaan. It always amused me to think that our interpreter was very likely related to our Shangaans living a mere twenty five miles away, and that had he lived on our side, Julio or Augustino would have been called July or August. The interpreting was quite complicated as the official spoke only Portuguese and Paul spoke only English with Augustino and myself battling on in a mixture of Shangaan and English. He would inquire where we were going and the length of our stay. "To the store for about half an hour" would satisfy him, and with an impatient wave of the hand, we would be dismissed. From there, we had to go to the Customs hall which generally looked like a schoolroom with about six officials, several of whom seemed to be home schooling their children. The procedure was much the same here and one felt one was a great imposition on these busy men's time.

In these depressing surroundings, with temperatures sometimes going up to 115° with no air conditioning, it was not surprising that some people went to pieces. The wife of a Rhodesia Railways employee had a breakdown, and in her muddled state, she decided to go home to Bulawayo on foot. No one paid much attention when she walked through to the Rhodesian side and through the police camp. Several hours later, her husband discovered her absence. Since no trains or vehicles had passed through the settlement, it was obvious she was on foot. A full-scale search was launched and she was found several miles into the Game Reserve.

On another occasion, a nineteen-year-old patrol officer from Vila Salazar got talking to one of the rare parties coming through Customs and Immigration into Rhodesia from Mozambique. There were two young women and two young men and they had driven up through Mozambique, camping along the way. He invited them to join him for a drink at the police club. Since it was by then quite late and they were self-contained, they decided to camp at Nyala siding and carry on in the morning. Later that evening, the policeman seemed to have gone to visit them and found them all asleep. The girls must have looked very attractive to him as they slept in the back of the vehicle because he decided to kidnap them. He immobilized his Land Rover by removing the rotor and then took off in their vehicle with the two girls, leaving their two companions in their tent. They were camped about five miles from VS and it would have been an easy matter for one of the men to have run back for help in the morning, but the night before they had seen a lion and some elephant, so they decided to flag down a train instead. The train was going in the wrong direction, but they took it and got off at Mbizi, 35 miles away, to report the matter. They were told the nearest police station was Vila Salazar. They took the next train back several hours later, but by now the kidnapper had an enormous start. A massive search was launched. They had aircraft and helicopters searching without success. It was not until several days later when he tried to cross into South Africa that he was picked up at Beit Bridge. It seems the girls were willing hostages and they insisted he had been kind and courteous and they had thoroughly enjoyed sightseeing with him. The young policeman was discharged from the police and sent for psychiatric evaluation, but it transpired he was just plain desperate for female company.

When I had to go to Nyala siding to pick up fruit trees I had ordered from Salisbury, I found the Warden had erected a boom where one left Gona-re-Zhou at the railway line. An attendant presented me with a book in which I had to write my name and business and he raised the barrier to let me pass. I arrived back to find the attendant gone. I walked around the little cluster of huts where the man was housed and found a woman. I asked her where the attendant was and she answered with a torrent of words which I couldn't understand. I examined the boom and found it unlocked. It was a cantilevered metal boom and I couldn't think of a way to keep it up. As soon as I let go it crashed down again. I went in search of the woman and was just in time to see her close the door. I knew she wouldn't emerge again until I had gone. I searched every corner of my civilized brain but I could not come up with a solution other than that foolish woman locked in her hut to hold the boom up for me. After twenty minutes, I was seething with anger and frustration and I was reminded of a story Mr. Palfrey had told us. They had gone through to Malvernia to make some purchases. Before the time of the imposing building at the railway station, the Portuguese Customs had an African manning a boom, and when anyone had to be processed, the African would go off and summon the official who would attend to the formalities on the spot. This day, the attendant had arrived back to say the boss was having his breakfast. An hour later, Mr. Palfrey sent the attendant off again. He returned to say the boss was still having his breakfast. Anyone who lives in the bush in Africa develops patience, if nothing else, because one is so often thwarted by circumstances and one learns to be philosophical, but even an old timer had a limit to his patience. The Palfreys were on the Portuguese side and wanting to leave. Mr. Palfrey backed his vehicle up to the boom that marked the border between Mozambique and Rhodesia. As he put his foot on the accelerator, the boom splintered, and with a cheery wave of his hand, Mr. Palfrey told the astonished African to tell his boss not to hurry. A few days later, an African from Malvernia came into Mr. Palfrey's store and told him he had been asked by the Portuguese to tell Mr. Palfrey that if he ever set foot on the Portuguese side again be would be arrested. If this boom had not been metal, I think I might have done the same. The fence was made of sturdy wooden posts but in between were lighter metal stakes. I drove to the four-strand fence running from either side of the boom and I aimed the one front wheel at one of the metal stakes. It flattened the fence and I drove over. I fully expected repercussions from the Warden, but if they were going to have a boom, it should have been manned at all reasonable times. The attendant must have repaired the damage himself rather than have to explain his absence to the Warden.

The Game Reserve boundary fences were somewhat more substantial than the one at the boom, but they still looked rather flimsy, in spite of the heavy mopani fence posts. It was strung with what looked like thin wash line and I often wondered whether an animal bumping into it at speed would not just snap the wire. It was in fact high tensile steel wire. On a trip back from Vila Salazar, we once encountered a herd of buffalo running along the other side of the fence. As we gained on them, a young bull broke away and obviously intended to run across our path, as they so often do. He was still young but he weighed easily 1,000 lbs. He hit the fence at full speed and bounced off as though he had hit a trampoline, and the fence was still intact. Fortunately he was unhurt and ran off with the herd. The gap between the wires was only about 12," yet we once saw an impala ram, with sizeable horns, leap through between the strands, hardly slowing his pace. He had put his horns right back and tucked his legs in as he went through.

Chapter 21

In May of 1972, we had a letter from an American agent making our first bookings for August. Now our venture was becoming a reality, but only two of the huts were completed. The remaining four still had to be thatched and had to have the interiors done. We had constant interruptions with an endless stream of visitors, and if Paul and I were not visible, work ground to a halt.

The missionaries brought down visiting Americans to see Malapati, and the Game Department and the Police brought down visiting VIPs to see what we were doing. They would spend the morning or the afternoon, each no doubt thinking they were our only callers. We enjoyed meeting them but it did mean we had to stop what we were doing to entertain them, and time was vital to us if we were to be ready by August. We also found we were inundated with friends and acquaintances coming to visit. During one three week period, we had nine friends to stay.

One of the government officials stopped by and asked us to judge at the handcraft section of the Sengwe Agricultural Show. It was held at the cattle sale pens and it had the same festive air. A group of four singers who had imbibed rather freely gave an impromptu concert.

At some stage, someone had introduced a type of 'curly' feathered fowl and they were very popular. They always looked as though they had been pulled through a bush backwards. Poultry specimens were shown in cages made of mopani sticks that looked rather like lobster pots. Two angry curly cocks standing next to each other were frantically trying to fight through the bars, accentuating their rumpled look.

A beautiful handmade wagon had been entered. It was made entirely of wood. The flatbed was made of beautifully hand-planed planks and the driver's seat was a magnificent bench that could have graced any living room. The wheels were round slices of mahogany. The axles went through a hole in the middle and they were held in place with wooden pegs. This piece was obviously not intended for use. It was kept as the only entry in its category every year.

William had exhibited one of the loaves of bread he had baked for me the previous day and James had one of the dining room chairs he had made for us on show. From the look on their faces, I knew they expected to win. To them, it would add to our prestige if they did, and we would surely see to it that they won first prize. The locals grew corn, pumpkin, and tomatoes and there were many entries of these, but Mishek stood grinning behind magnificent specimens of more unusual vegetables that I realized had come from our garden. He confidently told me he would win because no one else grew eggplant, green peppers or asparagus.

Roy Borlase came by and told us he had to go to the hospital at Chikombedzi. The previous night an African, on his way home from a beer drink, had encountered an elephant. It had knocked him to the ground, but it had been scared off when another straggler from the beer drink had come singing down the pathway. Fortunately, the man sustained no more than a few broken bones and, I hope, a new respect for elephants.

James' father approached us about employing his youngest son, Amato. He was intelligent and spoke English. The ability to drive was a great status symbol and he was prepared to work in any capacity if we would teach him to drive. Paul was reluctant to do this as no one really had the time to spare, and it was obvious that as soon as he had his license he would want to work as a driver. We had no use for a driver at this stage. Paul, Jack and I did the driving, but Amato's family had already spent a considerable amount on driving lessons in Fort Victoria and he still didn't have a license. Finally, we agreed to take him on as a gardener and move Mishek up a notch. The driving school had taught Amato very little because he couldn't remember to use the clutch to change gears, and if Paul told him to stop he would stand on the brake and stall the engine. Eventually, Paul's patience ran out and Amato was the first and last employee we tried to teach to drive. Amos, who used a very strong perfume that seemed to pervade the whole house, replaced Amato in the garden. One could smell where he had been. Like Charlie, he brushed his hair into an Afro halo that framed his face.

Bookings were coming in now and we were working at night to finish the building on time. We had based the design on the Shangaan huts which have a wide overhang of thatch, supported by poles standing about three feet from the walls. Instead of windows, we had brick piers that we screened against insects. Each bedroom had two beds, a teak bedside table and stool, built in cupboard, luggage stool, bedside mat, and a large mirror. Alternate huts were done in burnt orange and brown, and the remaining three were done in olive green with brown curtains, bed covers, and towels. Leading off the bedroom was the bathroom. An arched doorway connected the two rooms. Building the arch was quite a feat and cutting the door to fit was even more so. The front door was of local teak and made by James, as were all the wooden fittings and furniture, and although they were not always quite symmetrical, they had a certain rustic charm. Each hut had a Shangaan name. They were named for some of the animals that occurred in the area... NONGU - Kudu, HONGONI - Wildebeest, MHALA - Sable, NYALA - Nyala, PUTI - Duiker and MBVALA - Bushbuck. Inside each hut, we had a painting of the relevant buck and a pair of mounted horns.

I had wanted to have rings and rods for hanging the curtains, but they were so expensive that we decided to improvise, and the substitute was more interesting than the commercial ones would have been. We sliced the 2" PVC heavy gauge piping into 1/4" rings. We then screwed an eyelet into the bottom for the curtain to hook onto and, being an off-white color, most people took the rings for ivory. Jack carved the door handles out of Tambootie, a very hard local wood.

The huts had been built of hollow blocks and we plastered the outside with cement the way Africans use mud. We tried having the laborers do the plastering but, having had traumas over the standard of smooth plastering on the inside walls, they just could not grasp that we now wanted the rough, hand plastered look, so in the end we did it ourselves. We painted with a mud-colored cement wash halfway up the walls and used a lighter tone for the upper half as the Shangaans do. The whole effect was most pleasing. The huts had been built in a large semi-circle, all facing onto a large expanse of lawn.

The main building consisted of an office and storeroom, living room, and pub, which was called the Tiva - the waterhole or drinking place. The living room had three large arches in the front wall and a substantial fireplace in one corner. We faced the front of the pub counter with beautifully matched round river stones. We found a carpenter called Joseph who worked with Tambootie, a very hard and difficult wood with which to work. Joseph was a frail and gentle person and a very good craftsman. He made the top of our pub counter and he did a meticulous job of dovetailing. Behind the pub, we had a small room where we had a refrigerator and where we stored the soft drinks.

The dining room was just behind the main building. It was basically a thatched roof mopani pole structure with cement plastered on the outside to withstand the rain. The front had no wall at all and looked onto a small area of lawn, enclosed by massive weathered fence posts that we had brought from an old cattle-dipping tank. The enclosure was about eight-feet high and it gave one a feeling of security at night. In the center stood a large and very old Kigelia tree. Under this tree we made a raised, circular platform, about 12" high and 6' across, out of anthill mud. This was where we made the fire at night and the anthill baked hard. Being raised, the ashes were easy to clean away in the morning and the ledge was comfortable for resting one's feet.

Since all the other buildings had names, I tried to establish from William what the equivalent of an enclosure was in Shangaan. He was totally puzzled by the word 'enclosure.' I explained it would be like a place where one kept cattle. He went into paroxysms of laughter when he discovered I wanted to call our dining room a cattle enclosure. "Better make it Chiwava" which was the enclosure elders used for discussions. So Chiwava it was. The interior walls looked rather bare and dark. Since the Shangaans don't do decorative work on their huts, we had to borrow from the Ndebele tribal decor. We used a cement wash to simulate their muted pinks and yellowy earth colors, and we painted one of their designs in a band around the inside walls.

A pathway that ran behind the Chiwava led to the guest area. It must have been an old buffalo route because they continued to plod along this little path, considerably narrowed by the new building. We erected a barrier of mopani poles, leaving a gap for us to get through between the barrier and the corner of the building, but the buffalo continued to squeeze through and they eventually removed a sizeable chunk of cement from the building. They seemed determined to use that pathway. Elephants were much the same. There was an elephant path coming down from the airstrip and past the Lodge to the river. They used it only at night. Possibly our presence during the day kept them away. Walking along this pathway in the morning, with the mounds of droppings still fresh and shiny and distinctly aromatic, one was always filled with a sense of wonder that but a few hours before, those great gray giants had walked this same pathway in the dark with the same casual confidence with which we were now walking it in daylight. We would follow the tracks with each little crack in the soles of their feet clearly defined in the powdery sand. They would go down the bank onto the riverbed and then continue on up to the permanent pool, about a mile from us. Here they would dig for water, making a hole about 12" in diameter and sometimes two feet deep, allowing the water to filter into the hole. They generally used the pools for bathing but preferred clear water for drinking. An elephant can draw up to 2 1/2 gallons at a time and it needs about 50 gallons a day, although it drinks only about 80% of the water; the rest is for bathing.

A new problem now arose. The local bats discovered our house. It had been designed for outdoor living. The dining room was just an extension of the patio and had no doors. To the bats, this was the most desirable place to hang. Unfortunately they didn't just hang. They made a pungent mess that had to be cleaned up each morning and the floor had to be washed with disinfectant. We put up curtains that we could draw at night, closing off the dining room. For a few days this confused them. Then they hung from the eaves and messed up the patio. We made a giant 'bat curtain' as we had done for the kitchen. We used lengths of reed, alternating with PVC rings, strung onto fishing line and hung these six inches apart across the front of the patio. During the day we could hold them back. It took some time for the bats to discover they could fly over the top of the roof into the patio. Finally, we strung fishing line three inches apart across the top of the patio, like a giant harp! They were hardly visible… bat-proof yet not unsightly. It seems incredible to have gone to such lengths, but in summer without air conditioning and with the temperatures in the nineties, we enjoyed putting beds out on the patio at night. It now became clear to us why homes in the Lowveld were so stereotyped, all with screened verandas. I liked our distinctive house design, and our innovative measures to keep the bats out worked for us.

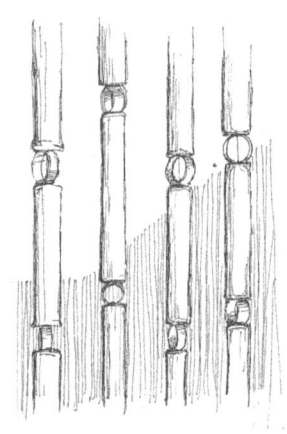

The reed 'curtains' worked so well we used them across the arches in the guest common areas and across the front of the Chiwava and anywhere we wanted to keep the bats out. They were not just functional; they were visually attractive and made a gentle, soothing noise, rather like wind chimes, as the slightest breeze moved them.

The mosquitoes were almost negligible. We had in fact installed fly screens on all the windows when we built the house, but they were superfluous as we generally slept with the doors open when we slept indoors. Sleeping on the patio was very pleasant. We would listen to the night sounds and look at the stars that were very bright in the darkness where they were not competing with city lights. We would invariably see a shooting star. The smells too seemed to take on an added dimension when the fierce heat of the day no longer diluted their distillation. As we lay there looking up at the night sky, we would see the inter-continental jets passing over, and for me they provided a physical manifestation of our link with civilization as though some invisible umbilical cord reached down to us.

When the boys were home, Jack would take them fishing. He was a keen bee keeper, which appealed to Christopher, and an authority on snakes, which appealed to both boys. On one fishing trip, Jack found a large python that the three of them set about catching. Jack held the head, Christopher the mid-section, and Simon the tail. Halfway up the hill, on the way back to the vehicle, they lost their grip on the python. In the ensuing struggle to hold it, the python was no doubt frightened and overcome by a bout of diarrhea of which Simon got the full blast. They managed to get the snake home, but Simon smelt as if a skunk had attacked him.

Jack wanted to keep the python as a pet. This seemed like insanity to me, but we could hardly object since this was his hobby. He kept it in his bedroom and we forgot about it. One morning, he announced that the python had escaped and was somewhere in the house. It took several hours to locate it, but we finally found it curled up in Jack's cupboard. We persuaded him to release it since both our cat and dog would make a tasty snack for the python. I could never feel any empathy for Jack's preoccupation with snakes. He really enjoyed handling them. He brought home a cobra that he wanted to take to a fellow snake lover in Fort Victoria. I was unaware of this and decided to go with him to Fort Vic to do some shopping. As we were about to leave, he rummaged around and brought out a pillowcase, securely tied at the top, but with a hole in the corner. It was then that he told me that his cobra had escaped. Even Jack was alarmed and we almost took the vehicle apart trying to find it, without success. I had a very unpleasant journey to town that trip, expecting at any moment to have the cobra appear.

On a trip to pick up timber one day, Jack spotted a monitor lizard up a tree. He and Mishek went up after it. I was surprised he had persuaded Mishek to help because Africans were generally terrified of reptiles. Even the harmless chameleon sent them running. However between them, they managed to dislodge it and brought it home. Small creatures we were nursing were generally put in with the chickens, which had by now become used to accept anything from yellow billed kite to duiker, but the monitor would eat them. Jack suggested we put it into one of the huts we were still working on until he could think of where to keep it. Being arboreal, the monitor climbed the walls and tore up the inside of the thatch as well as the screens over the windows. It was amazing how much damage that creature did in just a few days, so Jack decided to give it to the friend in Fort Victoria who had missed out on the cobra.

Chapter 22

One morning, an old man arrived and started pottering around in the garden. He was a weird apparition with an orange sack on his head, a yeast tin suspended from a string around his neck and a staff which had Coke bottle tops attached to it that made a rattle when he walked. On the front of his shirt, he had pinned part of a Lion beer pack: "Down a Lion and Feel Satisfied." I asked William about the old man and he said he was a local called Government. He had once worked on the gold mines. What obviously impressed William was that Government could speak English, and in William's words "then his mind changed." He was quite mad but harmless. His family had great difficulty in keeping him at home and he would wander from one village to another, staying for a few days and then wandering on. He carried a machete, which worried me, so I asked William to send him away. He turned on the hapless William with a choice selection of four letter words. He certainly spoke English!

We always knew when Government had been around because he would cut a blaze into the trees as he walked along. He also loved to make a fire with a stick and dry twigs. He would twiddle his stick until the first wisps of smoke appeared and he would blow until it flared up. He didn't ever put his fires out, and on several occasions they did considerable damage. But on the whole he was harmless and happy, wandering around in his fantasy world.

OXBOW

MANJINJI PAN

NUANETSI RIVER

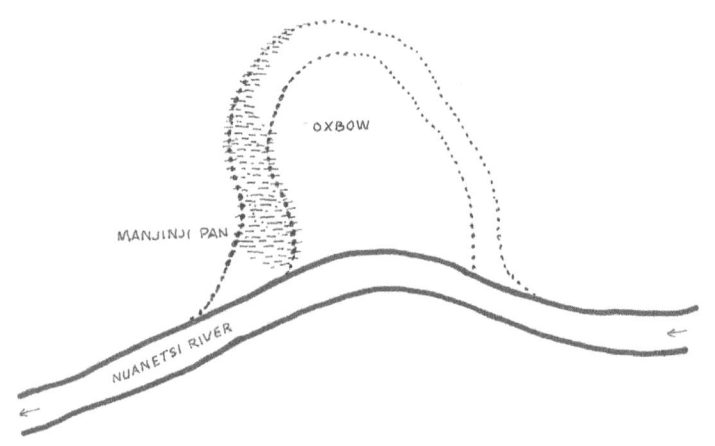

About five miles from us, in the Tribal Trust Lands, was Manjinji Pan. The approach was through some of the most beautiful riverine forest area which was unfortunately slowly being hacked down for firewood by the Africans. Once one left the Game Reserve, the difference was quite marked. There was considerable erosion. Cattle and goats were everywhere and there was almost no regeneration of the vegetation, from overgrazing.

Manjinji, however, was a proclaimed bird sanctuary and this included the vegetation immediately surrounding the Pan. As one approached it on the winding track, through a dense canopy of foliage, one had the feeling that this must have been how the early explorers had seen Africa. Manjinji was part of an old oxbow in the Nuanetsi River and had at some time been silted up and cut off from the river. It was seasonal; it filled during the floods and the water level slowly dropped until it was almost dry. The different water levels brought different species of birds and it was a fascinating place at any time of the year.

In summer, it was almost completely covered with water lilies. The banks were a mass of magnificent trees; the Kigelia (Sausage Tree) with its outsize fruits; Acacia Albida with its ferny branches swaying over the water; the Xanthophlea (Fever Tree); Afzelia Quanzensis (Natal Mahogany), with its fascinating red and black seeds; Combretum Imberbe, (Leadwood); and climbing up the stems of the trees, the beautiful liana, Combretum Microphyllum. These creepers sometimes have a stem 12-18" in diameter. They climb to the tops of the trees where they make a shower of red flowers. When the flowers drop, the masses of tiny winged yellow seedpods create an equally spectacular show.

All around the edge of the water grew the bulrushes and sedge, and the pan teemed with every type of waterfowl. There were saddlebill and spoonbill storks; various geese and ducks; herons and egrets; and the fascinating Jacanas, the lily trotters that nest on the lily pads. When they're alarmed, they leap up, clutching their young under their wings, with the little legs dangling.

With the prospect of guests that season, I felt I could no longer manage with only Esther to do the laundry. James brought a relative called Jane. She was a bright and cheerful person and she had worked in Bulawayo so she required very little training. She also spoke English, always a major asset. There could be so many misunderstandings without it.

Jack asked whether his family could come up and see Malapati. They wanted to bring their daughter and her husband and Jack's girlfriend from Johannesburg. Work on the Lodge would be suspended for the four days they were there, but it would be a valuable trial run before our first American clients arrived. We needed various items of hardware and Simon had a weekend, so Jack and Paul stayed to work on No. 3 hut while I went up to Fort Victoria for the weekend. Method wanted to come with me as he was having 'eye trouble' and thought he needed glasses. He would stay with friends in Fort Victoria and Simon and I would go to Le Rhone for the weekend.

The trip proved very interesting. Method was by far the most educated African with whom I had had contact at Malapati. He spoke fluent English and we were able to converse about a wide range of topics. When we passed Chitanga, just after the Lundi River, Method told me he too had been to boarding school like our boys. He had been to Chitanga School and not the local one-room Malaptai school because his father had wanted the best for his sons. I now understood why he and his brother James spoke such good English. He also told me it was named for Chief Chitanga who was chief of all the Shangaans. Method's family was Ndebele but he was well informed about the Shangaan people. Chitanga's was not a hereditary succession as I understood it, but on the death of a Chief, traditionally, a mere headman called Mpapa would appoint the next Chief Chitanga. Mpapa lived near Chikombedzi. How Mpapa's standing was established Method was not quite sure.

Method told me his family had been to Chikombedzi recently to see an 'African Doctor.' I was surprised because his family was so progressive and the men all educated, but it seemed even educated Africans would still resort to witchcraft. I asked him what the problem was. He told me a child in their village had died and it was thought that a childless woman living close by had wished the child ill! I scoffed at the idea but Method was amused at my skepticism. He kept repeating, "but of course it is so." The woman had been taken to the witch doctor to determine whether she was innocent or guilty. If she had been found guilty, she would have been shunned as an outcast and rejected even by her family. A few weeks later I inquired of the outcome and fortunately the woman had been found not guilty.

We were now stocked up for our first guests. We discussed with Method and Jane the possibility of having the minstrels who had performed at the Agricultural Show come to sing after dinner one evening when the Mudds were there. The minstrels were related to Method and Jane and they both seemed to think the standard of their performance would depend on the amount of liquor they had consumed. They thought the Malapati School choir would be a better idea.

Paul and Jack had almost completed number three hut while I was away. The brick piers had to be painted rather carefully as the huts were white on the inside and brown on the outside, and the white paint had to end at the edge of the brick piers. Renos, being one of the more skilled of the laborers, was briefed to do the job. He had helped paint the interior and one would assume he would know to use the PVA but instead he used white enamel and painted right around to the outside. Paul was upset by this and asked him to put everything away and they could sort it out some other time. For some reason, Renos decided to tip the remains of the can of enamel into a half empty can of PVA which Charlie then used to paint the inside walls of number 2 hut. This meant No. 2 had to be re-painted. One had to keep reminding oneself that one was dealing with people who had not had much exposure to civilization and the fact that they were willing workers counted for a lot.

The Mudds arrived on Saturday morning, and while we were getting them settled in we heard an aircraft buzz us and we heard it land. There had been considerable correspondence about a booking for this weekend, but as we were expecting the Mudds, we had written suggesting a later date. We had had no reply to our letter. It suddenly dawned on me that this might be the party who had wanted accommodation for eight people, but our letter may not have reached them. We only had three huts ready and I was doing mental gymnastics, trying to think of a way we could accommodate everybody. Paul drove up to the airstrip to meet them and found it was Osric Bristow and Sam Cawood, a rancher friend, who had decided to drop in and visit on their way to Mozambique.

They had lunch with us and Osric, who was an incredible raconteur, provided non-stop entertainment. After Osric and Sam, left we drove up to Mafuku, one of the artificial water holes in Gona-re-Zhou. An enormous herd of buffalo came down to drink. We had been able to show our visitors one of the 'big three' - lion, elephant and buffalo - which most people hoped to see. We had worked out a rough routine that we were trying out on the Mudds. Method had arranged with the headmaster of the local school to allow his choir to sing, but we had no idea of the size of the choir. It turned out to be thirty children whom we had to pick up and return to the school. When Paul arrived to pick up the children, he found there had been the inevitable misunderstanding. The headmaster, Mr. Shumba, had had the children waiting since 9 a.m. and he had finally dismissed them at 4 p.m., but he now insisted they go around to the various villages to pick up the children. Mr. Shumba brought two members of the School Board, one of whom was Faniel, whose brother Makenzie was the Internal Affairs driver. We offered them a drink and they joined our guests. To our staff, this now meant a free-for-all social evening, since their relatives were being entertained. Both Method and Jane were related to Faniel, and Jane did the rounds greeting all and shaking hands with her family, oblivious of the needs of our guests. I found Method sipping a bottle of beer.

The choir marched into the Chiwava and Mr. Shumba grouped and regrouped the children. He then tuned his choir, giving them each a note to sing. Finally they were ready and launched into hymns, with a lengthy explanation preceding each one, while the children waited patiently. It wasn't really what we had in mind and we asked whether they would sing a selection of their favorite traditional songs. Immediately they produced lovely harmonies with hand clapping and delightful rhythms. The songs were charming and the children sang beautifully, but we realized the organization involved in transporting them was just too much to have when we had paying guests.

At six the following morning, we had coffee and then went out for a game drive. The Land Rover had two rows of seats at the back and could comfortably seat six with another one in front next to the driver. The front passenger was usually the spotter who had to keep a look out for anything of interest. We had removed the tops of both Land Rovers as we ourselves enjoyed driving this way, and it proved popular with the guests. There weren't many places one could drive around like that in a Game Reserve.

The early morning drive was always exciting. There is something invigorating about the start of a day, especially in the bush with its fresh, clean smell when everything seems to take on new proportions. There is a feeling of newness, and of being one with Nature. We topped a rise and looked down onto the biggest herd of buffalo we were ever to see. We guessed about six hundred animals. It was an awe-inspiring sight. They milled around like cattle, with the young bulls dashing forward every now and again and churning up the sand until they were swathed in a cloud of dust, which, in the early morning light, gave the scene a subtle quality. On the way back, we saw a herd of elephant quietly browsing in the mopani scrub. We went back to a leisurely breakfast and then drove to Manjinji Pan as the Mudds were keen bird watchers. After lunch, we went for a walk up the river and pointed out the various tracks where the animals had come down to the river to drink at the pools. On foot, one was often able to get quite close to animals if the wind was coming from the right direction, and these walks proved to be the highlight of most people's stay at Malapati.

When it had cooled down in the late afternoon, we took them out for another game drive and came home in time to shower and change for dinner. We had three very pleasant days with the Mudds and it proved a valuable experience. We were able to establish how we would occupy our guests and we were able to eliminate what we thought would be impractical. On one of the game drives, we had done a considerable mileage in Gona-re-Zhou, and although we had seen a fair amount of game, we had seen no more than we could have seen driving around Malapati. Some of the best viewing was in fact between our house and the airstrip and we decided only to go into Gona-re-Zhou if there was something our guests had not been able to see in Malapati. The long drives into Gona-re-Zhou could become tedious.

In the mail, we had a booking from a South African couple from Johannesburg. Jack's parents offered to telephone on their return and confirm the booking. At this stage booking posed a problem. Our only means of communication was by mail and the mailbag was sent down twice a week on the African bus to a trading store about ten miles from us. Many times we went to meet the bus to pick up the mail only to find that the driver had gone through Nuanetsi on his way down from Fort Victoria and had not picked up our mailbag from the post office. At other times, the post office had been closed because the postmaster had gone to Fort Victoria for the day. Sometimes the bus just didn't come down to Malapati. The frustrations were endless.

The District Commissioner had an arrangement with the post office to send any telegrams for us to his office. They would radio the contents down to Manuel at the D.C.'s rest camp and he would come over on his bicycle to relay the message. By this time, the message was often quite garbled and sometimes very funny, but we were very grateful for this service, our only means of urgent communication.

During the Mudd's stay, there was considerable activity every night in the bush surrounding the guest accommodation - elephant browsing and trumpeting and buffalo droppings on the lawn, but not a sign of the lions - not until the night after they had left!

The buffalo were becoming a problem as they were coming each night to eat our banana plants that grew just outside our bedroom window. We hastily put up a mopani pole paddock fence, but the following night one of them crawled under the fence and chewed at the plants. Paul took a metal wastepaper basket and went out to the shower, just feet from the buffalo on the other side of the wall, and banged on the tin. The buffalo took off in such a rush that it took the fence with it.

Chapter 23

Once we decided to do more game viewing in Malapati we had to make the tracks. We started on the track between the airstrip and the house and we let it double back on itself, looping back and forth, without the previous track being visible from the next. In this way we were able to cover the entire area. This location was favored by the rare and elusive Nyala and in this way we could ensure that we would always see them.

It was August and grazing was becoming scarce. The game gravitated to the camp and every plant seemed to have an animal craving it. The buffalo had almost demolished all the banana plants by this stage and one of my precious cycads fell to the porcupines. The elephants came onto the lawn one night and tore down one of the creepers.

A parcel arrived via the african bus with three of the nine waiter's suits I had ordered. The rest were to follow. In the meantime, the waiters would just have to keep clean. Our first American client was due to arrive the following day. She had been booked through a New York tour operator who promised to bring us a great deal of business. As she was alone, chartering an aircraft had not been feasible and we had agreed to meet the scheduled flight from Salisbury to Buffalo Range, 120 miles away. Just before Paul left, we heard a leopard in the bush between the house and the camp and we fervently hoped he would return in the next few days while Melanie was with us.

The drive back from Buffalo Range was quite exciting for our client. It was dirt road all the way, in itself a novelty, and it took them through the granite hills and Baobab trees near Buffalo Range. They went through the heavily wooded cattle ranching country where the ranchers still jealously protected their game. They saw several giraffe and eland crossing the road before they were even in the Game Reserve. Then they came through the Mopani scrub of Chikombedzi, past the mission hospital, where they encountered several boys driving ox carts. They would always just bale out and abandon the cart and oxen at the approach of a vehicle. This was, of course, intensely interesting and new to our guest. There were also the inevitable herds of goats dashing out of the bush to cross the road just ahead of the vehicle. Numerous scrawny fowls, generally molting around the neck, would dash out and run ahead of the vehicle, as only fowls will do, to add to the atmosphere of the drive. Finally, they reached the Game Reserve and arrived at Malapati in time for lunch.

Melanie was an interesting and intelligent woman who had done a great deal of travelling. She had had a long and tiring drive and we thought a picnic lunch at Manjinji would help her to relax. It was looking superb and it simply teemed with every kind of waterfowl. We even saw a languid crocodile surface with a water lily on his head! It was one of those days when Nature was kind when we wanted to show off our bit of Africa.

The following morning, Manuel arrived with a telegram which had been radioed down from the D.C.'s office in Nuanetsi. As always, the telegram had been telephoned by the African clerk at the Post Office to the D.C.'s African radio clerk, who in turn had transmitted it to Manuel, who had then written it down and brought it to us. Although these clerks had a fairly high standard of English, there were many words that were not in their vocabulary, so it was not surprising that the messages were sometimes so garbled. This one read, "A merry man can date four by air on Friday." Melanie came to the rescue. Our American agent, Brien Merriman, was in Rhodesia on a visit and he had mentioned to her that he might fly down to see Malapati. Some days later when we received the confirmation copy of the telegram it read, "Can you accommodate four arriving by air on Friday. Merriman."

Melanie was in number 1 hut, the Paynes, from Johannesburg, would go into number 2, number 3 was free, though number 4 still had a fair amount to be done, we decided to accept and radioed the reply to Brien. Jack and Paul had to take turns to slip away to work on number 4. It had to be painted and had to have the curtain rods put up and the plumbing done. I also still had to make the curtains. Melanie enjoyed sitting around the fire chatting until after midnight and when we suggested she might like to turn in early, she would protest. "I love it. I can do all my sleeping when I get home."

The boys were due home for their school holidays on Thursday and Jack was to drive to Fort Victoria to pick them up and to do the shopping for the additional guests. I made detailed lists for him and prayed that he wouldn't forget anything. William came to tell me that Amos was "weak in the arms and hot in the stomach." This was generally a symptom of malingering among our staff and I would administer a heavy dose of anti-malarial tablets and put the ailing one off work for a few days. Invariably, the very person who had stood wan and listless before me earlier would suddenly emerge as the life and soul of the gathering when they were on their own.

Amos was our second waiter and Method would just have to manage on his own. He came to me just before lunch and said he had spilled beet root on his white trousers the previous evening. Amos was so slight, his trousers wouldn't fit Method. William was about the same size as Method but only about five foot tall and he had already altered his trouser legs to fit. I remembered two lengths of cotton traditional prints that I had. Tribal men wear them like a sarong and I thought Method could wear one instead of trousers with his white jacket and red fez. I gave them to Method and let him decide which one he wanted to wear. We were having a drink before lunch when I caught sight of Method. The sarong looked most exotic but he had replaced his fez with the second length of material. He wore it around his head like a turban but the extra yards make his head look three times its size. I suggested the fez might work better.

That afternoon the Paynes arrived. They were an easy and friendly couple who got on well with Melanie. Paul managed to finish the fourth hut that night and we were ready for the next party to arrive the following day with Brien Merriman. He had brought a courier whom he was going to employ, and a Rhodesian farming couple from Bindura, Freddie and Monica Johnson. They had flown the party down in their Cessna. They owned the Milibizi Fishing Lodge, and as Brien would be sending tourists to them as well, he had been to see their Lodge on Lake Kariba. The Johnsons were unassuming people and interesting to talk to with many of the same problems that we were experiencing.

We were having drinks that evening when Jack arrived back with the provisions and Christopher and Simon. They had a cage with a pair of white mice. Jack had done a mammoth job of shopping and he had managed to get everything. He vowed he would never do it again. "Felling trees, loading sand or cement, making bricks, plumbing ..... anything else is easy compared to the nightmare of worrying about remembering everything you're going to need for the next three weeks."

The Johnsons were in the newly finished number 4 hut and they were late arriving for drinks. Eventually Freddie came in, whispered something to Paul, and they both went off. One of the pipe joints on the hand basin was leaking and had flooded their hut. Kind people that they were, they hadn't wanted the other guests to know that anything was amiss. Paul managed to tighten the joint and we had the staff clean up.

Melanie was flying to Salisbury the following day and we were driving her back to Buffalo Range, but the Johnsons insisted on flying her there, a matter of half an hour by air. They arrived back with the met. report that the following day would be heavy 'guti' - heavy mist or light rain. It cleared up by noon and they were able to leave after lunch.

It was now just the Paynes and ourselves. Mr. Payne told me that his trousers, which he had sent to the laundry, had been ironed, and as they were drip dry, ironing could ruin their drip-dry quality. He suggested I mention to my ironing lady to check the labels on garments. I apologized to him and suppressed my smile as I thought of dear old Esther who wouldn't have recognized her own name had it been written on his pants. I asked Jane to check laundry labels before giving anything to Esther to wash.

After dinner that night, the Paynes said they would prefer to sleep late the next morning rather than go for an early morning game drive. They were such thoughtful guests, they insisted on sleeping late despite our protests. We felt sure they were doing it for our sakes. Our first batch of guests had been fun and good company and we looked forward to the next batch. We were really sorry to see them leave after four days.

On our next shopping trip to Fort Victoria, Paul attended to the hardware requirements while I bought the provisions. The supermarket was about to close for lunch when I finished my purchases. Rather than wait until two o'clock to pick everything up, I had all the packages put out on the sidewalk and waited for Paul. When he arrived, we packed all the frozen foods and perishables into the cool boxes and drove off home. It was only when I was unpacking that I realized we had left the remainder of the grocery order sitting on the sidewalk in Fort Victoria. It is a tribute to the honesty of Rhodesians that the next time we were in Fort Victoria, I found that my groceries had been handed in to the supermarket, they had listed them, and gave me a refund.

With the lull between bookings, Jack drove down to Johannesburg. Much as he enjoyed the bush, he missed female company. When he arrived back he was jubilant. He and Ellen had become engaged. He had also brought a generator which Len and Naiomi Wilson, who had been to stay with us, had given us. It was a wonderful gift and I would now be able to have lights in the house and I would be able to use my electrical appliances. Paul knew nothing about electricity and he didn't want to attempt the wiring of the house. He had had a severe electric shock as a child and 220 volts was not something he was prepared to tackle. We would have to get an electrician down to do it for us. A few weeks later, before we had done anything about it, Len Wilson and Jeff Smith, a mutual friend, arrived one Friday afternoon. Having given us the generator, they wanted to be sure we were using it and they had come up to install it for us. They brought all the necessary tools, wire, and provisions of every description, in case we were short of anything because of their unannounced arrival. We were quite overwhelmed by their generosity. The wiring seemed to go very quickly and two days later we were able to start the motor and have lights. We decided to have electricity in the house only as all our guests seemed to enjoy the simplicity of the Lodge as it was. Fortunately, game viewing was at its best because all but a few large pools in the river had dried up. The game now concentrated near the water. Apart from Len and Jeff, we had clients staying, and after dinner one evening, we took them down to the river. A large herd of elephants came down to browse on the acacias. It was bright moonlight and we were able to see them quite clearly and our guests were really excited about this experience. Just the walk back to the Lodge, through the bush in the moonlight, was a thrilling experience for them.

 A few days later, a policeman arrived and Jack announced, "The Fuzz are here." Mr. du Pont, the State President, was down in the area, staying in the D.C.'s rest house and he wanted to see our Lodge. Fortunately, we had no guests at the time and we invited them to tea the following morning. We were asked not to mention their visit to anyone, not even to our staff, and we were not to take any photographs. Their security detail would arrive half an hour earlier and check everything out. We were in quite a tizzy by the time they arrived, but they immediately put us at ease. Mrs. du Pont was a most attractive lady with an exquisite complexion. She was considerably younger than her husband. Always in the background was their armed escort. We showed them over the camp and they spent most of the morning with us. We had seen them on television often enough and, as with most celebrities I guess, it seemed surprising that they were so normal and unaffected.

Our first tourist season was almost at a close. We had at the outset decided to operate only from May to November. One could expect rain at any time after November and that could be disastrous with open vehicles for game viewing. Also, with the first rains, the pans filled and the game dispersed, free to drink anywhere. The grass became so luxuriant that one couldn't see the game even if they were there. Occasionally, after the rains, we saw zebra in the long grass with only their ears showing. It wasn't until May that the grass dried out again and became trampled down by the animals and one could once again be assured of seeing game.

Now that Jack was engaged, the lure of the city proved too strong and he decided to move back to Johannesburg. Our bookings for the next season were promising and we thought it was time to have a brochure printed. Len and Naiomi Wilson had a printing shop and they offered to do the brochure and stationery for us. We went down to Johannesburg for two weeks before Christopher and Simon came home for the Christmas holidays.

It was some time since I had visited my friends and I was amazed to find that I could have forgotten how much money went into living in a city. Everything seemed so opulent compared to the simplicity of our life at Malapati. They were all surrounded by a host of appliances, expensive cars, fur coats, and all the trappings of wealth. In turn, each asked me whether I was happy "tucked away in the wilds" and I'm sure they didn't believe I could be. I knew I was living a far richer life than I had ever done in the city. I wouldn't have traded for anything. It was far too hot ever to be able to wear a fur coat at Malapati, even had I wanted to, and a jazzy sports car wouldn't have got me out of our driveway during the rains.

Paul and Len spent a great deal of time on the brochure and finally we had what we wanted. We came home really feeling officially in business, now that we had a letterhead and brochure. We had chosen an elephant as our symbol.

Chapter 24

Early on Christmas morning we went up to the Palfreys. As always, they were bright and cheerful and delighted to see us. Mr. Palfrey told us an interesting story. Just before World War I, an African had come to his store with a rough stone which Mr. Palfrey thought might be a diamond. The man had agreed to show him where he had found it. They went on foot through very rough country and finally located the place. Shortly after he returned home, war was declared and in the excitement he forgot all about staking a claim. He enlisted, and four years later when he returned from the war, he came across the stone the African had brought him and he sent it to the Assay Office. It turned out to be a high quality diamond. He had tried on numerous occasions to relocate the spot, but it was too long ago - he had forgotten the landmarks. Diamonds eventually were discovered in that area. From the early 1980s DeBeers held an exclusive prospecting order which didn't last long. As of February 2014, the fields are operated by seven private entities, all of which are partnered by the Zimbabwe government.

The new Warden of Gona-re-Zhou, Tommy Orford, and his wife invited us to have Christmas dinner with them. They were pleasant people and we enjoyed meeting them. They had two young sons, one who was five and another who was three. The younger child, Patrick, had a Shona boy of about twelve who walked after him to ensure he didn't wander off into the bush. As they spent a great deal of time together, the little boy could speak only Shona, which at times made it difficult for his parents to understand what he was saying. When Patrick contracted cerebral malaria, he had to be hospitalized in Fort Victoria. His mother suggested it might be as well to have the 'umfaan' at hand, but the hospital came down with a firm NO. This was a European hospital! However, early the next morning the hospital called the hotel and asked the Orfords to please bring the umfaan to the hospital. They were unable to wash, feed, or dress Patrick because they couldn't communicate with him and he was uncooperative.

The guineafowl we had hatched out the previous season had attracted a great many wild ones and they had gradually paired off and gone into the bush. Periodically, a flock would move in cautiously to the old feeding place to eat the munga we put out each day. Munga was the bran-like residue from the African brew made from millet. The tribes people fed it to their poultry. Two of the original guineafowl had remained and mated. The female produced eighteen eggs in a nest quite close to the house and we were excited at having a new flock of guineafowl. When she began sitting on the eggs, we built a small wire cage which we put over her at night to protect her from the many predators which take ground birds at night. At midday each day, she would come off the eggs for half an hour and walk around with her mate, making a plaintive call. After about two weeks, I happened to look at the nest while she was out eating and I found there were only three eggs left. Some egg eater must have been watching the nest and had systematically plundered it during her short absence each day. From then on we kept a watch on the nest while she was away and she finally hatched out the three young. Obviously, the mortality rate is very high in the wilds which would account for the large clutch of eggs they lay. The hen is extremely vulnerable when she is incubating the eggs and when she has young. Even when they are roosting in a tree, a genet will frequently locate the roost from the droppings under the tree and come up after them. The guineafowl fly off with a shrill rattling call when they're alarmed, and at night they often end up on the ground where the genet catches them easily.

The Palfreys came to have dinner with us on New Year's Day. Mr. Palfrey told us that in the early days, one of the missionaries had used his hunting permit to shoot for the pot to provide meat for his congregation. If they were converted they got meat. Needless to say, he had a sizeable congregation. Mrs. Palfrey told us how one of the missionaries had been given a gasoline-driven saw with which to cut firewood. This is a wonderful implement to have when one had no electricity and one used wood for cooking and heating. One either had someone collecting firewood full time with a wheelbarrow or one did a weekly trip with a vehicle to stock up, and then it still had to be cut into suitable lengths. A Jewish well-wisher in the States had given these fortunate people a power saw. Unfortunately the donor had 'not been a Christian.' Mrs. Palfrey had been so incensed by this comment that in recounting the incident to us, she said in her charming, child-like way, " That night I asked God not to let him enjoy his saw if he drew such a fine distinction between Christians and the rest. And do you know, the next day he broke his saw and he never got it to work again. I think it was because he was unkind."

It was now 1973. The temperature hovered around the 100° mark. The rains were very late and it made the heat almost unbearable. Just being able to see the river flowing would normally make one feel cooler, but now it was still just sand. Paul's brother Adrian came out from England to see us. We took him to Manjinji Pan and we were horrified to find it was now just mud, and most of the waterfowl had gone elsewhere. It was so hot that one evening, when I had candles on the table, we came to dinner to find the tops of the candles had softened in the heat and bent over till they almost touched the table.

It was delightful showing Adrian everything. We had sent him regular progress reports and he was enthusiastic about what we had done. He missed Africa and the bush and he really enjoyed his time with us. He was acutely aware of the tremendous overseas interest in wildlife and everything related to it. He suggested Paul utilize his free time to film anything of interest that was available. This idea developed and we decided we should work to a theme. We roped in James Clark, a writer friend from Johannesburg, to do a script. Viv and Osric Bristow, who had all the animals at their disposal at Le Rhone, would also take footage whenever anything suitable presented itself. Viv had his own camera and Paul and Adrian decided to share the cost of another and they would provide the film between them.

The baboons generally slept in the enormous wild fig trees below the house and we thought they would be a good subject with which to start. We would have to get ourselves into position below the trees before dawn and then have them coming down in the morning. Paul went down the night before to make sure they were in fact sleeping in those trees that night. He shone a flashlight up into the branches. The baboons were there but they were so startled by this intrusion that baboon droppings rained down from above. This didn't seem a good idea, so Paul thought he would film them at the fishpond where their antics were a never-ending source of amusement. These clowns of the bush had universal appeal, perhaps because they were so human.

Paul set up a small tent nearby and despite my protestations he cut a hole in one side so that he could slip his camera through the aperture. However, the baboons were suspicious of this new erection and they stopped coming. Paul waited in the hot stuffy tent for several hours each day, but the baboons refused to return until we removed the tent that now had a hole in the side.

With the shortage of water, a great variety of animals came to drink from the fishpond until the elephants discovered it. For several nights running they drained it. Finally, one of them stood in it and it disintegrated. We filled it in with sand and built a small drinking trough, too small for the elephants to stand in, down on the riverbank. There was less human disturbance down there and we were able to watch the animals from above without being seen.

The fishing was always good when the water level dropped and the river formed pools. A party of young policemen from Vila Salazar called in one afternoon. They had been fishing at Rossi, a large permanent pool and a favorite spot for the fishermen. They had found some newly hatched crocodiles stranded in a small pool. They brought them to us, thinking we might like to have them for our guests to see. We decided to build a pond for them in an enclosure behind the public common area. In a year or two when they were large enough to be able to hold their own in the river, we could release them.

We had visited Tony Pooley's crocodile farm in Zululand some years previously to get material for a radio program we made for the South African Broadcasting Corporation, so we knew how to care for them. We kept the little crocs in our bath while we built their pool. They were not much larger than a large lizard. Like all small things, they were attractive, but not in a helpless, cuddlesome way. They looked like soapstone carvings, new and shiny. They settled into their pool happily. It was surprising to see how powerful they were even at that early age. A venturesome frog leapt into the pool and one of the little crocs grabbed it by a back leg. It shook the frog so forcibly that its entrails came out of its mouth. We thought we would legalize our crocs so we applied for a permit to keep them, explaining that they had been found by friends, stranded in a pool, and they would be released again. The local Warden contacted the Regional Warden, and far from considering our application for a permit, they decided to prosecute us under the relevant section of the Wildlife Act. The local Warden contacted one of the Section Officers at Vila Salazar who fortunately persuaded the Warden to drop the matter. It could have been very embarrassing, because this particular Section Officer had been one of the fishing party who brought us the crocodiles. A young ranger was sent to pick them up. We inquired as to what they were going to do with them and he told us he had been instructed to drop them into one of the pools anywhere in the river. In a strange pool, the adult crocodiles would almost certainly have devoured them, so it seemed to us quite perverse for them to be destroyed rather than allowing us to have them.

My sister, her husband, and teenage son came up to stay with us. Glenn, who was fifteen, wandered around the camp and down to the river but the moment he was out of sight, Edna became anxious. She was quite certain he would be eaten by some marauding animal. Glenn had a hut to himself, and when his parents went to bed one evening, he asked Paul whether we could play one of our recordings of lions roaring behind his parents' hut. Glenn stood in the middle of the lawn in the moonlight, and as the recording began to play, he called to his mother to come out and listen to the lions.

Edna appeared at the door and told him to go inside at once. He laughed and said he could hear better outside. She turned to Lou and said she thought the boy had taken leave of his senses. "Go outside and bring him in," she said, to which Lou wisely responded that she might then find herself a widow as well. He decided to use a coaxing tone and he very persuasively put it to Glenn that it might be safer to go into his hut and listen from there. He could in fact leave the top half of the door open. Edna was now so frantic that we could no longer torment her and we told her it was only a recording.

When the lions roared the following night, Edna and Lou rushed out and looked for us behind their hut. They returned hastily when they realized the volume was too great to be coming from a tape recorder.

Roy and Ann Borlase's cook, Masotch, came to apply for a job. I didn't need a cook, but I was curious, so I asked Ann about it and found they had to pay him off. Most Rhodesians had a 'spanner boy' who serviced the vehicles and usually accompanied one on any long distance trips. Roy's invaluable 'spanner boy' had a wife who had failed to produce children after many years of marriage. She had agreed to Phineas taking a second younger wife to bear children. According to custom, she had personally selected a wife for him, a sixteen year old relative of hers called Liza.

It would seem the problem lay with Phineas because Liza also failed to produce a child, and after one year she became desperate. The cook was young, attractive, and available but Phineas had discovered his young wife's infidelity. He had beaten Liza and threatened to leave unless Roy dismissed Masotch. Cooks were easy to find but a good mechanic was rare. So Masotch had to go. Our staff all knew about it and their sympathies seemed to be with Liza. Jane told me that the seventeen-year old Liza had said, "I want to have a baby before I die." A few weeks later, Jane told me Liza was pregnant and everyone was very happy.

There was still no sign of rain and there was now very little water around for the game. The temperature went up to 105° some days, and the nights were only slightly cooler. Even sleeping out on the patio we were uncomfortable. One morning, we saw lion tracks in the dew on the front lawn. They had wandered around the camp and had then come over to the house to drink from the birdbath, not twenty feet from where we had been sleeping.

During the floods the previous season, the force of the water had snapped the pipe connecting our well points to the motor. The whole contour of the river was so changed that we were unable to find the well points to connect again. Paul had to install another single well point as a temporary measure. Without rain to replenish the water supply, the water level had dropped so far down that our single pipe began to suck air, so we decided to look for the old well points. When Paul had originally installed them, he had taken them seventeen feet down from the top of the riverbed. Roy had twenty-six laborers who were temporarily idle, and rather than have them doing nothing, he sent them over to us to help in the search for the well points. It entailed a tremendous amount of digging and we moved tons of sand before we located them. They dug a hole thirty feet across and fifteen feet deep to uncover them. They then had to dig a forty-foot trench from the well points back to the riverbank. The previous connecting pipe which had been at right angles to the well points had been bent almost parallel by the force of the floods, and it was this which had confused us in our search for the pipe. We were then able to connect up to the much larger system again, drawing from five points instead of just one.

The drought was really severe and the water level in the sand dropped so low that we found pulling the water up from such a distance down and then pushing it up all the way to the house was ineffective. The pump had to be lowered. We had a concrete slab to which the motor was bolted up on the riverbank. We now had to make another on the riverbed to use when the water level was low. It had to be substantial or it would have washed away in the next floods. Paul made it five feet deep and four feet long and level with the sand so that it would offer no resistance and we could easily unearth it again after the floods each year. Without a good water supply, we could not have survived at Malapati and water, either too much or too little, seemed to be our most constant problem each year.

Chapter 25

Mike Clark, the Animal Health Inspector from Vila Salazar, told us there had been an outbreak of foot and mouth disease in the Lowveld and they had erected a cordon between Nuanetsi and ourselves. We had forgotten this by the time we next went to town. We noticed a rough shelter made of thatching grass and a uniformed African emerged and flagged us down. He asked whether we were carrying any meat or meat products and then told us our wheels would have to be disinfected. I got out to watch the procedure and I noticed they had a bucket of milky liquid and a bundle of leaves that they used as a brush to 'paint' the wheels. It seemed a very unsophisticated method and I thought it was probably just a token effort by the Veterinary Department to avoid being told they were doing nothing about it. The man then asked us to dip our feet in the bucket. I started to remove my good 'city' shoes, but he said it had to go in shoe and all. I was about to object when Paul reminded me that these men had powers of arrest. I plunged my imported shoes into the murky liquid, fuming at myself for not having remembered about the cordon. I could have worn old shoes or taken them off before I got out. I squelched back to the Land Rover, vowing to take up this matter of the foot in the bucket with the Veterinary Department. Just then Amon Mpepu's Super Bus arrived disgorging its eighty odd boisterous, bare footed passengers, and Paul told me to thank Providence that we had arrived when the bucket still had a milky look to it. I found that little consolation - clean or dirty water would have had the same effect on my shoes. Fortunately they dried out, none the worse for the immersion.

Thatching grass is tough and, on the whole, not edible, but in their search for grazing, the animals had either trampled it or eaten it as a last resort. The thatch we needed for the remaining two huts was not forthcoming. Until the thatching was complete, the plastering, fittings, and painting couldn't be done. The shortage of water also attracted the game to the camp where the gardens were still lush and green. They dug up the lawn; the baboons ripped up the aloe garden and the porcupines gnawed at the bulbs, the succulent young Baobab trees, the impala lilies and the precious Cycads I had planted. It was very sad to witness this struggle for survival.

At about this time, the attack at Victoria Falls occurred when three young Canadians were shot at from Zambia and one of them was killed. Almost immediately, cancellations began to arrive from South Africans booked into Malapati for the coming season. Our American agent had been so impressed with the bird life at Manjinji that most of our American clients were ornithologists, but Manjinji was now completely dry. We could have driven the Land Rover across the caked mud that had been such an exotic stretch of water, crowded with water lilies and the gathering place of so many species of birds. Even the lush look of the surrounding vegetation had disappeared. Manjinji had become a skeleton.

Around the camp, the undergrowth died away and everything turned to dust. It was heartbreaking to see it like this. With the building not completed, the gardens devastated by the animals, and Manjinji dried out, we felt we could not have any tourists for the coming season. It was a sad decision, but we wrote to our various agents and asked them to cancel all bookings as we would not be opening the Lodge until the following year. This was a tremendous blow as it meant living without income for another year.

With nothing to do for the remainder of the year, Paul occupied himself with painting. Being among the animals, he chose to do wildlife. He had studied portraiture as part of his art training, but had never done animals. His first study of a lion was excellent and it encouraged him to carry on. He worked in pastel, a medium he enjoyed and had used extensively while in advertising. He sent two paintings down to Johannesburg and the gallery bought them and asked for more. He thought he should have a show rather than selling the pictures as he did them, so he arranged for a one-man show in Johannesburg. Periodically he was plagued by self-doubt. If the show was not a success, we would have the additional expense of framing and gallery fees, but at other times he was buoyant. He could do it and we would take a trip to Europe to celebrate. In fact, in a moment of positive thinking, we booked the trip.

We still had the constant interruption of callers. Paul couldn't work with an audience, so he would pack up when he heard a vehicle approaching. For me the visitors provided an interesting diversion. One policeman who was on patrol and staying at the government rest camp, arrived to borrow a wrench and eventually stayed for lunch and then to dinner. He was a great talker and stayed until after midnight. He arrived again the following morning to borrow the wrench he had come for the previous day.

The road grader who was doing the roads in the Game Reserve called in to see us. He never took anti-malarial tablets because he said they lowered one's resistance, and if one forgot to take just one dose, one came down with malaria. Not taking the tablets didn't do much for his resistance because he was recovering from a bout of malaria. These callers often covered a vast area in the course of their duties and they were able to fill us in on all the local news from the Lundi River to the Limpopo.

Lack of communication was a tremendous problem. Many times a letter or telegram would arrive after the friends who had tried to warn us of their visit had already arrived. A new driver on Amon Mpepu's Super Bus would sometimes leave our mailbag at the wrong store and we would then have to drive miles to retrieve it.

Once when the mailbag had been on one of its round trips, we found a letter telling us that one of the Salisbury Agents would be coming down to discuss business with us for the following year. By the time we received the letter, they were due the following morning. The Salisbury Manager and his wife and the Managing Director and his wife planned to spend the night with their local representative in Chiredzi and then all drive down to us the following morning. We had previously given them a detailed road map and it was only a three-hour drive from Chiredzi, so when they hadn't arrived by lunchtime, we became anxious. If they had taken a wrong turn they could end up on the Limpopo River. Paul went to look for them. He went through the Game Reserve, up to Chikombedzi where he checked for tracks going the other way, but there was no sign of them. He arrived home late that afternoon. We were feeling rather flat after all the preparations. Just at sunset they arrived full of apologies. They had had a change of plans and had only left Salisbury that morning, and had not even gone to Chiredzi, but had been unable to let us know.

Frank had a Chinese wife called Paula. She was small and enchanting - very cosmopolitan and poised. Her father had been a diplomat and she spoke several languages. Robert and Rosemary Forester were young, attractive people. Robert was English and had a languid manner that belied his ability. He was Managing Director of a company that was expanding rapidly. Rosemary was tall, willowy, and vivacious. She was interested and knowledgeable about most things, but her particular interest was in birds and she always asked pertinent questions. They were all pleasant and charming people and I was glad that we might be doing business with them when conditions improved.

We took them around and fervently hoped they could visualize Malapati as it would be in a good season. Fortunately, they were long time Rhodesians and had experienced drought before. In the late afternoon, we all went off to shower and change and agreed to meet for drinks. We were waiting for Frank and Paula when they seemed to embark on an argument in their hut which was the nearest to where we were sitting. The sounds carried over the quiet evening air. We all four talked at once in our embarrassment and kept up a steady stream of conversation to cover their altercation that by now had become violent. When at last Frank and Paula arrived, she looked cool and poised and it was difficult to imagine either of them had ever raised their voices at each other. Frank sat down with a sigh and said jokingly, "Never marry an Oriental. No matter how sophisticated, some taboos remain with them." One of them it seems was that a bat sitting on a woman's head would make her hair fall out. They had left the top half of the door to their hut open during the day and when they returned, they had undressed to have a shower when a bat swooped from the rafters and Paula made for the door, stark naked. The thought of his wife running around the camp without clothes on had activated Frank to take a swipe at the bat with a towel. Paula crept under the bed and with each swipe the agile bat swooped low to avoid the blow, low enough to give Paula a glimpse of it and this would bring forth an agonized howl. At last Frank, had opened the door and the bat flew out.

They had three days with us, and despite the drought conditions, they were impressed with the facilities. We later heard they had an eventful trip back. A few miles after leaving us, an impala had bounded across the road in front of them followed by two lionesses in chase. A little further, just inside the Gona-re-Zhou Game Reserve, they rounded a corner just as a Nyala ran out. They were unable to stop and collided with it. It was still alive but obviously seriously injured. Apart from the fact that these are rare and Royal Game, they were concerned that it might be in pain and unable to move. They drove to the Park office and told the Warden what had happened, expecting them to go immediately to put the animal out of its misery. Instead, he kept them an hour questioning them about the speed they had been travelling, reading the section of the Wildlife Act relating to Nyala, penalties for speeding within a Game Reserve, and generally dressing them down. We were angry when we heard about this because it would have been so easy for them to have dragged the animal a little way into the bush and to have driven away without a word.

Over the years, we met so many really pleasant people in National Parks and made lifetime friends of some, but it seemed in our area we were destined to always have the type of individual who was determined to exercise authority at all costs. We sometimes wondered whether they were not posted to Gona-re-Zhou to get them out of the way. A fact that seemed to aggravate their antagonism towards us was that our Game Reserve butted onto Gona-re-Zhou and they had no jurisdiction over us.

Shortly after the Salisbury party had been to see us, we heard a vehicle one Friday afternoon. Every government official was out of the area by midday on a Friday so as to be in town that evening, so it could only be visitors for us. We were delighted when we saw Peter Wright, the Warden from the Zimbabwe Ruins Park, and his wife Pat and their two little girls. They had come to see us and had brought Simon home from school for the weekend as a surprise. We really enjoyed showing them around. It was so pleasant being with people who just enjoyed the sound and smell of the bush and who didn't necessarily want to see lions or elephants. It can be rather a strain when one has guests who want to see something specific and the animals don't materialize on demand.

They had to leave again after lunch on Sunday and Simon was very close to tears. My heart went out to him as I smiled back cheerfully. The boys going back to school was always the most difficult thing for me to handle during our time at Malapati. Occasionally they would ask, "Can't we do correspondence?" referring to the system most Rhodesian farming parents used for the first few years. The Education Department sent out weekly lessons that were returned for correction and comments. Each day there was a group session on the radio. I was once at the Borlace's house when School of the Air came on. Angela settled herself and duly answered "Good Morning" in a solitary little voice and responded promptly to all the questions as though she were in a classroom of children.

At the beginning of each year, they were able to go up to Bulawayo or Salisbury and meet their teacher and the rest of their classmates. Birthdays were noted and read over the air. These lessons carried on until they had completed elementary school, but most people sent their children to boarding school after the first two years. They needed the physical contact with other children and the group activities a regular school offered. Ann Borlase taught both Angela and Tony this way for the first two years before sending them to boarding school in Fort Victoria. An elementary school teacher told me that children who had been home schooled initially showed greater concentration and interest in schoolwork than most other children did. She felt it was the result of having individual tuition for the grounding.

Most of the American missionaries used the American correspondence system for their children right through high school. They all said the children had no emotional problems and they had no difficulty in relating to other people when they returned to the States, but their circumstances were mostly somewhat different. They were often on a remote mission station, but there were several families and people of all ages, outside their families, with whom they could communicate.

We went up to Gwelo for Christopher's Sports Weekend. He was developing as a long distance runner and came in third in his event. We cheered ourselves hoarse. At the dinner that night, we were seated next to a couple whose name would probably have meant something to us had we been Rhodesians. Since it obviously didn't, the lady told us how her husband had hurt his back while fishing at Kariba with the P.M. and how he had been flown back to Salisbury in the P.M.'s helicopter. It took me some time to realize she was talking about the Prime Minister. I thought it odd that when one doesn't know the Prime Minister, one refers to him as Ian Smith, but when one does know him, one refers to him as the P.M.

Chapter 26

We heard that the Palfrey's children had prevailed on their parents to move to Fort Victoria. Neither of them wanted to leave but they had run out of excuses. At first they couldn't go during the summer, as the roads would be impassable. Then they couldn't go during the winter as the Highveld winter was too severe to go into from the Lowveld. "Perhaps next summer, before the rains...." and now it was summer again and their children had bought them a compact little house in Fort Victoria. They had sold two of their three stores, the remaining one being at their homestead. I could understand their children's concern, but I wondered how happy these two old people would be removed from their present environment and all they had known for the greater part of their lives.

Mrs. Palfrey collected river stones that she tumbled till they were smooth and then made into jewelry. She used a contraption rigged up by Mr. Palfrey. The stones were put into a motorcar tire and the axle was turned by a diesel engine. The noise was deafening but as we were their nearest neighbors, fifteen miles away, it didn't matter. In a half-acre suburban garden she wouldn't be able to do that. She was also kept busy with the store and the book keeping. Mr. Palfrey attended to the store, picked up supplies from Nyala Siding, and worked on his vehicles. They enjoyed the neighborliness of life in the bush where a detour of fifteen miles was quite natural "to say hello to the

Palfreys." Even in a small town like Fort Victoria, life would be very different and they could easily become just another elderly couple, indistinguishable from the rest.

We provided our domestic staff with rations which consisted of corn meal, whatever vegetables we had in the garden, sugar, tea, salt, and meat. Of these, meat was the biggest problem. Jane didn't eat mutton because it made her stomach "boil," so it had to be goat. Every Shangaan kept a herd of goats and William had a sizeable herd but for some reason a goat could never be had locally. Whenever William announced it was time for meat, I would ask whether they knew of one for sale. They would all four stand and scratch their heads and look puzzled for a while and then one of them would volunteer a name, usually from the other end of the Tribal Trust Lands.

This time there was one near Manjinji. Late that afternoon when the herds came home from their daily grazing, William and I went to conclude the transaction. When we returned, William was securing the goat to a tree for the night when it galloped off. William, seeing his meat disappear, gave chase with Christopher close behind. After ten minutes I became anxious. I had visions of Christopher and William running headlong into a pride of lions in pursuit of the goat and all for a few dollars. Simon and I drove some distance down the road and called but heard nothing. We went all the way to the river crossing and called again. We thought they might have found the goat and be home by now, but there was still no sign of them. We went up to the airstrip and finally heard Christopher reply. We drove down along the game fence and found Christopher with the goat that he had rugby tackled, very close to the place the lions had pulled down a zebra the week before. William arrived shortly after, puffing and panting. The following day the staff had a feast, as always eating almost all the meat in one day. At first I had offered to freeze some of it for them, but they preferred it this way.

As always, the boys were reluctant to go back to school. Life at Malapati was devoid of schedules and the numerous rules imposed at boarding school. When we took them back, we called in to see the Palfreys. They had a charming little house in Fort Victoria and Mrs. Palfrey was very happy with all the amenities of town life. Mr. Palfrey was rather glum, on principle I think. He had his irascible reputation to consider! It must have been very much easier for him to have modern amenities. … having electric light and not having to worry about the generator; having water come out of a tap, not having to pump water; having a telephone for the first time in their lives and not having to rely on a 'boy on a bicycle' in an emergency. Above all, having a service station to work on his ancient and constantly ailing vehicle.

Mr. and Mrs. Capp from the Lundi Mission came down to see us with an American architect who was charmed by the 'ethnic' design of the Lodge. He felt it was the first time he had seen indigenous architecture used by white people in the whole of southern Africa. Shortly after they left, a party of students from Pretoria University arrived. A mutual friend in Johannesburg had given them our name and they had promised to visit. They wanted to spend the night sleeping out and we suggested they walk up the river to the 'Tower' at Makonde Pool and spend the night in the safety of the Tower and walk back again the following day. They left their vehicle with us and had a most rewarding night at Makonde. Numerous herds of elephants had come down to drink and lions had roared all round them. They had hardly slept at all for all the activity.

Alan Wright had constructed this game-viewing tower at Makonde Pool, a permanent pool in the river about a mile from the Sub Office, north of us. The Tower, as it came to be called (or Wright's Erection by his detractors), was a very solid structure made of cement blocks and looked like a small fort. It was roofed and a steep flight of steps up one side took one to the platform that was seventeen feet from the ground. On the wall was a notice that read:

Always remember that you are an unwanted intruder at this watering place and many of the elephants that drink here have a legitimate grudge against all humanity. The reach of a bull elephant is such that, should your actions provoke him, he would have no difficulty at all in removing you from this platform.
Alan Wright, District Commissioner, Nuanetsi

We spent many evenings at the Tower. In the absolute stillness of the night we would hear the shy, clipped call of the scops owl … crook, crook; the pearl spotted owl with his call of rising notes, ending with a swift slide down the scale again; the fiery necked nightjar, which to me symbolized Malapati at night. His continuous litany would be taken up by others of his kind, seeming like an echo down the river. We would hear the baboons grumbling and squabbling away in the trees where they slept. Occasionally one would bark sharply, possibly in irritation at a neighbor who had jostled him. Sometimes others would take up the bark and occasionally we would hear the grunting of a leopard that had disturbed them.

We would sit in the Tower, straining our eyes in the darkness, staring at the trees on the opposite bank, until their dark shapes began to look like elephants. Silently, the first elephant would glide onto the riverbank, trunk raised, testing the wind. Just as quietly the remainder of the herd would arrive and drift towards the pool, ghostly in the moonlight. Some would dig in the soft sand with a gentle swinging of the foot and then drink the water that seeped into the hole they had dug.

One would first hear the swish of water as they waded into the Pool. Then the splashing as they bathed became so loud it was like a waterfall. Then too the trumpeting would start, whether from exuberance or irritation with each other, I don't know, but it became quite shrill and deafening at times. They would drink and play for about an hour and then withdraw with the same quiet grace as they had arrived.

Paul had noticed a small leak in one of our PVC water pipes going to the camp. Before he got around to repairing the leak, the baboons noticed the wet patch and dug up the pipe and bit through it to get at the water, so during the night the tanks had drained completely. Paul mended the leak and covered the hole with dry sand to discourage any further digging by the baboons. We filled the tanks again but the next morning we were out of water again. An inspection of the camp proved negative. Later in the day, he sent John to get some piping stored under a bush near the staff huts. John stepped into a squelchy patch and there was the leak. Three thousand gallons of water had drained into that clump of bushes and it might have taken us days to find the spot. A tunneling mole had found the only bit of soft black plastic piping Paul had used to take a lead off to the staff quarters. They replaced it with PVC and we were with water again.

We were expecting three friends from Johannesburg for four days. With the Lodge now closed, we thought it would be a good opportunity to put the staff through their paces again so we had invited these friends. We had only just refilled the tanks when Robin, Rosemary, and Charles arrived. It was fun seeing them again. They were witty and very stimulating company.

We were having a drink before dinner that evening when we heard a vehicle approaching. Next thing a man appeared on the patio. He was about our age and immaculately dressed in a white safari suit. I'll call him Claude Patrick but I was most intrigued by the way he introduced himself. "I'm Buddy Patrick's brother, Claude." His brother was a well-known environmentalist and hunter but Claude was equally well known, or perhaps I should say notorious. We had heard of him but had never met him. I wondered whether introducing himself as Buddy's brother he felt he might add a glossier image to himself. He had just driven down from Nuanetsi and he wanted accommodation. I couldn't believe that impeccable safari suit had done that dusty drive from Nuanetsi. I told him we were closed for the season and that these were personal friends we were entertaining. He then offered to buy the Lodge! He was so insistent and persuasive that we eventually agreed to let him stay for the night. It then transpired that he had a girlfriend in the truck. They joined us for drinks.

His girlfriend, Nella, was an extremely well-endowed girl physically but she hardly spoke. She was obviously overwhelmed by Claude and she was the perfect foil for this exotic extrovert. Periodically he would turn to her for confirmation "You've seen it in my house," or "You were there," and she would nod in reply. We heard one hunting story after another, liberally illustrated by an exhibition of scars on his stomach (where a leopard had clawed him), a damaged thumb from an encounter with a lion, and injuries on his rear, and inflicted by a buffalo. Nothing was too personal to show. Our Johannesburg friends sat agape, as much by the wondrous stories as by his contortions in showing us the scars. I don't think they had expected entertainment of this high order on their first night at Malapati. I got so engrossed in the stories I almost forgot to ask William to serve dinner.

On one of his trips to the Far East, Claude had been on a tiger hunt in Thailand. In the course of his story, he turned to Charles, jabbed him in the ribs with his elbow, and said, "There I was in Bangkok station - you know Bangkok station..." Charles looked mildly surprised and then said, "No, actually I don't." That didn't impede the story. In telling of a hunting safari in South West Africa, Claude mentioned a pair of shoes he had had made out of zebra skin from an animal he had shot. When Claude went to retrieve something from his truck, Nella suddenly uttered the only thing she was to say all evening. "When he wears his zebra skin shoes, he's all feet." When his stories became really involved, he would turn to Paul and say, "I've got that in my scrapbook - I'll show it to you one day." His stories ranged from moving currency illegally to easy ways of 'getting' things through Customs. He told how he had left a parcel of money in a hotel safe in Rhodesia. At Customs in Beit Bridge he had been searched and had even had his car up on a jack and the hubcaps removed. He had been very indignant and had fussed over the inconvenience, quite certain they would find nothing. He spent the night on the South African side of the border and the following morning he had gone back across, picked up his money from the hotel safe, and then went through Customs without a question from the now cautious Customs officials.

We went to bed late and were up early. Claude appeared again in another impeccably pressed outfit. He asked me whether I wanted to buy a kerosene freezer, something always in demand in remote areas, away from an electricity supply. I told him I had one too many and it was temperamental at that. We had used a level to get it absolutely level, stood it upside down for twenty four hours, and had even taken it for a ride on the back of a Land Rover, all standard treatments for an ailing kerosene freezer, but it still behaved erratically. Claude was certain he could make it work (or no doubt find an unsuspecting buyer for it) and offered to buy it. I hastily accepted. He loaded it onto the back of his truck and then produced a large bag of money from behind the seat and peeled off the notes. He must have had several thousand Rhodesian dollars in that bag. He was obviously on one of his currency moving trips and it surprised me that he was so overt about it all. This was at a time and place when one had to apply to the Reserve Bank to move funds from one country to another. They were going through to Malvernia, thirty miles from us on the Portuguese side of the border, to have a lunch of prawns. A few days later we heard from one of our police acquaintances that Customs at Vila Salazar, on the Rhodesian side, had been alerted and they had been waiting for Claude. He was relieved of his bag of money and a freezer, and was prosecuted for illegal transportation of currency. We often wondered where our freezer had ended up.

The next two days were great fun. Robin, Rosemary and Charles were easy people to have as guests. We managed to see most things except lions and we didn't even hear them roar. We did see a sable antelope close up though and this delighted Robin as she had never seen one. She was an Africana collector and had concentrated on the work of Cornwallis Harris. The sable was first recorded by Harris and was formerly known as the Harris Buck, so the Sable was of particular interest to her.

On their last day, Paul took Charles on a walk through the bush to the permanent pool about a mile up the river from us. Before they set out, Paul had given him the usual instruction of "try not to talk. The sound carries and scares everything away". Paul tended to forget he was an exceptionally fast walker and Charles had great difficulty in keeping up with him. On the way back he had felt the call of Nature, but he later told us he had been reluctant to ask Paul to stop. He been told not to talk, and he had felt rather like a puppy, trotting on behind and unable even to lift his leg on a passing tree. We really enjoyed having them and were sorry to see them leave.

Chapter 27

We had to go to town for Christopher's mid-term long weekend. We left at 5:30 a.m. as it was our turn to do the car pooling from Christopher's school and either Paul or I would have to drive up to Gwelo to pick up Christopher and the other boys. At Nuanetsi we found we had a puncture. We changed the wheel and then called in at the post office for our mailbag. We had arranged with the Postmaster to have our bag left in the telephone exchange as we thought we would pass through Nuanetsi before the post office was open. The mailbag wasn't in the exchange and the post office was locked although it was 8:45. We went to the Post Master's house and his cook told us the boss was still asleep. We sent the cook to wake him and he hurriedly dressed and apologized profusely for having forgotten to leave the mailbag. His forgetfulness caused us no end of trouble at times, but he was also extremely obliging when he did remember, and we appreciated this. He did small favors for us that we would never have had from a larger post office. Living in a remote area with few amenities and where even the simplest thing could take hours to accomplish was sometimes very frustrating for us. A small part of us was still on city wavelength, expecting everything to just flow as planned, but they seldom did and one had to accept this and anticipate it.

In Fort Victoria we had the puncture repaired and Paul left for Gwelo, leaving me to pick Simon up at lunchtime. Paul arrived back at 4 p.m., exhausted after almost eleven hours of driving. We had arranged to meet at the garage we always used and Paul pulled up with a loud bang. We had had another puncture and I thanked the powers that be that he was almost stationary when it happened. We spent the weekend at Le Rhone, on Lake Kyle. These weekends involved a great deal of travelling, but they were very important to us. Being together as a family was something very special for us and when we had spent time with each other again we all felt recharged.

One of the Bristow's lionesses was about to have cubs, and Paul and Viv were going to film the birth. They had fenced off one corner of the lions' sleeping enclosure into a cage about 8' x 10'. The chain link enclosure was covered by thatching grass, inside and outside. They planted tufts of grass and sticks to give it a natural effect. The lioness, known as Lazy, was encouraged to sleep in this cage to get her accustomed to it. We needed very strong lights for the filming and out there in the lions' enclosure; we would have to generate any power we needed for light.

Osric had predicted the birth for about June 20. Paul and I pitched a tent about two miles from the lion enclosure under a large wild fig tree. Paul took the vehicle each day to allow him to come back for meals easily. Early one morning I thought I would walk up to the enclosure to see how things were going. When I reached the fence, I whistled and called to attract attention but I got no response. The lions had already been released from their sleeping enclosure and were somewhere in the twenty-acre enclosure they roamed around in each day. The gates connecting their sleeping enclosure to the larger one were closed and I decided with the lions in the next encampment it was safe to climb the ten-foot wire fence. As I got to the top it began to wobble, and at that moment I looked down to see the lions in the adjoining enclosure approaching stealthily, almost flat on the ground in the stalking posture. I knew they couldn't get at me but I was horrified just the same. I gave a horrified howl. Why were they stalking me? Then I saw the reason. Piccolo had followed me and she was dashing up and down trying to get in! My Tarzan-like howl brought everyone to my rescue and I was able to come down.

Lazy was now permanently ensconced in the cage, and the generator had been positioned as far from her as possible to minimize the noise. There were three cameras - Paul and Viv each filming and a professional cameraman named Peter operating the third. They cut holes in the wire just large enough to allow the lenses through and at different levels to secure different angles. At first, Lazy was anxious when the cameras began to whir and she would rush at the cameras and tear hunks of grass away. The two lower cameramen had to be on the alert for these moments when she would put her ears back, before the rush. Gradually she came to accept the noise and the lights.

During the day when the lions were in the main enclosure, they were overcome with curiosity at all the activity and they would crouch in the grass and edge forward until they could see us. Osric had to drive them away continually, but in no time they would be back again. It was mid-winter and bitterly cold at night. The three cameramen sat huddled in blankets, taking turns to watch for the first sign of the onset of labor. Osric was four days out in his calculations. Labor began at 9 a.m. on the fourth day and Lazy produced her first cub with very little difficulty. She lifted her leg, there was a slight show of blood, and then out popped the cub, looking like an avocado. She licked away the covering membrane, bit the cord and then, seemingly thinking it too long, she bit it shorter. Finally satisfied, she licked her baby clean then ate the afterbirth. This was Nature's way of keeping everything clean to avoid attracting scavengers. She produced three at hourly intervals and then settled down to allow them to drink. Immediately they were jostling and pushing each other away, vying for the best position, and in no time it became obvious which would be the more dominant animals. Within an hour of being born, they dried out and turned into fluffy dun colored little creatures with prominent dark rosettes that faded as they matured. The tails were ringed in the same dark color but lacked the distinctive tuft of the adult lion. Although cubs are born with their eyes partially open, they appear not to see very well for the first week or two. We were very excited at having this unusual sequence on film.

We returned to Malapati to find the baboons had discovered the croc pond we had built behind the camp pub. Despite the fact that we no longer had the crocs, it was still kept filled as one couldn't have enough drinking places for birds. The baboons had come to drink via the roof and had pulled out great footfulls of thatch as they came scaling down. The monkeys had eaten all the tomatoes and the Francolin had stripped the beans. I couldn't blame them - there was so little left in the bush for them to eat.

One of the Rangers stationed at Mabalauta came around to see us. He and his wife were interesting people. When we had got to know them better, they laughingly told us that when he had first arrived, the Warden had forbidden him to have any social contact with us! He was an independent minded individual and had made a special effort to get to know us. He asked whether we would buy him a small calculator, unavailable in Rhodesia, when next we were in Johannesburg. We asked for exact specifications because experience had taught us that it was very easy to buy the wrong thing. On one occasion we had been asked to buy drip dry double bed sheets. I shopped around and finally found the exact color and bought them, only to find they were intended for a king size bed - "I'm sure I told you king size." On another occasion, a set of electric curlers I had bought for someone had developed trouble and I had to return them on a subsequent trip.

We went up to Fort Victoria for Rhodes and Founders weekend. It was the biggest thing on the Rhodesian calendar, apart from Christmas. Friends brought Christopher down from Gwelo and we had four days together at Le Rhone. Some time previously, a flock of determined crows had attacked Osric's light aircraft. They had torn the fabric so badly that it had to have a new skin put on in Johannesburg. He had been advised that the aircraft was now ready and Viv and Carol were motoring down to pick it up. Paul had business to attend to in Johannesburg, so on the spur of the moment he decided to go down with them and drive back with Carol leaving Viv to fly the Cessna back to Le Rhone. By that time the cubs would be ready for the next phase of the filming. In the meantime, I would go down to Malapati to make sure all was well and to give instructions for the week we planned to be away. Carol and Paul would pick me up on the way back.

Paul always seemed to be unduly worried about my doing a trip on my own and he asked me to have the vehicle checked before leaving Fort Vic. This seemed so unnecessary, but to please him I agreed to do so. Christopher returned to Gwelo on the Tuesday afternoon, but Mr. Horsfall, the principal of Simon's school, had early on said we could bring him back in time for school in the morning after a weekend because we lived so far away.

As we left for town the following morning, the engine of the Land Rover began to cough and sputter. We managed to crawl into town and Simon dashed off to class. At the garage, I found the battery terminals were frayed and the timing was out. It had mercifully happened within reach of a garage and I never again took it lightly when setting out on a trip.

William, Jane, and Method normally stayed at Malapati during the week, but the rest of the staff went home every evening. I let William, Jane, and Method go home for a few days as I frequently had to ask them to stay on if we had unexpected guests. so I used this time to let them have some leisure time with their families. I could manage very well on my own. At the end of the day, I would sit out on the patio and enjoy the total solitude with the sounds of the bush all around me.

One evening, I was sitting out on the patio at dusk when I heard the thudding of hooves as some large animal crashed through the bush in front of the house. I ran out to see a Kudu bull stop in the clearing behind the house. He stood for a moment looking around and then bounded off towards the river. Moments later, several impala came from the same direction and again dashed off towards the river. Something was obviously chasing them. I walked very quietly to the top of the driveway where I would have a clear view of anything crossing the track that ran down to the river crossing. As I watched, several more impala leapt across the road and then a pack of wild dogs appeared. They looked so very like underfed German shepherds.

They stopped to look at me and suddenly my insides turned to jelly. I knew about lions. I had been told often enough "always stand, never run." Wild dogs were another matter. I knew very little about them and what I did know were all horror stories. Now the pack was not 50 yards from me. A few of them stood up on their hind legs with a peculiar 'Yip, yip...'as if to get a better view. They watched me for a while and then continued their chase and disappeared around the side of the house. The adrenaline that had been building up now propelled me, and I shot into the house and stayed there. The following morning, I found the remains of an impala on the camp lawn.

The speed at which wild dogs eat is quite incredible. Once when Paul and I were driving to the river crossing, we saw a pack of wild dogs pull down a Kudu quite close to the house. We went back for a camera but got back to find they had totally devoured it and only the skull remained.

In the mailbag, I received a letter from Mr. Downey our insurance broker. On a previous trip to Salisbury, we had met him and he had suggested coming down sometime to make a personal assessment of our insurance needs. We said he could come anytime, just to give us about a week's warning. His letter said he would be flying down and arriving on Friday which was now only two days away. This lack of speedy communication was very frustrating. Paul and Carol were due to pick me up on Friday so I had to try to reach him to postpone the trip. I drove over to Manuel with a carefully worded telegram to transmit by radiotelephone to Nuanetsi with a request that they have the telegram sent for me. I fervently hoped it would reach Mr. Downey in time.

At 4:30 the following afternoon, I heard an aircraft buzz the house and then land at the strip. My heart sank. I drove up to the strip and to my surprise I found Viv there in the newly done up Cessna. They had bought another truck in Johannesburg and with Paul there they were able to have him drive it up. Paul and Carol had gone straight back to Le Rhone. It was now too late to carry on, so Viv spent the night at Malapati.

Just before dawn we went up to the airstrip. Several herds of impala and zebra were quietly grazing and only spared us a glance as we drove over to the aircraft. I dropped Viv off to do his pre-flight check and I then drove up and down several times, checking for new antbear holes and trying to scare the animals off, but they sauntered back as soon as I passed. The noise of the aircraft engine finally sent them running. We took off as the first light of dawn touched the bush. Gradually I was able to pick out the various landmarks. It was glorious being up there at sunrise. The red orb of the sun appeared over the horizon, spilling its light onto the African bush. From up there it looked so different, with miles of wilderness unfolding in every direction to the horizon. It gave me a glimmer of what infinity could mean. It seemed so still and uninhabited, untouched by Man. One was unaware of the game; the clusters of huts of the African villages, their thatched roofs and mud walls blending into the surrounding vegetation and forming the tapestry of color we saw from above. As the sun rose I could see the game paths, converging onto some water hole, like the spokes of a wheel.

Flying has always been a sort of spiritual experience to me, making me aware of my own insignificance in the Cosmos. On the ground, one's vision of Life seems to become limited to one's own limited point of view and specific needs. Trivial problems take on great importance and become engrossing. Looking down on it all from a few thousand feet, I often had the thought that those little dots, each representing a homestead, filled with their own concerns and aspirations, might, to some Greater Life Force, be no more than ants are to us. It was always a humbling thought.

We crossed the Lundi River in no time at all and I was able to see the smoke from cooking fires of the African villages. The country changed dramatically here where the Lowveld meets the Highveld. It was now a mass of granite outcrops, the rocks seeming incredibly smooth, like some gargantuan bubble that had erupted from the center of the earth in the mists of time. Sometimes several rocks were balanced on top of each other, as though placed there by some giant hand, and they looked as though just a touch could send them hurtling down. These granite outcrops are very typical of Rhodesia.

As the country became more undulating, the vegetation too changed. It was now those exquisite mountain acacias with their flat canopy that give the hills and mountains a soft, ferny look. Here too were the Msasa trees whose leaves are the most brilliant shades of red and brown when they first appear. In the distance we could see the shimmer of Lake Kyle. We flew over Morgenster Mission with the Zimbabwe Ruins to the left, and we were at Le Rhone. It was a most awkward landing strip, as one had to approach it up a valley and then do a tight turn to approach the strip that was uphill.

Carol and Paul were waiting for us. It had taken an hour by air to do a trip that took us five and a half hours by Land Rover. The first thing I did was to telephone our insurance broker's office in Salisbury, only to be told Mr. Downey was away on business. I hoped it was business other than Malapati.

Paul and Viv filmed Lazy carrying her cubs around. She had made a nest for them in the main enclosure. They were now almost three weeks old and she took them to introduce to the pride. Unlike the domestic cat which carries its kittens by the scruff of the neck, the lioness grips the cub across the shoulders with just the head and hindquarters showing. She took the first cub and put it down in front of the dominant male of the pride. He sniffed it with the disdainful air of a Victorian father for his young. When the stumbling cub came too close, he withdrew and the females of the pride moved in. Lazy, who had gone to pick up the next cub, rushed back to her baby among the females. She seemed hesitant about leaving it, but reluctantly went back to get the next cub. They went through the same procedure until all three cubs had been presented. The adolescents who approached were sent running by Lazy who became quite agitated by them. One by one she removed the cubs again, back to their nest. When the cubs were about two months old, she rejoined the pride.

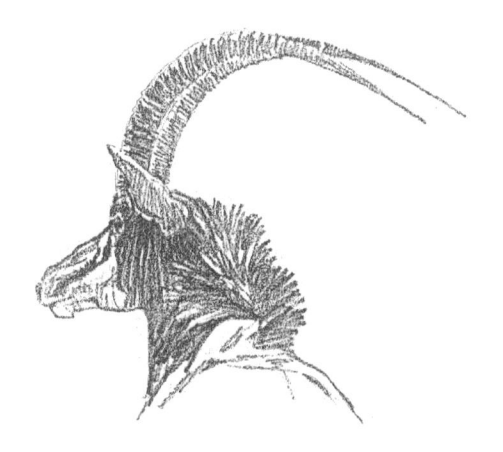

Chapter 28

Osric was going up to Salisbury and then on to Hartley to pick up a young sable. Hartley was predominantly a ranching area now, and local ranchers were darting the Sable and selling them to game farmers. Not enough was known about the stress factor of these beautiful creatures and most of those darted went into shock and died almost immediately. A young male had survived the capture and was now waiting in an enclosure for Osric to pick up.

We decided to go with Osric. He was stopping off in Salisbury and we needed to have a meeting with a tour operator who had contacted us. We also needed a telephone and wanted to go into the feasibility of this with the Post Office. It turned out that a telephone was out of the question. Since we were the only ones requiring the line, we would have had to bear the cost of bringing it down from Chikombedzi which was roughly thirty-five miles away. The cost of the poles and cable would be prohibitive. Also the elephants would probably have pushed the poles over. We were advised to apply for a radio-telephone, which we did.

The tour operator was a man I'll call Mr. Boyle. He had written to us explaining that his wife had been in the tourist business in East Africa where she had been the 'Queen Bee' in a safari business. They were planning to start an enormous safari organization and they wanted to include us in their itinerary next season. Something about the tone of the letter did not appeal to me. However, Paul felt we should discuss possible business with him personally. We met with Mr. Boyle at Meikle's Hotel in Salisbury. He was a large blustering man, ruddy faced and very British. He dropped all the right names - school, army regiment - which I found rather boring and distasteful. He felt he and his wife would have to come down to see Malapati before he could commit himself. This seemed reasonable enough and we agreed that he should let us know when it would be convenient to come down.

We also went to Mr. Downey's office. We found him there and heard his account of what had happened. My telegram had arrived in time, but he hadn't been into the office the previous afternoon and no one had thought to open it in his absence. He had flown down with his wife on the Friday morning as Viv and I were on our way to Le Rhone. He had done business at Triangle on the way and then come to Malapati. He had buzzed the Lodge as we had suggested and then landed. After fifteen minutes he had taken off again and once again buzzed the camp. William heard him and had gone up to the airstrip on his bicycle to meet them. He told them we were away. It was now too late for them to go anywhere else.

William had suggested they spend the night at Malapati. He told them it was not far to the camp - they could walk. It was only about a mile and a pleasant stroll for someone accustomed to the bush. For Mr. Downey and his young wife, it was quite an experience walking along a dirt track through the bush. Even the mild impala darting off had set their hearts pounding. They noticed a herd of buffalo and paused, but William just plodded on ahead pushing his bicycle, so they had followed. Jane had settled them into one of the huts and William had made dinner for them. Lions roared around the camp that night just to remind them what could be lurking in the long grass on the way back to the airstrip next morning. It had been frightening for them at the time, but as always with something like this, it had been an exciting experience in retrospect.

At Hartley, we spent the night with Cammy and Ben Brackenridge at their ranch. It was one of those mellow old homesteads going back to the early pioneer days. It had a welcoming aura of comfort. The rooms were enormous and were furnished with items inherited by successive generations and added to over time. Comfortable armchairs flanked the fireplace in the living room. The distinctive smell of thatch permeated everything. It was a rambling house and one knew it took a fleet of domestic help to maintain. The veranda, which wound around three sides of the house, had every imaginable kind of pot plant. Like the house, the garden was a happy, casual arrangement of flowerbeds and trees.

The sable Ben had for us was not yet mature but he already had good horns. He traveled well until we stopped at Fort Victoria, twenty-five miles from his final destination, to pick up gas. Several Africans crowded around the trailer with much jostling and shouting which eventually startled the animal. He thrashed round in the crate and broke one of his beautiful horns right off. This was a great tragedy as they don't grow again and the graceful symmetry of the backward sweep of the horns is what makes the sable the beautiful creature it is.

We told Osric about our guinea fowl losing so many of its eggs to a predator. He thought it might have been a monitor lizard, although baboons also plunder nests, but he felt they would have been more blatant, taken all the eggs at once and left ample evidence of their visit. Paul thought an incident like this would make interesting footage for our now budding film on wildlife, but it would be almost impossible to conceal oneself from the sharp-eyed baboons. Osric said he could arrange the sequence with his tame baboons and a tame guineafowl. The only problem was finding eggs at this time of the year. It was July and guinea fowl only breed after the first rains, from December to February. We contacted our friend Paula McWilliam who had one addled egg and we used this as a model for our clutch of eggs. Paul painted eighteen chicken eggs the pale coffee color and then lightly flecked them with brown. When he was finished, it was difficult to tell them from the original one.

Osric's business was providing wild animals for films and it was fascinating to see him in action. He laid a trail of raisins. These are inconspicuous on the film, but they would keep the baboons busy and interested and at the same time it leads them naturally to the nest of eggs. He settled the guinea fowl on the nest and tucked her head under her wing. For some reason when one does this even to a domestic fowl, it sits like that for about thirty seconds before removing its head. The hen sat quite still. The baboons were released and Osric showed them the first of the raisins as the cameras began to roll. They hurriedly worked their way up to the nest just as the hen raised her head and looked round. She flew off with a flurry as she saw the baboons approaching.

They were like naughty boys at a party - one egg in the mouth and one in each hand. Unable to eat the egg, they would drop one for another baboon to snatch. They shoved and pushed and squealed in frustration until they had broken every egg. Then they tried picking up the broken eggs. It was a mess but an hilarious spectacle. It had obviously not been baboons that had raided our hen's nest last season.

When we finally got home, we found that Manuel, from the District Commissioners' rest camp, had brought a telegram which had been radioed to him. It was from Mr. Boyle. "Arriving by air Friday with your son and a friend." I felt very ashamed for having judged him an opinionated bore. He had obviously arranged with the school to have Simon brought to the airport in Fort Victoria where they could pick him up on the way down to spend the weekend with us. I felt anyone who could be that thoughtful was entitled to his eccentricities.

I helped Jane prepare the Boyle's hut as I wanted everything perfect. I had matching towels and Kleenex to go with the color scheme of each hut, but to Jane the more multi-colored it was, the more attractive. I put out an emergency mending kit and other amenities and a copy of Focus on Fauna. This concise wildlife handbook by James Clarke was written in layman's terms with interesting asides. I hoped it was what the Boyle's were expecting.

We prepared the boys bedroom for Simon and his friend, putting up the bows and arrows, feathers, quills, and skins which made the bedroom theirs but which were just dust collectors while they were away. From the center of the ceiling we suspended the old hornbill and the room was then just as they had left it, like a lived-in museum workshop.

The Boyles arrived at 6:30 that evening and as they stepped out of their car with their son and a friend, I realized an error had crept into the telegram along the way. I felt inclined to put their son into Simon's room with its flying hornbill, but I realized they were in no way responsible for my disappointment at finding it was not Simon. We hastily prepared two more huts for the son and his girlfriend.

Mrs. Boyle was a pleasant, homely English woman who seemed to have little interest in her husband's project. She was far more concerned with her son whom she very obviously felt was being led astray by his older girlfriend who was encouraging him to quit university. This created a rather hostile atmosphere. Mr. Boyle was oblivious of this and pored over scrolls of graph paper indicating hypothetical tourist movements.

The following morning, we showed them around Malapati in the open Land Rover. Mother, son, and girlfriend continued their controlled quarreling in heavy undertones while Father lay back in a rather bored fashion. When Paul asked whether they would like to drive up to one of the Pans to look for elephants, his comment was "When you've seen one, you've seen the lot," and he welcomed the suggestion to return to camp. For a safari operator, he seemed more interested in the logistics of his operation than in the wildlife.

I tried to analyze why I disliked the man so and I decided it was his pretentious attitude. His conversation was liberally laced with foreign phrases which could only have been intended to impress since "my best friend" would have been much simpler than my "alter ego" and "on a friendly basis" much easier than "pro amico" and we had to "rendezvous" for drinks. One had to concentrate to translate it all. "The e.t.a. would be 1900 hours." Apart from all the abbreviations and foreign phrases, I had to be constantly doing mental calculations to work out his times. I didn't feel the weekend had been particularly constructive or productive and it was quite a relief to see them leave.

We had heard rumors that there was to be an impala-culling program in Malapati on the new District Commissioner's instructions. When it started, it turned out to be the most haphazard operation ever conceived. The Game Department shot four hundred animals which they loaded onto trucks and then sold to the local Africans at fifty cents each. Some of them bought as many as ten carcasses. The Game Department advised another one thousand should be shot. Fifty cents had been a ridiculous price to charge and the next batch that they sent up to Chikombedzi were one dollar each. This was still cheap, but in dealing with primitive people, one cannot suddenly double the price of a commodity. The Africans just refused to buy them.

An earlier District Commissioner had given us permission to shoot one impala a week for rations, but our unfriendly Warden had warned us that we required a culling permit. On a trip to Salisbury, we went to see the Director of National Parks and we were referred to an elderly underling who was most unhelpful. Most of the interview was spent quoting the Wildlife Act to us. In the end, we decided we would continue to buy meat for our staff. This massive culling operation now made nonsense of the obstructive attitude in letting us take just one impala a week.

Nearly half the animals shot were taken off on our boundary. We felt incensed that as local residents we had not been advised of the impending culling and that when they started, the two rangers concerned drove right past our house and started shooting without even calling in to tell us. They used telescopic sights and lights and they shot from six in the evening until three in the morning. On one occasion, when they dropped an impala one hundred yards from our house at 6:30 in the evening, we went after them and pointed out that at that time, we or our staff were still frequently walking around outside.

Our antagonism was largely due to the difficulties we had experienced over being allowed to shoot just one impala a week for our staff. We felt the meat could have been better utilized with a sustained yield rather than the mass shooting like this. So much of what National Parks did in those days seemed inexplicable and unjustifiable to rational people.

These rangers were shooting under pressure to complete a quota and they were obviously quite often unable to locate a wounded animal. Every day we would find carcasses of animals that had eventually died from misplaced shots. What really angered us was when we began to find the carcasses of nyala does, rare and gentle antelope, whose breeding ground was in this riverine area. One could be forgiven for wounding the occasional animal in the dark, but a National Parks ranger should have been able to distinguish an nyala from an impala. We wrote and complained to Salisbury and suddenly the whole operation was called off. We were never able to get confirmation of this, but we were told that the decision to reduce the impala population had been made by an individual who was very uninformed in these matters. He was a District Commissioner newly transferred to the area who had been persuaded by the local Warden, who was known to be gun happy, to embark on the culling operation. This was done without either of them consulting their respective Head Offices in Salisbury.

Unlike the elephants, the impala were still very much in evidence after the culling, although there was a marked lack of young the following lambing season. I don't know whether this was a natural birth control due to the scarcity of food during the drought, or whether the ewes aborted during the harassment of the culling.

Paul had a month to go before his show and he had to use every moment to finish. We planned to leave for the U.K. immediately after the show and to return just before the Christmas vacation. I arranged with friends to have Christopher and Simon for their mid-term long weekends while we were away. I gave William and Jane detailed instructions about the care of the animals while we were gone and Roy Borlase promised to look in every day on his way to work to see that all was well and to deal with any emergencies.

We left Malapati at the end of September so as to have ten days in Johannesburg for the framing of the twenty-eight paintings. Two days before the show, we took them to the gallery and the Director helped Paul decide on what prices to charge. One third of the sales would go to gallery commission. We also had to pay for the printing of the invitations to the opening night and the catalogue. I fervently hoped Paul would sell enough to cover the expenses to give him the incentive to continue. He enjoyed it and he had an unlimited source of material at Malapati.

My fears were groundless. The opening was a whirl of excitement. All but two of the paintings were sold that night. We hardly touched ground for the next two weeks. To add to the excitement, I discovered I was pregnant again after a gap of thirteen years.

We left for England, our first trip back since before we were married. It was a homecoming of sorts. We had both studied, lived, and worked in London, where Paul and I, both visiting South Africans, had first met. We found London vastly changed with its high-rise buildings and its cosmopolitan population. But in spite of it all, it was still the same old London where one felt mentally stimulated and excited by just being there. Many years before, I had been at the Cordon Bleu culinary school and I was now doing a refresher course. We had to pay for the ingredients we used each day and I was horrified to find how expensive everything was. At Malapati I could buy a whole sheep for less than the price of a chicken in London. We had to pay ten shillings, at that time about a dollar, to have the feathers removed. I don't think one could have bought an unplucked fowl in a store in Rhodesia if one wanted to.

One of my fellow students was an Australian lady my age whose husband was specializing in surgery and they were in London for two years. There were two men, one who was blond, bearded and who wore flowing caftans. The other was a Moroccan who was small and dark and I always thought of them as Peter and Judas, although this was no reflection of their personalities. 'Peter' kept very much to himself while 'Judas' kept up a steady stream of conversation. He was Moroccan and ran a restaurant in the West End. The remainder of the students were girls who had just left school and were qualifying with a view to taking jobs at ski resorts in Switzerland or on luxury yachts. Paul spent his time visiting tour operators and travel agents and doing the round of art galleries.

Chapter 29

When we got back to Malapati, the animals were overjoyed as always to see us. Piccolo, who was now twelve years old, had developed a growth on her mouth. We went to pick up the boys from school for the Christmas vacation and we had a joyous reunion. It was the longest period of time we had ever been away from them. I was surprised that they were so delighted at the news that there was to be an addition to the family.

We had brought Piccolo with us to see the veterinarian. He diagnosed incipient cancer. Riddled with cancer as she was, the kindest thing seemed to have the vet euthanize her. The boys were distressed at the loss of their constant companion in their forages through the bush. She had been so much a part of our lives. I thought of her as pup when Simon, as a baby, would lie on her until she squealed. How quickly she had grown and got her own back by catching him from behind by the pants and holding on till she pulled them off. We mourned for the passing of an old friend. The vet suggested we get a new puppy right away. He thought it would help fill the void, but we felt we loved her so much, we didn't want another dog to eclipse her memory. The decision was taken out of our hands. On our way home, we stopped at Nuanetsi and the Postmaster told us of a litter of pups at the police camp. They were also of terrier origin. The father was called Shovel and he was well known in the Lowveld. As so often happens in country districts, they would sometimes be short a man for a game of cricket and Shovel had been trained to field a ball. We chose a little bitch that looked most like Piccolo and she proved a worthy successor. She was very quick to learn and she had a tremendous personality. The only problem was a name. She was so like Piccolo that we kept calling her that. Eventually we hit on the idea of abbreviating it to Pick, since her father was called Shovel. She soon learnt to walk sedately in the bush instead of chasing after everything that moved. The river was a problem. She loved the water and would have been a tasty morsel for a crocodile. The long awaited rains had come and the river was flowing again.

One afternoon, we were sitting down by the river, watching a troop of baboons on the opposite bank. They felt secure with the stretch of water between us and they were apparently oblivious of us as they sat sunning themselves and scratching idly in the sand like a group of sunbathers. Pick went too close to the edge of the bank, which was very soft river sand, and we decided to let her learn by falling into the water. Suddenly, the bank gave way and she plunged into the fast flowing water. Paul lunged out and grabbed her before she was swept away. As he did so, a roar went up from the baboons, rather like a crowd cheering at a rugby tackle. It must have been their reaction to a predator pouncing on its prey. From then on Pick respected the water.

Method asked for time off to go to Umtali for a few weeks. I agreed and fixed a date when he would return. William asked me whether he should get me a replacement, but I told him Method was only taking his annual vacation. Something about the unconvincing way he nodded his head prompted me to question him, but he was not prepared to volunteer further information and shrugged it off with "I don't know Madam." Method didn't return on the appointed day and William again asked whether he should bring a replacement. Method had obviously not intended to return and had not wanted to upset me by saying he was leaving. This seemed to be a characteristic, regardless of their background. I later heard a prominent African journalist being interviewed during a talk show. He told how, as a young boy, both his parents had died. He had been taken in and educated by a family of white missionaries in a rural area. He was intelligent and the family had decided to send him away to university. After he graduated, he went back and worked at the mission for a short time. He felt this was expected of him, but he hankered to do something else. He could not bring himself to tell them how he felt, so in the middle of the night, he left without saying anything to his benefactors. He did not want to upset them. Similarly when a worker intended to leave, they would never tell one if they were not coming back, no matter how justifiable the reason.

William brought Wilson, who was also one of the Chauke family, to work in Method's place. He was a lay preacher and a very pleasant man. He spoke some English and had at one time been one of Mr. Palfrey's storekeepers. Renos brought his brother Maxwell as a second waiter. Renos was officially the gardener but could turn his hand to anything. He worked with Paul and was quick to learn. He was soon able to attend to minor plumbing jobs. He could help with the servicing of the vehicles and he had become Paul's general maintenance assistant. He could understand a little English but he had great difficulty in speaking it. His brother Maxwell, on the other hand, spoke very good mission English. I asked Maxwell why he was able to speak English and Renos was not able to do so and he said, "Renos was always very dull at school." This augured well for Maxwell but it soon turned out that his only talent was speaking English. He was incredibly clumsy and he was always stepping backwards onto one's toes, but like Renos he was very amiable.

I persevered with training Maxwell as a waiter, then tried him in the kitchen as an assistant to William. The little cook eventually complained about Maxwell's breakages. I tried him in the camp, helping Jane, but she too complained. Finally, he ended up as assistant to the assistant gardener with Renos overseeing the pair of them. I felt he could do the least damage in the garden, but even here he was not beyond triggering a disaster. His problem was his enthusiasm. He was so eager to please that even when he was digging, he didn't just dig. He dug so deep that he once severed the main PVC water pipe taking the water supply to the camp. He carried on furiously, not questioning the enormous muddy puddle that suddenly appeared. Renos, his 'dull' brother, spotted the leak and repaired the damage.

On another occasion I was unable to find the granulated fertilizer. We fed the chickens a small amount of crushed shell each day as a supplement to their food. When we had run out of it, Maxwell decided to add fertilizer to their food. It didn't seem to make much difference to the chickens.

Jane wanted to go home for a while to help with the building of their new village near the Mahozi River. William brought a young girl named Miriam to replace her. Miriam could not have been more than sixteen, but she was quick and bright, although she spoke no English. This didn't bother me but could be a disadvantage in dealing with visitors who might ask her for something or give her a message. We thought she might need help in this regard, so we took on Nays to help her work in the camp. He was also young but he did speak English. He had a military bearing which we discovered was because he was a military reservist. Samuel, a slight young fellow, had joined us as a second waiter. I was now satisfied that this team could cope with a full camp. They were all Shangaans, and all related to William in some way. They worked well together and the atmosphere was congenial.

The National Parks Warden was away on extended vacation and Tim Paulett had been sent down to Gona-re-Zhou as Warden in his absence. He came to visit us with Gill, his fiancé. They were an interesting couple and we enjoyed meeting them. A few days after Christmas, they were back and told us of their recent experience. They had decided, on the spur of the moment, to get married on Christmas Eve. They set off for Chiredzi and arrived to find the river in flood and the bridge under water. Determined to go through with their wedding plans, they crossed on the high-level railway bridge on foot, then hitched a ride to Chiredzi to get a special license. They were a very bedraggled pair but they were able to get married on Christmas Eve. We saw a great deal of them while they were at Mabalauta and we kept in touch with them after they left.

One of the missionaries, who frequently called in, stopped by and told us he felt he had neglected our spiritual needs. Would we like him to pray with us? Paul immediately remembered something urgent he had to do. I explained to the well-meaning missionary that I preferred to pray alone. To me prayer was a personal thing. Orthodox religion had long ago scared me off. I didn't see God as a vengeful being who sat in judgment. I saw God as a life force to which I could tune in to recharge. I prayed as I went about my chores, not on my knees with my eyes closed. I would start each day by thinking, "It's a new day. Help me to spend it wisely and as profitably as possible. You know my needs, attend to them as you think fit." I didn't want to offend this good man who was devoting his life to his beliefs, but I felt it would have been hypocritical to have knelt down in his kind of prayer. Perhaps he didn't see my prayers as spiritual communion, because he never again called in to see us. On the whole we had a very good relationship with the missionaries.

The various government departments were allocated funds, which, if not used before the end of the year, fell away, rather than being carried forward to the next year. On the other hand, if they ran short before the end of the year, there was no more forthcoming until next year's allocation. This led to very careful administration of funds until December when there was a spending spree!

Both Internal Affairs and National parks would grade their roads in December. For a few weeks, the roads in the district would be magnificent until the onset of the summer rains at the beginning of the year. If only the money could have been spent during the winter months, it would have made a tremendous difference to traveling on those dirt roads.

The damage to the roads during the rains became so serious that the new District Commissioner stopped Amon Mpepu's buses from using them in summer. They were allowed to go as far as Chicombedzi, but no further, so our mailbag could not come all the way down. We had to depend on people passing through Nuanetsi, coming down our way, to bring our mailbag. Trucks and tractors belonging to the local Africans still churned up the roads until the surface would be like driving across miles of railway tracks.

The Borlases were having a party to which we were invited on Saturday night. Several people were coming down from Nuanetsi and would be staying in the District Commissioner's rest house, near the Borlases. Tim and

Gill and another ranger and his wife were also coming. As we were about to leave home, I tried on a short curly wig I had bought in England. I thought it would be a fun change from my long hair. Paul laughingly told me I looked like a Shangaan 'curly' fowl. He put it on himself to show me how unattractive it was and we were both convulsed with laughter. Bearded as he was, only his nose showed under the heavy, curly bangs. I dared him to go to the party wearing the wig. I felt certain no one would notice. At various times, Paul had worn the local African motor car sandals, Bermuda shorts, and generally departed from the Rhodesian bush attire of very long khaki shorts with knee length socks and lace up shoes. I'm sure they had always thought us rather strange. One would have to be strange to voluntarily abandon the comforts of living in a big city and set up home, miles from anywhere, and to have no desire to head for the bright lights at weekends.

We set off for the party, our first major social encounter since returning from Europe. I tried not to look at Paul because even in the half-light of the vehicle, his profile brought on a fit of laughter. We arrived and everyone was sitting out on the lawn with lights strung between the trees. Not a soul commented on Paul's appearance. I watched his bobbing curls as he talked animatedly to someone. After about ten minutes, Paul removed the wig and expressed his surprise that no one had noticed. Of course they had noticed, they said, but they thought it was the latest hair fashion from London!

The high level bridge at the D.C's rest camp was completely submerged and the water level was higher that it had been during the previous floods. The giant wild fig trees down on the riverbank below our house had their lower branches almost touching the water. The turbulent water was most impressive when the Nuanetsi River was in flood, but when the water level dropped again, one was able to stand on the river bed and look up at the debris which marked the high water line. I was always awestruck then at the volume of water which had come down. The bridge at the Sub-Office withstood the onslaught, but when the water subsided, we found the churning water had scoured away the western approach to the bridge. Roy brought in several loads of sand and rock to repair the damage so we were able to cross the river again. Our own riverbank had changed its shape and we had a tremendous deposit of new silt which created the alluvial soil of the riverbank. Recharged, the soil now gave sustenance to every seed that dropped and which would eventually contribute to the dense riverine canopy. The growth was almost tangible. It had the feel and smell of a hothouse and the mossy smell of eager growth.

The Ministry of Information wrote to say they would like to do a feature article on Malapati for their magazine, Rhodesia Calls. Their writer and photographer did a magnificent article with color pictures and they included reproductions of some of Paul's paintings. This publication was sent all over the world and we had a tremendous reaction. We not only got bookings for the Lodge but we had many inquiries about Paul's paintings. One of these resulted in having three of his works included in a show at the Royal Ontario Museum in Toronto - Animals in Art Through the Ages. When Reader's Digest wrote up the show, they in turn mentioned Paul and reproduced one of his works.

With a baby on the way and Paul already preparing for his next show, we realized we would have to get someone to help with the running of the Lodge. We had a huge file of applications from various people who had written to us from time to time wanting to be rangers, housekeepers, or secretaries. We were trying to decide how to set about selecting a suitable couple when we heard of Richard and Brita Harland who had a ranch near Que Que where they grew summer crops. Richard had been a ranger with National Parks and had in fact at one time been stationed at Mabalauta, so he knew the area well.

We wrote to Richard and Brita, putting a proposition to them and suggested, if they were interested, that they should come down for a few days. They were just what we had in mind. Richard was a fund of information on most aspects of wildlife, but birds were his specialty. He was particularly attracted to Malapati because of the fact that we had Pygmy Geese at Manjinji

Pan. He was doing a study on these birds and he had hand reared some young from which he managed to breed in captivity.

He had a quiet and unassuming manner about him but he had an extensive knowledge on most subjects. Additionally, both he and Brita had a lively sense of humor. Brita was a delicate looking girl with enormous blue eyes. We felt an immediate bond with them. The idea was that Richard would take half of the guests out game viewing and Paul would take the other half. Brita would see to the catering and supervise the running of the camp. Richard and Brita were to come to us during the tourist season and then go back to Que Que for the summer months when we were closed. Brita had no catering experience, but as a Rhodesian housewife she had domestic help, including a very experienced cook called Tsuro, who had worked for Richard before Richard married Brita. As with most Rhodesian housewives, although Tsuro did the cooking, Brita planned the meals and gave dishes their finishing touch. She could do the same with William. She and I would work together for the first month and then I would hand over to her. They agreed to join us the following April.

We had a telegram from Mr. Boyle saying they would be flying down to Malapati to finalize arrangements for their tours. They arrived in a luxurious aircraft, complete with their own pilot. William was away and I had to make lunch myself. When Mr. Boyle began to discuss business matters, I asked whether we could wait until after lunch when I would be free to join in the discussion. He gave me a cool stare and continued as though I had not spoken. After lunch I joined them but I was obviously not to be included in the planning. It became quite embarrassing. He commented on the tremendous finances involved in his operation, using a million-dollar aircraft, and having full time couriers and staff to fly and accompany his parties. These couriers would rouse guests at 0.600 hours and at 6.10 they would 'rendezvous' in the public lounge for an early morning cup of coffee. At 6.25 the Land Rovers would depart on their game drives. The whole day was accounted for in this way, leaving no leeway for the extra time one might wish to sit at a waterhole to watch game come to drink, or for a day when they might prefer to go for an early morning walk and go to Manjinj for a picnic breakfast.

Since I was not to be included in the discussion and Mrs. Boyle was idly leafing through a magazine, I went to talk to the pilot. I asked him how long he had been working for the Boyles. With a look of surprise he told me the aircraft belonged to him and they had chartered it for the day.

Two weeks later, we had a long letter from Mr. Boyle listing, among other things, the lack of space in our kitchen (which was huge by any standards). I in fact had two kitchens, one where the cooking was done and another where the food was prepared. He expressed his concern over Brita's lack of qualifications. Also included was a list of suggested menus and the various ways potatoes could be prepared! I realized this operation was going to give us trouble. We had started Malapati to enjoy our surroundings in a leisurely way and to share our experience with others in as painless a way as possible. Experience had shown that treating people as one would treat guests in one's own home worked well. Everyone who had come to Malapati seemed to relax and enjoy themselves. We had no desire to start our own private rat race in the bush where I would be nervous and anxious every time this tour operator's party was due to fly in. Paul and I discussed the matter and we decided we could do without their business. We wrote and asked them not to include Malapati in their itinerary.

Chapter 30

Richard and Brita arrived and we soon realized we had made a wise choice. We worked well together and we had a great deal of fun in the process. Brita suggested that since we would be spending all our time with our guests during the winter, we dispense with our dining room in the house and turn it into an office where we could eventually have the radiotelephone. Our living room furniture could be moved into the public common area and we could use the room as a second dining room where we could have breakfast and lunch, leaving the chiwava for dinner at night. This meant that only the two bedrooms and bathroom remained for our use, but experience had proved that when we had people to stay, we had very little leisure anyway. In the cold light of day the chiwava lost its magic, but at night it had the feel of Africa with the one side open and looking onto a crackling log fire.

Not long after the Harlands arrived, we were having dinner one night when Paul bit his tongue. We laughed at first but when it wouldn't stop bleeding I had a look at it. He had somehow managed to just about bite a piece out of the middle surface of his tongue. Short of having his tongue doubled up, I couldn't imagine how he had accomplished this. My first aid knowledge extended to pressure points to stop bleeding but it hadn't covered something like the tongue. It was very difficult for us spectators to keep a straight face, but when it didn't stop bleeding after ten minutes, we thought he might have severed something serious and visions of driving to Chikombedzi came to mind. Richard suggested making a pad for him to bite on. We renewed the pad several times and gradually the bleeding stopped. It was quite a relief to see him with his mouth closed again. For several days after that, one or another of us would remind Paul at mealtimes to "mind your tongue".

We applied for a radiotelephone and pretty soon two technicians arrived from Fort Victoria. We had the mast and stays and various other items they had specified and under their direction we rigged these up. The set itself was an enormous transmitter, which looked like a sizeable switchboard but with a handset attached. Our number was ZEE 19 and our call up period was 9:30 to 10 a.m. We had to switch on every day at this time and incoming calls received at any other time were notified by Salisbury telephone exchange that the call could only be placed during our call-up time. We could ring out at any other time, provided no one else was on the air.

Just before 9:30, we had to start the motor for our house power supply to have the electricity to use the phone. We then had to give Salisbury our call signal. They would then reply and connect any incoming calls. After that, they placed any calls we wanted to make. This was laborious compared to a regular telephone, but to us it was absolute bliss to have an immediate means of communication with the outside world. It would cut down on so many of our trips and misunderstandings We had decided to link up with Salisbury because most of our calls were to tour operators and agents based in Salisbury and our calls were then considered local calls, although we lived down on the South African border.

We once had rather an amusing experience when we telephoned the Immigration Department at Vila Salazar. They also had a radiotelephone but they were linked to Bulawayo. Our call went up to Salisbury, who telephoned Bulawayo, who linked up to V.S. and we were able to speak to them. The call had been routed several hundred miles to enable us to talk to someone who in bush terms was almost a neighbor!

Paul and I returned from a trip to Fort Victoria to find one of the Salisbury tour operators had called to tell Richard they would be flying down the next day. Everything had to be just right because their decision to bring clients might depend on the impression we made. Fortunately, we had just stocked up on provisions. It was late when we arrived home and we unpacked the perishables but we left the bulk of the shopping in the Land Rover to unpack in daylight. Among other things, we had bought a fifty pound bag of lime wash with which to spruce up the name and markers on the airstrip.

Early the next morning Maxwell unloaded the vehicle, dumping everything onto the patio. In his enthusiasm to complete the task before we appeared, he had pulled out the bag of lime wash and hurled it onto the patio where the packet had burst, spilling the contents over a large area. Fortunately, I arrived before Maxwell could do further damage by turning on the garden hose, which seems to have been his intention. The patio surface was brick and I'm quite sure with water, the patio surface would have been permanently white. I have often found when one doesn't want something to work, it does beyond the manufacturer's wildest dreams. Some of my most durable dyeing has been done accidentally in a washing machine when one small red item has turned all the whites pink and which withstood all attempts to whiten them again.

The whitewash was a disaster of the type which only Maxwell could create. The tour operator and his entourage would be arriving within a few hours. We could explain that it was an accident, but we wanted the first impression to be one of well-managed efficiency. A vacuum cleaner would have done the job in minutes, but such a thing was unknown at Malapati, so we set to work with every available broom and brush. We managed to remove most of the powder and then carefully dusted the cement between the bricks. The patio had an overall grey look, but we managed to remove this by hosing it down and scrubbing the surface. By the time our party arrived, the patio was dry and looking particularly clean.

We had our first guests in April and from then on we were pretty busy. When we had a lull, Richard and Brita would go home to Que Que for a few days to see if all was well there. Our guests were varied and came from almost every corner of the globe. Strangely, they were mostly very similar people which was perhaps why they all got on well together and why we enjoyed having them. Many of them have kept in touch with us.

Only once did we have anyone I could happily have wished away. We had a call from a Salisbury tour operator asking us to book a party of five, three guests, two couriers and pilot for three days. We didn't charge for the couriers or pilot. When the aircraft landed, Richard went up to the airstrip to meet them and was dumbfounded to find Mr. Boyle and his wife, two lady 'couriers in training,' and an American surgeon who announced that he had heard about Malapati and had insisted on having it included in his tour. Mr. Boyle had obviously realized he couldn't book directly with us, but since this was a personalized safari, he couldn't miss out on it. He had used the client's name to make the reservation and had gone through another agent. We had the satisfaction of knowing he'd had to pay the agent's commission and he'd had to pay for himself and his wife.

I hadn't met the party until just before dinner when I went into the pub. The men all stood up when I came in except for Mr. Boyle who pretended not to notice me. Whenever I made any comment to our guests Mr. Boyle would snort contemptuously. I was appalled by his lack of manners but I was determined to let his client have a memorable stay. He persisted in making derisive comments in an undertone until eventually his usually taciturn wife said, "Ronnie, please do stop now."

At dinner, I said they should just sit where they wanted to, but he said they were training the girls who should arrange the seating. With each course, Mr. Boyle would take one mouthful and then gently push his plate away, clearly indicating that it was not to his liking. Brita had cooked 'nimus,' which she served with a vinaigrette sauce. They were a type of locally grown nut which the Africans boil and then mash. Since our guests had not seen them before, it generally interested them to try something different and indigenous. One of the couriers commented that they tasted like the chestnut stuffing for a Christmas turkey. Mr. Boyle growled, "and that's where it belongs."

When we went to Manjinji Pan, Brita packed a thermos of tea and another of coffee and cookies and we took along cold drinks in a cooler. Mr. Boyle inquired whether the tea was China or Ceylon. Since it was Ceylon, he said he would have it with lemon, knowing we would not have taken lemon on a picnic. On their last night at Malapati, the girls were busy arranging the seating when our American guest decided he would rather sit next to Richard to continue his conversation with him. In the ensuing confusion of 'you sit there,' Mr. Boyle was left to sit next to me or between Christopher and Simon on the opposite side of the table. He chose to sit between the two boys. They had detected his antagonism and when he turned to one of them and got a monosyllabic reply, he responded with "Children really have no place in an establishment like this." I leant over and with a charming smile I told him very quietly that when they were home, our children were very much a part of the establishment, that I was determined his client should enjoy his stay, and he might as well too because it was the very last time he would set foot in Malapati. Their client survived the regimentation. He later wrote to say how much he had enjoyed his stay. He had enjoyed talking to our sons and had found them so well informed that he was sending them a subscription to the San Diego Zoo News.

That May we experimented with having a short foot safari, with guests spending one night in a very simple camp, sleeping out. We selected a site under a huge Baobab tree, fairly near Makonde Pool, where large numbers of animals came to drink at night. In the afternoon, Richard would drive the party to the bridge where they would leave the Land Rover and walk the remaining distance through the bush. This was only a distance of about two miles, but it gave them a taste of wandering through a wilderness area. They would stop to look at animals' tracks and droppings, identifying the birds and vegetation, and end up at Makonde Pool, opposite the Tower. They would sit there until sunset, quietly watching the game come down to the pool. We would take camp beds, sleeping bags, grass mats, and folding chairs in a separate vehicle by another route and set up camp, leaving Maxwell to make a fire. We deliberately kept this camp simple. When the party arrived, they would have a drink and then a barbecue with salad and baked potato. They slept under the night sky to the sounds of the bush ... elephants trumpeting at the pool as they splashed around, the impala browsing all around the camp with an occasional male snorting his superiority. The harsh snort of an impala is quite frightening when one doesn't know what it is. More than once, Richard was woken with the urgent whisper, "There are lions close by."

The first people Richard took out were a couple from Johannesburg. They arrived back the next morning delighted with the experience and asked to go again the following night. The same people, both medical doctors and both smokers, had rather an amusing incident when they ran out of cigarettes on their last day. They were on their way to Manjinji to go bird watching with Paul and Richard, so they stopped at Palfrey's old store. It had been bought by one of Renos' brothers. The store was down to their last packet of fifty cigarettes, which had been opened, as tribal people will frequently buy them one at a time. The cigarettes were shaken out onto the counter top and slowly counted with frequent fresh starts as the storekeeper lost count. Finally, the number was established and the arithmetic done on the back of the box to calculate the cost of twenty-nine cigarettes. They were then again carefully packed back into the box and the transaction was complete. I'm sure these doctors had never made such an unhygienic purchase, but I suppose the urge to smoke overrides all else.

On one trip with a party who was going to sleep out, Richard noticed some vultures sitting a little distance ahead. He thought it might be a kill and stopped to investigate. He left the party sitting in the Land Rover while he went to see whether it was safe to approach. Curiosity overcame them and they cautiously followed him. He looked around and waved his hand, indicating they should wait. They construed this as a danger signal and headed back for the Land Rover. Robin, who was not in the least bit athletic, vaulted right into the open Land Rover. It turned out to be an ailing buffalo which the vultures seemingly had pronounced incurable.

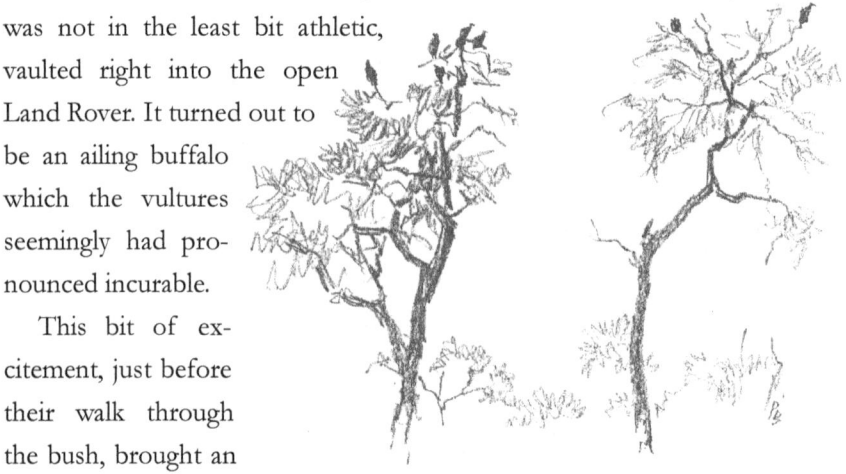

This bit of excitement, just before their walk through the bush, brought an added dimension to the walk to Makonde. Robin announced she was having the camp bed next to Richard, the man with the gun. In the morning, Richard found what he at first thought had been an elephant urinating at the foot of Robin's bed, but she explained she always made frequent trips to the bathroom during the night, and no way had she been prepared to take the flashlight and leave the safety of the campfire.

Chapter 31

Tamba still continued to go for daily walks with me but he was obviously very lonely. Occasionally I would put Pick into his enclosure and they would romp for a while and then Tamba would settle down to groom the pup. Pick would sit with her eyes half closed, enjoying the attention for a while, but she would eventually get bored. Christopher wrote to say he knew of someone who had a little female they were prepared to let us have, and it seemed a good idea to have a mate for Tamba. When we next went to pick Christopher up from school, we went to Tebekwe, a chrome mine near Gwelo, to get the little female which turned out to be a male. He was kept in a very small cage and not used to being handled. By this time I had thanked the family profusely and given them a gift for parting with it. I could think of no way of handing it back graciously but I also felt desperately sorry for the poor little fellow. Yet I could think of no way two males would get on together.

My fears proved groundless because when I put him into the cage with Tamba, they leapt around joyfully and played non-stop. At night they huddled up together in the sleeping box. I had always wondered whether the way Tamba slept was normal for a monkey. He slept on his stomach, with his head and legs tucked in, but Tebekwe slept the same way. There were some obvious differences between the two. Unlike Tamba, Tebekwe would not make eye contact with me and would only look at me when he thought I wasn't looking. He accepted me but would not let me handle him.

Tamba, although the larger of the two, did not dominate Tebekwe, as they generally do, making the younger one quite submissive. They seemed to be equals. Tamba also continued to enjoy drinking milk which he did by pursing his lips and drawing it up. Tebekwe drank only water. After their walk, I would leave them to play around in the tree in front of the house and they would leap around and swing from the topmost branches with incredible ease. One afternoon, Paul was painting on the patio when I heard the monkeys chatter in alarm. At first I thought there was a snake on the roof, so I climbed up, but I could see nothing. The two monkeys edged forward and peered onto the patio. Tebekwe rushed off screeching and chattering. Paul was doing a painting of a leopard, which is one of their predators, but it seemed inconceivable that Tebekwe could recognize a picture. When Paul took it inside, Tebekwe went back to playing in the tree with Tamba. As soon as Paul brought it onto the patio again, Tebekwe again began his chattering. Tamba was unmoved by it all. He had had no contact with his mother, but his fear of predators seemed to be instinctive where birds of prey were concerned. I could not find an explanation for this. Occasionally, the two monkeys just decided they wanted to carry on playing and no amount of coaxing would entice them back into their cage. Generally I could put food in the cage and they would leap in or if that failed I would start the engine of the Land Rover and Tamba just could not resist going for a drive with me. In the vehicle it was a simple matter to grab him after we had done a turn around the driveway. Once I had him back in, Tebekwe seemed to feel insecure on the outside and he would cling to the outside of the cage trying to get in. On one occasion, a troop of wild monkeys had been hanging around for days and when I let Tamba and Tebekwe out, nothing would persuade them to return. One of the smaller wild monkeys, whom I took to be a female, romped around with Tamba, leading him to the riverine vegetation where the troop sat chattering. Tebekwe followed him. I watched them go with a certain amount of sadness. I was particularly attached to Tamba, whom I'd had since birth, but if it meant they could be re-introduced to the wild and have the freedom of the bush, I would be glad. The following morning, the two bachelors lay outside their cage. Tebekwe had his arms and legs badly ripped and Tamba had a deep wound in the abdomen. An adult vervet monkey has ferocious fangs. Although Tamba and Tebekwe were now both adult, they had been no match for the dominant male of the wild troop. For once Tebekwe allowed me to handle him. I fed them both penicillin and dressed the wounds. The two of them huddled together dejectedly in their sleeping box. They lay like that for several days, accepting my ministrations and gradually they recovered, slightly the wiser about the ways of their wild relatives, I hoped.

Paul and I went down to Johannesburg for me to visit my doctor and for him to get some paintings framed. We took the Mazda truck since we wouldn't need four wheel drive. The rainy season was now over and it was a softer ride than the Land Rovers. At this stage of my pregnancy I didn't think I should have too much bouncing. We went through Gona re Zhou as we had a message for the Warden. Just before we reached Mabalauta, we saw vultures dotted around in the trees. We stopped and saw two elephant cows, one of whom had just given birth to an absolutely minute calf. They all three looked very well, so we assumed the vultures were waiting to clean up after the birth. I was soon to go through the birthing process and I was driving five hundred miles to consult with a gynecologist; I would be in hospital for ten days and everything would be very sterile and complex. I couldn't help but marvel at the simple way nature handles these things. On our way back, we arrived at Nuanetsi and found there had been late rains while we were away. We had ninety miles of dirt road to cover in the Mazda, which was very low slung. If the roads had not already been churned up by traffic, it would be possible to get through, so we decided to try. All went well until we got to the basalt, the black "cotton soil" that became a quagmire with just 1/4" of rain. It required skillful driving. One had to know when to go slowly to avoid skidding and when to accelerate to avoid getting stuck. It looked as though we might get through. Just one bad stretch remained, but one of Amon Mpepu's buses had been through and had churned the road into deep ruts. It was 11 p.m. and we stumbled around in the mud, laying sticks and mopani branches in the ruts. When the flashlight batteries gave out, we realized we would have to wait until daylight. There were tremendous advantages to living in the wilderness but at times like this I was very aware of the disadvantages. In my advanced state of pregnancy I even had trouble getting comfortable in my own bed. To add to my misery, it started to rain and we had to bring the luggage into the cab with us. It was quite one of the most uncomfortable nights I have ever spent. When daylight came, we were soon able to extricate ourselves and we arrived home tired, muddy, and disheveled. It was one of those times when I thought to myself "lucky my city friends can't see me now."

On the way down to the river one morning, I noticed an enormous solitary old baboon, high up in a wild fig tree. He seemed oblivious of me as I approached and he continued eating the figs. I stood very still watching him for a while. Suddenly he saw me. He made no attempt to climb down - he just bailed out from a height of about twenty feet and landed with a thud, which should have left him winded, but he didn't hesitate. He loped off on all fours, looking at me over his shoulder as he went. A surprising number of animals were taken, mostly by lions, quite close to the lodge. A short distance from us was what the boys called the Malapati stream, but this name only applied during the rainy season when it was quite magnificent. It wound its way through the dense riverine vegetation, cascading over the rocks in a little waterfall and finally running into the Nuanetsi River. For the rest of the year it was just a dry wash with massive trees on either side, their gnarled roots exposed by successive floods. Just before it entered the river, it was quite wide, as the river pushed back up the gully during the floods. At this point, the banks on either side were almost twenty feet high and it made an ideal place for a lion to pounce onto an unsuspecting animal below. Several times we found buffalo carcasses here with the distinctive claw marks on the shoulders. At one carcass we found a vulture skeleton inside the buffalo skeleton. Presumably it had crept too far up the chest cavity and had been unable to extricate itself again.

One morning I found a freshly killed impala within a stone's throw of the house. It had been disemboweled but otherwise untouched. There were pugmarks around but I couldn't tell whether it was cheetah or leopard. Paul identified it as leopard since they disembowel the carcass before eating. I had very likely disturbed it and he thought it likely that it was still around. It was interesting that in all our innocent wanderings, no one ever came to any harm. Once, shortly after we arrived at Malapati, we had gone for a walk with Christopher and Simon. I was in the lead and I became aware of a rumbling noise which sounded somewhat like a distant engine. Suddenly, an elephant trumpeted just ahead of me and I turned to run. My family had already taken flight. When I finally caught up with them, breathless and shaken, they patted me on the back like a triumphant marathon runner and declared they hadn't been aware I was capable of such a burst of speed! Another time, Simon was in the lead and as he rounded an enormous termite mound, he turned to face us with his mouth agape, unable to speak. When we caught up with him we saw what at first looked like a rolled up sleeping bag but it was in fact a large python that had ingested a buck and was disinclined or unable to move during the digestive process. It proved to us all by first hand experience the importance of "walk, don't run." Puff adders lie in a game path waiting for small rodents and approaching at a walk gives them time to get away. Wandering through the bush, I was constantly startled as some creature broke cover and dashed off. If I stood still, they seemed reassured and invariably stopped some distance away, graceful and statuesque, and surveyed me with that gentle animal stare, with just an occasional flick of the ear. Walking in the bush was never just physical. We exercised all our senses. We smelled the animals that had passed that way; the strong herbal scent of the elephant dung; we identified the plants; we heard and watched the myriad types of birds as they fluttered around in the vegetation overhead; we tasted the various wild fruits; we handled the driftwood, fashioned in nature's workshop; the brightly colored river stones, tumbled by the force of the water. A tantalizingly familiar smell would waft over the air like newly cut raw potatoes and then it would be gone. We later learned it was the Phyllanthus reticulatus whose miniature fruit emits the elusive aroma like newly cut potatoes. All this sharpened our senses and we came back from a walk refreshed and invigorated.

Paul's next show was to be in Johannesburg in June when I went down to have the baby. He was working at top speed to finish in time but he frequently had to stop for several days to help Richard if we had a full complement of guests. When they arrived back from a game drive in the late afternoon, some people would want to shower and change for dinner while others preferred to have a drink before going to change. This meant Richard had to go straight to the pub, but he also had to shower and change for dinner, but by then the next batch of people would have arrived for a drink. When guests slept out, a second person had to drive a Land Rover to the campsite with Maxwell, the equipment, and food. We realized we would have to take on someone else to help. Our advertisement brought an avalanche of replies and we made a short list. When there was a lull in the bookings, Richard and Brita went up to Salisbury to interview the most likely sounding people. They decided on Robin Johnson, a young bachelor who had been to hotel school and who was keen on wildlife, although he had no practical experience. Robin was a pleasant young man and quite prepared to do anything. He could drive the Land Rover, play barman, and generally be useful to both Richard and Brita.

Paul was now able to devote himself to his painting, and to avoid interruptions, he carried his easel and table with his equipment down to one of the massive old trees near the river, away from our guests. He came up to the house one morning to have tea with us and when he returned he found the wild monkeys had raided his pastels. They sat up in the tree drooling multi colored saliva. From then on he had to pack everything away whenever he left it.

Christopher and Simon had a long weekend coming up and as we had a full camp that week, I offered to go up to Fort Victoria to do the shopping. I had difficulty fitting behind the steering wheel so Robin went with me. We did the shopping and picked up Simon and then drove to Shabani where Christopher was being dropped off. We went back to Fort Victoria to pick up the meat and perishables and we eventually left for home at 5 p.m. We had a five hour trip ahead of us and we would be travelling through elephant country in the dark. About twenty miles from Chikombedzi we had a flat tire! I realized with exasperation that I had never seen how the spare wheel on the Mazda was removed. It was recessed into the underside of the chassis and a metal plate, which nothing would dislodge, covered it. I was so frustrated that had I had the means I would have forcibly removed that wheel. As it was, there was nothing we could do but wait for help. This was a lonely stretch of road and anyone likely to travel it would have gone to town by now. The likelihood of another car passing this way at this time of night was very remote.

We made a small fire and settled ourselves for the night on the side of the road. At three a.m., we heard a vehicle approaching and sure enough it was Paul. When we hadn't returned by midnight, he realized something had happened. He deftly removed a long rod from behind the seat, stuck it into a slot, and the spare wheel dropped out. We changed the wheel and were ready to go within ten minutes. The following morning, Paul discovered Robin had removed the tool kit while trying to dislodge the wheel and it had been left on the side of the road. Three days later when we returned the boys to school, we found it placed on a prominent stone, at the side of the road, near where we had left it!

A friend of Brita's came to stay for a few days and Richard thought it would be good experience for Robin to take her out for a walk along the riverbank to the permanent pool about a mile up the river. They had no sooner left than they were back. Robin breathlessly told how a short distance from the Lodge they had found a huge lion footprint in the sand. It was quite the largest he had ever seen, larger even than the plaster cast we had in the pub. We all set out to inspect it and found it was the imprint of a young hippo which had gone that way during the night. Robin was most embarrassed and we couldn't resist teasing him whenever we saw hippo in one of the pools "six lions in that pool Robin" and he found it as amusing as we did. We had a most interesting call at this time. The Ministry of Information telephoned to say a National Geographic team was due to come to Rhodesia and they wanted Tom Nebbia, the photographer, to come down to Malapati. However, just before he was due to arrive, his trip to us was cancelled in favor of an interview with Ian Smith, the Prime Minister, which I guess made a more interesting story.

Chapter 32

When Christopher and Simon next came home on holiday, they prevailed on Richard to take them floating down the river. The original top of one the Land Rovers made a perfect flat-bottomed boat. They took it up to the bridge at the Sub-Office and the three of them drifted down on the current to the Lodge and they saw an enormous amount of game, totally unaware of them, being completely unused to looking for anything on the water. They saw a herd of buffalo, which continued drinking as they floated past and impala, Kudu, and Nyala.

I woke one morning to find my feet grotesquely swollen. Paul, Richard, Brita and Robin were out with the guests and they would be away for some time. I remembered Floyd Hicks telling me Mina at the Superstore had developed 'toxemia' during pregnancy and had nearly died. I looked it up in the medical dictionary… "Ill-understood condition of pregnancy in which there is oedema and raised blood pressure. If ignored there is danger of eclampsia." If I had thought to ignore the symptoms, "eclampsia" changed my mind. "Eclampsia…Complication of late pregnancy in which the mother suffers convulsions, which may be fatal."

By now I was sure I was seriously ill and I was certainly not going to wait for the party to return later in the day by which time I might have had the fatal convulsions. I could no longer fit behind the steering wheel, but Simon volunteered to drive me to the hospital. He was twelve and still had difficulty in seeing over the top of the steering wheel, but we set off at high speed for the Mission Hospital at Chikombedzi. Every now and again, Christopher would look down at my feet and say, "It's getting worse. Your feet are bulging over the tops of your sandals now." After a severe jolt when Simon hit a bump in the road, he said, "Perhaps this driving will make the baby get born on the way and then you won't have to worry about your feet." I was not about to have the baby on the side of the road and I tried not to think of what might happen. It was a great relief when we arrived at the hospital. The doctor confirmed it was toxemia and gave me medication and assured me I was a long way from developing eclampsia.

On the way home, we stopped at Mina's store to buy Cokes. One had to be very thirsty to drink Cokes from Mina's store. They were always tepid. Straws were a luxury Chikombedzi didn't know about. The bottles smelled of that long ago time when the storeroom Mina now used had been a 'butchery' and the meat had spoiled. Mina watched us pull up outside the store and gazed wonderingly at Simon. "Mybabo, you can drive. Can you swim also?" To her, these two things were obviously the highest accomplishments. Mina was so impressed with this feat that she presented him with a baby goat which he proudly bore back to Malapati. He was the most pathetic bundle and he had such a pungent smell that we called him Pooh. The smell fortunately disappeared when they shampooed him.

Pooh was intimidated by Pick who loved nothing more than to nudge him from behind. After several weeks of vitamin enriched milk, he lost his hangdog look and he would turn on Pick and lower his head defensively. He trotted about the house and he would browse around in the pantry, helping himself to treats.

He stood on his hind legs to reach the higher shelves. He was omnivorous and he infuriated William who would shoo him out, shaking his dishcloth at him. Pooh would back away but he would make a show of butting William with his non-existent horns. He finally learnt that it was the telltale clip, clop of his little hooves on the floor which gave him away, and he would step gingerly through the kitchen door and stop to listen, advancing a few paces and waiting for a reaction. This way he would work his way into the pantry and while William was outside he could wreak havoc in there.

I was now eight months pregnant and we planned to go down to Johannesburg. The baby's arrival would coincide with Paul's show. One evening, Samuel came into the pub with the message that Brita wanted me urgently in the kitchen. There had been a minor disaster with the soup and Brita wondered what she should serve in its place. I knew I had a case of tomato soup on the top shelf of the pantry, but there were also tinned tomatoes, tomato sauce and tomato puree and I thought it would be quickest to go myself as I would recognize the soup. I got up on the kitchen step stool and handed the case of soup down. I was wearing a full-length terrace dress and as I stepped backwards my heel caught in the hem of the dress. I tumbled from the top of the stool and landed on my behind in a pool of water. Brita had no children but William's wife had five or six and before Brita or I could react, William took charge. "Call the Boss - baby's coming," he called urgently to the bystanders and Samuel went off to make the announcement. I felt fine, just a trifle bruised and wet, but Brita insisted I go to bed. Paul and the guests arrived to find it had been a false alarm. I realized the baby must have been standing on my bladder when I landed and I had just had an accident.

The incident made me realize it was now time to get down to Johannesburg. Our daughter Kate was born three weeks later on June 13, 1974, and ten days later Paul had his second show, which was sold out. We brought Kate home when she was a month old. At the border, we were told we had ten days to get a residence permit for her. They gave us the forms to complete. In the excitement of coming home the forms were forgotten.

We had an ingenious 'bush cot' which Pat Wright had lent us. It had an aluminum frame and the top and sides were mosquito gauze. The top zipped closed to keep everything out. Tamba was intrigued with the new addition and he would gaze at her lovingly in her secure little cot. "Lovingly' I thought until the day I put her out without closing the top. He leapt in with her and in a flash he had her pacifier which he took to the top of the tree. Perhaps remembering his own baby days and his feeding bottle, he sat and sucked it for a while. When nothing came out, he gripped it in his teeth and stretched it to its limits before letting it go with a snap. Paul stood below ranting at him and vowing that if Tamba ever got in with Kate again, he would be shot. Tamba sat unconcernedly destroying the precious pacifier, only stopping occasionally to waggle his scalp and lower his eyelids defiantly at Paul.

This was a busy period and we had some delightful people come to stay. Lt. Col. and Mrs. Everard were booked in for ten days. He was the former General Manager of the Rhodesia Railways and was now the Acting State President. At the same time we had two American hunters from Oklahoma and two Rhodesians. The Everards were driving themselves down from Bulawayo but they didn't arrive the afternoon they were due. The following day they arrived in a National Parks vehicle. Mrs. Everard was in a very bruised state but still cheerful. They had missed their turn in Gona-re-Zhou and headed straight for Mozambique. When they realized they were on the wrong road, they retraced their steps. Mrs. Everard who was driving had "driven an ambulance through the Blitz in London without a single scratch." Now the poor lady, exhausted by the long and arduous drive on unpaved roads, had fallen asleep and their car had left the road, cutting a swathe through the bush before hitting a tree. They spent a horrible night and the following morning Col. Everard set off on foot to get help. They were in the middle of the Game Reserve on a very lonely stretch of road, but by pure chance he met a Game Ranger from Mabalauta who brought them down to us. The Game Department arranged for their car to be towed to Nyala Siding and for the Railways to take it to Bulawayo. Col. Everard was none the worse for the experience but we put Mrs. Everard to bed where she stayed. We gave her a radio and lots to read and all made frequent visits to her during the day to keep her up to date on what was happening in the camp. She was a vital lady and didn't miss a thing that happened.

The Americans were Zac T. Miller and his friend Glen, whose last name I never discovered. Zac was a dynamic man and everything one imagined a Southerner to be. He had that fascinating drawl and everything he said was hilarious. He had paid $1,000.00 in excess baggage which consisted mostly of firearms. He had come out on a hunting safari to Kazuma near Victoria Falls and he had brought several extra guns as gifts. He owned the 101 Ranch which at one time had employed Buffalo Bill Cody as a cowboy. Zac had an enormous gun collection which it seems ran to several hundred, some of which had never been unpacked. He had people on the Ranch who hand loaded his bullets and he had 'town loads' and 'country loads.' We asked about the difference and he said country loads were to kill but town loads were just to "make 'em bleed 'n cry."

Apart from the fact that Glen was a wheat farmer, we discovered very little about him because he was as retiring as Zac was extroverted. Zac had a thing about firearms and he wouldn't move without his Colt which he always wore in a holster on his hip. When he went out game viewing, his fingers itched as he looked at a fine specimen. Even looking at baboons, which no one would ever shoot, Zac would take an imaginary aim. This horrified Col. Everard who I am sure was a member of the Humane Society, the Anti-Cruelty League, and every other Animal Rights group. We had to have them sit at opposite ends of the living room at night and engage them in separate conversations. Zac would invariably start on some hunting exploit and we would talk loudly to try to cover the conversation, but Zac had a loud voice which carried well. "Bloody murder, that's what I call it," Col. Everard would mutter. He had mentioned that they would be returning to Bulawayo by train since they had no car and Zac thought he would like to try Rhodesian Railways rather than flying back. We made the necessary arrangements, and on the morning they were due to leave, Zac was ready and packed and pacing up and down outside their hut. "You just take your tahm Glen. No hurry. You just take your tahm". How Glen could have packed under that repeated barrage of assurances, I don't know, but they finally set off with Richard with ample time to spare. At Malvernia, Richard put them into a luxurious air-conditioned coach and they were off.

I think Col. Everard relished the ensuing quiet, but we missed the voluble Zac with his constant stream of commentary, very little of which seemed to have escaped Mrs. Everard's ears as she lay resting!

Among our recent guests had been an Australian Member of Parliament and his wife. Although they had both been born in Australia they had hardly a trace of an accent. They were well traveled and interesting to talk to. During a discussion one evening, I mentioned the war in Rhodesia and he was taken aback that we should consider it a war. When I mentioned that the World Council of Churches was making large donations to assist the anti-government forces, he refused to believe it. He felt no Christian organization would ever contribute to bloodshed. I thought it unwise to continue this discussion but it surprised me that so little was known about the Rhodesian situation internationally that this intelligent man could be so naive.

In conversation with Col. Everard, I had asked him whether Rhodesia would get majority rule and he replied, "Yes of course." Being involved with the government, it was interesting to us to know what the prevailing government feeling was. When I pressed him for a time frame, he astounded me by saying "Fifty to a hundred years." This was even more surprising than Ian Smith's response to a reporter had been …. his now famous "Not in my lifetime." How wrong they all were.

When we took the Everards to Malvernia, they got the full treatment with all the Rhodesia Railways staff to see them off, as befitted the former General Manager and Acting President of the country.

In all the excitement of arriving back with Kate, we had forgotten to apply for a Residence Permit for our little alien. In the mail, we received a letter addressed to Miss Kate Bosman advising her that she was subject to deportation for not complying. We could fill in the form easily but we had to have a photograph of her and at two months she looked like every other baby so I used one of Christopher's baby photographs. It amused me that no one had checked this non-resident's age so I wrote them a letter purporting to come from Kate. "My parents have been negligent by not complying with your original request to complete this form, but I could not get the photograph taken because we live two hundred miles from the nearest town with ninety miles of very bad road. Please do not deport me, it would cause me and my parents great hardship since I am only two months old." Someone with a sense of humor replied. "Dear Miss Bosman: We certainly will not deport you. It would cause us great hardship too, travelling on ninety miles of very bad road to come and pick you up. Herewith your Residence Permit".

I went out with Richard on a game drive one morning. We hadn't seen the usual amount of game but Richard made it so interesting that one really didn't need to see much. He stopped to show us a tree where a pair of African Hawk Eagles was nesting. The male sat in the tree and the female rose from the nest as we stopped. Richard pointed out the disparity in size and told us this allowed them to prey on different creatures. The larger female catches guinea fowl while the male catches the francolin, which are smaller.

Further along we stopped and he pointed out a lone elephant and her calf. He thought it strange that a cow with a calf should be on her own. Through binoculars he noticed that she had lost the end of her trunk, but she seemed in good condition. The wound had healed. He pointed out that an elephant uses its trunk to draw up water, which is squirted into its mouth, and it used the prehensile tip to pick up food when it grazed or browsed. She wouldn't be able to nibble the tips off the acacia trees because elephants have only molars, the tusks being the equivalent of extended incisors. An unobservant person might have passed the cow and calf, but Richard made it the highlight of the morning drive. He could think of no reason she was not with the herd. He told us of an interesting scene he had once witnessed when a cow had a damaged trunk. The herd would graze and periodically one or other of them would pass a mouthful back to the disabled cow. She too had been in good condition. It was just another reminder of the way these giants of the wilderness cared for one another. Stories were legion of elephants trying to support an ailing calf or a dying matriarch. It made one realize the horror they must have experienced during the culling, seeing family members going down, and unable to do anything about it.

Whenever we noticed vultures on a game drive, Richard would check it out. The remains of a kill always had a gory fascination for people and one could usually work out what had killed the animal. Frequently there were still scavengers around and this made people feel they had almost witnessed a kill. When Richard found a Kudu carcass near the Sub Office, he stopped to examine the footprints. It had been taken by a lion. The following day he stopped to show another group the remains and to his surprise, he found a dead leopard under a bush close by. It had been shot since Richard had been there the previous day. It was an absolute mystery. This was private property and the general public was not allowed here for game viewing and was certainly not allowed to enter the area with a weapon. Only an Internal Affairs official or a Parks Ranger would have been here with a rifle. Africans did not have firearms. It was strange that anyone would want to shoot a leopard in a game reserve and yet make no attempt to take the skin, which could be the only reason for shooting it. We never did figure out the answer.

At one stage, there was a spate of poaching in Gona-re-Zhou and they went for elephants and they always hacked out the ivory. There were various theories, mostly that they were Portuguese hunters from Mozambique crossing the border illegally and going back the same way. There were wild accusations ... possibly the mechanic from Chiredzi who had been down the previous day, but fortunately for him, when the next elephant was shot, he was safely at home. The Warden, in a heated moment, told someone he thought it was a policeman from Nuanetsi who was frequently in the area and who was known to be a crack shot. Word sped back to Nuanetsi and the policeman demanded an apology. And so it went on with us on the sidelines, watching it all and eagerly waiting for the latest developments. Eight or nine elephants were shot but the culprit was never caught.

Chapter 33

At almost any time there was some controversy in the district and the parties concerned became very heated over quite trivial matters. People passing through would relay details to us and we would wait for the next phase. At this time, the same policeman who had been mentioned as a possible poacher became the center of a storm again.

At the time, a new District Commissioner had been appointed to the Nuanetsi District. These people were always beyond reproach, rather aloof, and did everything by the book. Entertaining was of a very formal nature. Much to everyone's surprise, the new D.C. was totally different. He was divorced and living on his own, so he never entertained. It seems his wife had kept the furniture because his home was furnished very sparsely.

The clubhouse, pool, and tennis courts at Nuanetsi had been erected by Internal Affairs for the use of the local residents which included the person running the post office, the police, and Internal Affairs, and these amenities were under the control of the D.C. For some reason, their status as the most senior official of their department seemed to make most of the District Commissioners assume a proprietary attitude to anything the government owned. It always amused us to hear a D.C. talk about his bridge, his trucks, his tennis court, and his club. This one was no different. The policeman in question had a very attractive girlfriend visiting him from Fort Victoria and he took her to the Club for a drink. Attractive, single, young females were rare in Nuanetsi and after a few drinks the D.C. forgot all protocol and made advances to the policeman's girlfriend. Soon a very angry boyfriend confronted him and told him in no uncertain manner to lay off. Taken aback at being spoken to like this, the D.C. forbade the policeman ever to enter 'his' club again.

For some reason, this D.C. drove a large and old American car. The gear stick had to be held firmly in place or it would jump out, and the exhaust had long since dropped off and the car made enough noise to have been jet propelled. The policeman and his friend left the club, but he let it be known that if he heard the D.C.'s car just once again, he would lay a charge of disturbing the peace. The D.C. was forced to have his car repaired. It escalated in this village of about twenty families until it was decided that someone higher up should intervene and the policeman was transferred to Fort Victoria which probably suited him better anyway.

On a trip to Manjinji, Richard noticed openbill storks nesting in the trees. It was later confirmed by the Ornithological Society that it was the most southerly known nesting place for these birds at that time. Paul had his camera with him and he was determined to get pictures of the Storks on their nests, but they were in some old dead trees some distance into the water. He waded out despite my protestations. Every time he stood on a submerged log and stumbled, I was certain he was being taken by a croc. Fortunately he came to no harm and he got his pictures.

Renos asked to go home for a while and he brought a replacement called Amon. Although he was a Shangaan, he had difficulty understanding me. When I asked him to kill ten ducks for me and to clean them, he brought them in beautifully plucked but with their enormous yellow, muddy feet still attached. The previous day, he had dressed a sheep for me and he had removed the head and the feet and I explained with much gesticulating that he should do it the same way. He went off smiling and later returned with the ducks which now had their feet and wings removed. He told me he thought I wanted all the appendages removed as with the sheep. I was grateful that he hadn't removed the skin on the ducks!

At the end of the season Richard and Brita returned to their farm at Que Que for the summer. At the same time, Roy and Ann Borlase were transferred to Bikita, east of Fort Victoria. They had been kind and thoughtful neighbors. They had lived only four miles from us and by bush standards that was close. We generally didn't see much of them socially while we had guests, but during our closed season we enjoyed having them to dinner or spending an evening at their house. If either of us had a glut of a particular fruit or vegetable, we shared it. We exchanged books and magazines. Whoever was going to town would do emergency shopping for the other and in between times we borrowed from one another. We missed them greatly when they left.

On a visit to Le Rhone, we found another newborn vervet monkey had just arrived. Like Tamba, it had been removed by Caesarian section after a dog had savaged its mother and the Umtali Museum had sent it down. Carol was too busy to undertake the four-hourly feeds and, under protest from Paul, I took him back to Malapati with us. We called him Tali. He was only a few days old and he was a most pitiful little bundle. Since I had to handle Kate constantly I couldn't have him clinging to me as I had with Tamba, so I made him a rag doll which he clung to. A few days later, Brita sent us a very young civet cat which also still had to be bottle-fed. We called her Musky. She was a dear little black and white creature with a shiny black nose and very bright eyes. I put them into Pick's basket in the kitchen for warmth that night. During the night Pick joined them in the basket. She was only nine months old and had never had puppies. In the morning, we found her lying like a newly delivered mother with the monkey and the civet nursing. She came into full milk and spent long hours grooming her two strange babies.

Whenever Pick got up, Tali leapt onto her back and Musky padded on behind her. She was a good mother and successfully reared them both. They were a strange trio. When Pick sat down Tali would jump off and play with Musky. If Pick barked and dashed off after something, Musky would follow at high speed, but Tali would lie down on the ground shrieking with rage. It seemed as though the mother monkey would have grabbed her offspring before running, and it frustrated Tali no end to have his mother dash off without him. When he got no reaction from Pick, he would scamper off after her and leap onto her back with a contented chatter.

With summer now in full swing, the temperatures sometimes reached over 100 and Kate had a constant heat rash. Osric and Joyce Bristow were now living at their new game park near Salisbury and their house was available. When they offered us the use of their house on Le Rhone, we accepted. It seemed senseless for this infant to have to endure the discomfort needlessly. The house was furnished, so we only had to take very little with us. As it turned out, 'very' little became a fair amount.

As we were going to be away for several months, the menagerie had to accompany us. There was Pooh who was now a sizeable goat, Pick and her two hangers on, the two older monkeys, and of course MacGregor. We looked like a circus on the move. The stay at Le Rhone in the higher altitude was a refreshing change after the hothouse atmosphere of the Lowveld in summer. Shopping was a simple matter of a short drive into Fort Victoria.

Paul arrived back from a trip to town one afternoon with two young Australians, Mike Hogan and Diana Ozolins, who had been hitch hiking round Rhodesia for a week. He suggested they have dinner with us. They were really roughing it and they had been sleeping out of doors in their sleeping bags most nights and welcomed the offer of a home cooked meal. Pick and her two strange children who wandered in and out of the living room fascinated them. They were now both weaned and although Tali still clung to Pick, Musky often went off for days at a time. Being a nocturnal animal, she went out at night and seemingly would just sleep where she found herself in the morning.

After dinner, Paul drove Mike and Diana to the Zimbabwe Ruins where they planned to spend the night camping, before returning to South Africa the following day. A short while later, we had an urgent call from the Medical Officer of Health for Rhodesia telling us that a team of medical researchers would be coming out to see us. We were not to leave the house or make contact with anyone until they arrived. The following day the team arrived. Among them were Dr. Margaret Isaacson from the Medical Research Institute in Johannesburg and Dr. Lyle Conrad from the Center for Disease Control in Atlanta, Georgia. He had been flown out from the States.

They told us that when Mike and Diana arrived in Johannesburg, Mike had complained of a violent headache. He had had a swelling in the groin some days before coming to us and at the time they had attributed it to a tick bite. It was wrongly diagnosed as malaria and he was transferred to an isolation hospital. When he didn't respond to treatment, he was treated for hepatitis, but he had died before they could diagnose his illness. An autopsy revealed that it was a virus very similar to the Marburg strain, a virulent virus that had broken out in Marburg, Germany when twenty-five research workers had become ill. They had been working with tissue from green monkeys imported from Uganda and seven of the team had died. The green monkeys were later found to be victims too, and not the reservoir hosts. The symptoms were horrible. First high fever, headache and vomiting, followed by skin eruptions and internal bleeding, and finally destruction of the liver and kidneys.

Diana had mentioned under questioning that they had handled both the monkey and the civet the night they were with us. The nurse who had cared for Mike had also contracted the disease but she recovered, and when Diana went down with it, they were able to use the nurse's blood to make a vaccine. It would seem that each virus has its own particular shape and can only be combated by an antibody corresponding to the shape of the virus. Only a specific antibody can do this because it is like a negative cast of the virus it combats. It is able to latch onto the surface of the virus and seal the crack on its surface, rendering it harmless. Anyone who recovers from a virus develops antibodies, which are ready to attack should the same virus strike again.

We felt quite sick at what we might have precipitated. They took blood from us all and from Pick and Tali, whose veins were no larger than spaghetti, and they wanted blood from Musky, but she hadn't been home for several days. We offered a reward to anyone finding her with the express instruction that they were not to touch her. Carol's young son Tony found her asleep under a tree and Paul brought her home. He carried her as though she was an unexploded bomb and they were able to take a blood sample from her.

Seeing the doctors gowned and masked, wearing gloves and knee-high rubber boots, one realized the virulence of the virus. They were taking no chances. We had a few horrifying days until all the tests were proved negative.

Lyle Conrad later sent us a copy of a book called "FEVER," a true medical detective thriller with all the drama of the "Andromeda Strain." It told the story of the Lassa virus, which broke out in Nigeria in 1969, and bats and rats were thought to have been the vectors. It was a sobering thought that someone carrying such a lethal virus had been in close contact with us. When Mike had come to us, he was still in the incubating stage and a victim only becomes infectious after a week of incubation. Another day or two and we could have picked up the virus and precipitated an epidemic. This outbreak went no further because he had been placed in isolation, but in Zaire and Sudan, a similar outbreak had claimed almost six hundred lives.

An Italian film unit arrived at Le Rhone to make a film using some of Viv's animals. The script called for a tourist in a game park to be filming lions and in his enthusiasm he climbs out of the vehicle and is attacked by the lions and devoured, watched by horrified fellow tourists, including his wife and child.

It was interesting to see a movie being made. The two lions to be used had been hand reared and Viv was able to handle them and they enjoyed romping with him. A manikin of Viv's build had been brought out from Italy and meat was tucked into the stomach cavity. The manikin was dressed in clothes identical to those Viv would be wearing. It was topped off with a wig of sandy hair and the finished prop looked just like Viv.

The lions were not fed the day before filming this sequence. We had been roped in as extras and I had to sit in the back of the car with Carol, the distraught wife, in the front seat. Paul sat in another vehicle. Christopher and Simon were upset at not being used, but they were returning to school shortly and they wouldn't have been available for re-takes. They didn't know how lucky they were. Re-takes, I was to discover, could go on for days until one felt one had lost all spontaneity. Carol had to have glycerin applied to her face every time she had to lean out of the window, screaming her grief.

Viv played with the lions and they swarmed all over him. Finally, the manikin replaced him and the lions spoiled it by immediately pulling the wig off. Another re-take. Eventually they discovered the meat under the clothes and they clawed at the flailing manikin. A bag of 'blood' broke and it was a gory and convincing scene indeed, culminating with the lions once again apparently scalping him.

Some months later we were amazed to see a gruesome story in a South African Sunday newspaper. A lion had mauled and eaten a tourist in Angola (where strife between the F.N.L.A. and M.P.L.A. precluded anyone from checking the facts). There were photographs of the attack and there we all were! They were stills from the film and the story had been sold as factual and it had been syndicated all over the world.

Chapter 34

A visiting American bought one of Paul's paintings, but as it was not quite ready, we agreed to ship it to him. When it arrived in the States, it was confiscated under the terms of the embargo placed on Rhodesian goods. The buyer only escaped prosecution because he had influence in high places and he agreed to return the painting. This posed a problem as Paul was due to exhibit at Game Conservation International in San Antonio, Texas. We made inquiries and found that we could legitimately export to South Africa and then to the States, but under the South African currency regulations, the proceeds would then have to remain in South Africa.

This was ironic, in view of the fact that South Africa practiced unadulterated apartheid at that time and had made no attempt, as Rhodesia had, to try to find a solution to the racial problem. In Rhodesia, the western world was determined to foist majority rule on a country not yet ready for it. However, the hard facts were that Paul's art market was in South Africa and if he was going to export his work it could only be done from South Africa. Rhodesia did not have a large enough population. The white population, at that time, numbered 375,000 and of those only a small percentage would be art buyers.

Just at that time, Paul was commissioned by the South African Government to do a series of postage stamps. One of them, a pair of lions, later won an international award as the most beautiful stamp of the year. We now had to make a difficult decision. He either had to paint for pleasure only and continue with Malapati as our source of income, or we had to move to South Africa. Malapati was so much a part of us. In a few short years Christopher would be drafted into the Rhodesian army. Kate was an infant who could at any moment need immediate medical attention. It was not an easy decision. We finally decided to sell Malapati and return to South Africa.

The National Monuments Commission which controlled Museums approached us about buying the Lodge. The area was ecologically suitable for research work having a wide spectrum of Rhodesian wildlife as well as having some small mammals which didn't occur anywhere else.

At the same time Clive Harding contacted us. He was a member of a South African pop group called Four Jacks and a Jill. When he heard Malapati was for sale, he immediately chartered an aircraft and with the pilot and his business manager, he landed at our airstrip unannounced. William met him and explained we were in Fort Victoria. Like Mr. Downey before him, they had accompanied him and looked over the Lodge. He wanted to use it for tourists, a retreat for themselves as well as having sound recording facilities for the group.

William gave him our telephone number at Le Rhone and told him that our radiotelephone had been disconnected, but there was a telephone at the Sub Office. It was not far. To an African who is accustomed to going everywhere on foot, anything up to twenty miles is 'not far,' and the three of them in their fancy boots set off with William for the Sub Office. Before they were halfway, they had removed their uncomfortable and unsuitable footwear and were stumbling along on tender feet unused to this kind of abuse. At the Sub-Office, they found William's telephone to be a two way radio which could in any case only make contact with the D.C.'s office at Nuanetsi. They had no option but to retrace their steps to the airstrip and fly to Fort Victoria. Once there they telephoned us and we picked them up from town. They were all real 'townies' and as I surveyed their long hair and way-out gear, I tried to imagine them walking the tracks at Malapati and my imagination failed me. Clive was blond and blue eyed and surprisingly impassive for the leader of a pop group. He was more like an amiable St. Bernard. Both Paul and I liked him immediately. He was gentle and quiet spoken and he had been bowled over by Malapati. He loved every aspect of it. Perhaps Malapati would work its magic on him and transform this urban creature as it had me.

When we advised Museums of Clive's offer, they decided to withdraw in favor of the sale to a South African who would bring in the much-needed foreign currency. Sad as we were to part with this niche we had carved for ourselves from the wilderness, we were glad it would continue as a retreat for tourists owned by others who would enjoy it as we had.

Malapati had done many things for us. It had allowed Paul to withdraw from the competitive commercial world. He had proved that he was indeed a practical person who could build a house and a safari lodge from scratch; a person who could in fact do anything he set his mind to. It also served as the springboard for his successful art career. It transformed me from a city dweller to someone who was not only comfortable in the bush, but one who grew to know and love it. It taught us to be self-reliant and to discover qualities in ourselves we hadn't known existed. It had provided a wonderful environment for Christopher and Simon to grow up in and instilled in them a love of Nature. Above all, it had given us a perspective on Life and a set of values which I hope will remain with us always. Now it had opened up this new phase which we were entering.

The sale of Malapati took some time to go through, and when Paul was in the United States a few weeks later, Christopher and Simon prevailed on me to go down to Malapati for the school vacation. As always, it was wonderful to be home. The staff, who were all on retainer while we were away, didn't show up as they usually did when we returned. Only Renos was there. It seemed everyone had urgent business to attend to.

Pick was overjoyed to be back at Malapati and Simon and Christopher wandered around all day long. On a trip to Manjinji we had noticed William at the store. I knew he had seen us, and I expected him to show up for work the following day, but he didn't. That night when I went to bed I was suddenly gripped by fear. I felt vulnerable and helpless. It was a feeling quite alien to me. Even in the city I had never been a nervous person. None of the doors at Malapati even had keys. We had never had use for them before.

I thought of the many times I had been quite alone at Malapati and how I had enjoyed the solitude, letting the quiet roll over me in tranquilizing waves. Now the quiet was somehow ominous. My fear was something almost palpable. At midnight I could bear it no longer and I woke Christopher to have someone to talk to. We sat up until Simon and Kate woke. We hastily packed and returned to Le Rhone.

Perhaps the strange behavior of the staff had triggered off my fear. Perhaps I had subconsciously noticed something amiss. Or perhaps it was just a premonition of what was to come. A few months later the whole southeastern area of Rhodesia erupted into a battleground. It was closed to the public and Clive's manager was moved out. The Lodge was mortared and the roads were land mined by the anti-government forces.

We recently read in a conservation brochure "Mabalauta's wild beauty attracts all sorts of people. Paul Bosman, the artist, constructed a secluded hideaway home in the Malapati area, in the riverine woodland of the Mwenzi, the untamed beauty providing an inspiration for his work …The dwelling still stands today, now within the park, empty and overgrown." In another publication we read of elephants being darted and moved out of the Game Reserve after the drought of 1992 and found reference to the airstrip we had made. It's nice to know that in spite of all the devastation the area suffered during the war, it still exists.

The D.C.'s rest camp was used as a military base. The village of Nuanetsi was security fenced and traffic between Fort Victoria and Beit Bridge had to travel in convoy with a heavily armed escort. Vila Salazar was bombarded almost daily from Mozambique.

Lindsay Bell, who had first interested Christopher in bees, lost his older brother in the war. The Palfreys didn't survive long in Fort Victoria. Mr. Palfrey died of a heart attack and Mrs. Palfrey died shortly after. Quiet and gentle Piet Kok contracted a fatal kidney infection. The flamboyant Osric Bristow, our guide and mentor in our early days in the bush, always ready to lend assistance in any way, was killed by a train on his own ranch. His trusted 'spanner boy' Johannes died two days later of no apparent cause. The Africans said he went to join the boss. Graham and Denise Millar were posted to Concession in the northeastern area of the country into the thick of anti-government activity where their personal transport was a fortified vehicle called a 'crocodile.' They later emigrated to South Africa as did Roy and Ann Borlase. Their son Tony stayed on in Rhodesia and bought a farm close to Harare where he ran a profitable business growing roses and soy beans for export. When the homestead was obviously too attractive, he was issued a Section 8 to vacate the property and crops as it had been allocated to a cabinet minister. Tamba, Tebekwe and Tali joined the Bristow menagerie of domesticated wild animals working in films. Our Siamese cat MacGregor died of old age at twenty-three and Pick enjoyed a long and happy life, eventually emigrating with us to the U.S. Many of the ranchers we knew were killed or ambushed so often, they lost their nerve and abandoned their ranches to move to South Africa.

Christopher and Simon stayed on in Rhodesia to finish their schooling after we returned to South Africa. There seemed to be no way the system in South Africa would ever change. We decided to emigrate to the U.S. not realizing what a lengthy and complicated process it would be, perhaps the most daunting undertaking of our lives. After graduating, Christopher had to do two years of compulsory military training in the South African army in a parachute battalion and then worked in Botswana as a game ranger until we emigrated. Simon trained to do art restoration and framing and continued to do that later with a gallery in the U.S. Kate, who was less than a year old when we left Malapati, has heard our stories so often, she could recount them verbatim. She was seven when we left South Africa for the U.S. but she remembers a great deal about it. She graduated as an Art major at the University of Arizona in Tucson, following in her father's footsteps.

We emigrated in 1982 and visit Africa to keep in touch with our roots; both Paul and my families had been in Africa since the 1700s. We became U.S. citizens in 1988. At the naturalization ceremony, I suddenly thought of the wars our forebears had fought in Africa for their right to be there; the hardships they had endured to make Africa the place we knew and enjoyed, and I was overcome with guilt at turning my back on it all. I wondered whether a candidate for citizenship had ever run out of the swearing-in ceremony. Just then I heard a speaker from the Daughters of the American Revolution, "We welcome you. Bring with you your memories, your culture and your traditions and incorporate it into the rich tapestry, which has made this country what it is. Don't ever forget your roots." At that moment, I knew that an early ancestor had done just what we were doing - gone to another continent to establish a new branch of the family. I realized I need never lose my African-ness.

I often think back to those days at Malapati when life was simple and had a gentler quality for us…when war and strife was something that happened elsewhere…when elephants were so abundant they could cull two thousand. It was an experience few people will ever know and while I'm glad I am of Africa, I am also glad that I am no longer a part of it, with the turbulence of its transition.

We were told that Mina, who ran the Super Store at Chikombedzi, was killed during the struggle for independence in a land mine explosion, another innocent victim of the war. I like to think, when I consider our good fortune today, that Mina's constant wish for us has come true "All God's luck be with you."

Acknowledgments

I would like to thank the many friends who read my manuscript over the years and made useful comments. I would particularly like to thank Bill Quimby who edited the first few chapters which showed me how to do it and encouraged me to persevere.

I would like to thank my sons Christopher and Simon who played such a large part in its making and for carefully keeping my letters to them and to which I was later able to refer when writing about it. I am also grateful to them for keeping at me to "do your book". To my daughter Kate, who had to endure life in a wilderness area as an infant and who later, as a graphic designer, helped me put it all together in book form and get it published.

While we were living in Rhodesia life just seemed ordinary for us. There didn't seem to be a need to take many photographs. Fortunately, Paul was able to beautifully recreate, with his line drawings, so many of the incidents that really needed a photograph. Paul, who was the cause of it all and to whom his family will always be grateful for a wonderful phase of our lives, died in December 2011.